The National Outdoor Leadership School's Wilderness Guide

by Peter Simer,
Executive Director

and John Sullivan

Illustrations by Walter Cumming

A FIRESIDE BOOK
Published by Simon & Schuster
New York London Toronto Sydney Tokyo Singapore

Portions of the text in Chapter Four, "Cooking for Nutrition
and Pleasure" and the Appendix on NOLS recipes were
originally published in NOLS COOKERY by The National
Outdoor Leadership School.

First Fireside Edition, 1985
Published by Simon & Schuster, Inc.
Simon & Schuster Building
Rockefeller Center
1230 Avenue of the Americas
New York, New York 10020
FIRESIDE and colophon are registered trademarks
of Simon & Schuster, Inc.

Manufactured in the United States of America

20 19 18 17 16 15 14

Library of Congress Cataloging in Publication Data

ISBN: 0-671-61821-0

While both the authors and NOLS believe that this Guide
provides sound and accurate information concerning
wilderness camping and hiking techniques, they regretfully
cannot guarantee that utilizing the techniques herein
described will assure you a risk-free experience. The
inherent uncertainties in each wilderness trip, and in each
individual's physiological and psychological response to
wilderness situations, mean that there will always be some
risk.

Acknowledgments

MANY PEOPLE have contributed to the shape and content of *The National Outdoor Leadership School's Wilderness Guide.* We are grateful for their knowledge of the backcountry and their precise critiques of our work which have enriched the book throughout its development. We want to thank Sherrod Beall, Q. Belk. D. C. Carr, Tony Cullen, Willy and Tina Cunningham, Doug Dalquist, Don and Donna Ford, Dave Gipe, Lannie Hamilton, Kevin Hildebrandt, Jim and Julie Huntley, Shari Kearney, Jon Kusel, Claudia Lindholm, Len Pagliaro, Jim Ratz, George Schunk, Cyndy Simer, Lucy Smith, Dan Tillemans, Don Webber, and Louisa Willcox for sharing with us their store of wilderness knowledge. A special thanks to Randy Cerf and Tod Schimelpfenig, who read and reread the text and made many suggestions which have sharpened the book's focus.

Suzanne Hawley, Peggy Smith, Mónica Sullivan, Dan Whipple, and Louisa Willcox have ably assisted us with both research and editing; and Honore Ashcraft and Nita Loper typed late into many nights in order to prepare the final manuscript. We are indebted for their commitment and skills.

We are particularly thankful for Geoff O'Gara's fine writing and editorial abilities. Geoff has helped us in so many ways, and his friendship, encouragement, and willingness to "take another look at that chapter" have been essential to the completion of this book.

The knowledge contained in this book is the result of a collective effort on the part of all NOLS instructors who developed and tested new ideas and techniques in the evolution of the unique curriculum and methods of the National Outdoor Leadership School. We'd like to thank them all, and especially Don Adams, Jim Allen, Mike Allison, Steve Anderson, Steve Antosca, Scott Antrim, Mary Arthur, Randy Aton, Del Bachert, Ed Baker, Myles Bakke, Phil Barnett, Bruce Barrus, Mike Becherer, Jack Bellorado, Linda Black, Peter Blessing, Mike Blumenthal, Kathy Bogan, Ross Brown, Bill Brudigam, Jim Buline, Paul Calver, Ann Cannon, Candice Carpenter, Andy and Nancy Carson, Abby Caul, Peter Chance, Dave Chrislip, Ken Clanton, Frosty Claypool, Dirk Cochran, Tim Conlan, Jim Conners, Pat Conners, John Day, Molly Doran, Polly Fabian, Scott Fischer, Walter Fish, Tom Flavin, Frank

6 Acknowledgments

Florence, Ben Franklin, Tim Fritz, Bob Gathercole, Ian Gersten, Steve Gipe, Lewis Glenn, Diane Godschalx, Pookie Godvin, Glenn Goodrich, Steve Goryl, Jim Halfpenney, Chalmers Hall, John Hamren, Jeff Hardesty, Steve Harper, Gary Hauk, Rob Hellyer, Eric Hosek, Dave Hubbard, George and Paula Hunker, Tony Jewell, David Kallgren, Stephanie Kessler, Rob Kirkpatrick, Kelly Kissock, Sarah Knowles, Wally Krall, Wes Krause, Jim Landmann, Mickey Landry, Steve Lawrence, Drew Leemon, Rick Lemmer, Paul Link, Tim Loften, Rusty Logan, Taylor Lumia, Dave McGovern, Brian MacLean, Brendon McNamee, Steve Matson, Walter Meeker, Stacy Michaels, Peter Morse, Bill Murdock, Mike Murdock, Carolyn and Dave Neary, George and Mary Jo Newbury, Jack Niggemyer, Vinnie Norris, Herbie Ogden, Rick and Nancy Pallister, Cody Paulson, Kurt Petersen, Alan Pohl, Tim Rawson, Louise Richardson, Janet Ross, Mark Roy, Tom Ryan, Steve Ryder, Jon Salisbury, Nels and Brenda Sanddal, Georgia Saviers, Bill Scott, Craig Seasholes, Sandy Shea, Matt Sheldon, Don Sherrill, Skip Shoutis, Dave Slovisky, Adelle Smith, Jim Smith, Mark Soukup, Dick Stokes, Mike Strong, Roger Taylor, Brad Throssell, Rob Thurston, Ben Toland, Peg Trowbridge, Leslie Van Barselaar, Tom and Connie Vanderhyden, Pat Viani, Steve Waldrip, Tom and Dorothy Warren, Will Waterman, Bill Webster, Rob Weller, Rusty Wells, Pete Williams, NeNe Wolfe, Bart Womack, Jeff Woods, and Greg Ziegler.

Finally, to Dan Johnson, our editor at Simon & Schuster—who has thoughtfully asked the right questions, ably corrected our copy, and like every good wilderness leader exercised the right combination of patience and prodding to keep us moving in the right direction—many thanks.

For Cyndy, Kurt, Mónica, and Peter

Contents

FINDING A MINIMUM-IMPACT CAMPSITE • SETTING UP CAMP · The Sleeping Area · Camp Kitchens · Catholes and Latrines · GOOD WATER, GOOD HEALTH · BREAKING CAMP

HEAT LOSS: HOW IT WORKS • FABRICS AND INSULATORS • Insulating Fabrics · Insulating Fills · Shell Fabrics · BACKCOUNTRY CLOTHING • Against the Skin · Middle-Layer Clothing · The Outer Shell · Head, Hands, and Feet · Accessories · CHOOSING, FITTING, AND CARING FOR BOOTS • Parts of the Boot · Fitting Boots · Breaking In Boots · Boot Care · Specialized Boots · Boots by Mail Order · The Foot Is the Important Equipment · PUTTING THE PIECES TOGETHER

SLEEPING BAGS • Loft • Insulators · Sleeping Bag Design · Shells · Zippers · Internal Construction · Sleeping Pads · New Waves · Sleeping Bag Care · Tips for Sleeping Warm · BACKPACKS • The Softpack · The External Frame Pack · The

Suspension System: Shoulder Strap, Hip Belt, and
Backband · The Bag · How to Fit a Backpack ·
Getting into a Heavy Pack · Packing the Backpack ·
Caring for Your Pack · SHELTERS • Buying a Tent:
What to Look For · Setting Up Your Tent · Tent Care
· Lightweight Shelters · STOVES • How Stoves Work
· The Burning Issues · LET EXPERIENCE GUIDE
YOU

FOOD FOR ENERGY • RATION PLANNING •
RATIONING FOR HIGH ALTITUDE AND COLD
WEATHER • THE OUTDOOR KITCHEN • PUTTING
THE POT ON THE FIRE

FOOT CARE • PERSONAL ENERGY
CONSERVATION • Rhythmic Breathing · Pace · The
Rest Step · Layering for Climate Control · The
Effective Rest Break · ORGANIZATION FOR THE
TRAIL • TIPS ON TERRAIN • Trails · Off-Trail ·
Walking Uphill · Walking Downhill · Contouring ·
Crossing a Slope · Walking Over Boulders · Crossing
a Snowfield · River Crossings · TIME CONTROL
PLANS

BACKCOUNTRY ILLNESS AND PREVENTION •
Mountain Sickness · Cold Injuries · Snow Blindness
· Sunburn · Heat Exhaustion and Heat Stroke ·
DEALING WITH ACCIDENTS • Approaching an
Accident Victim · Immediate First Aid · The
Physical Exam · Evacuations · WOMEN'S MEDICAL
CONCERNS • FIRST-AID KITS

List of Illustrations

Foreword

IN 1974, in the exhilaration of having just achieved a personal goal of climbing the Grand Teton, I made a serious commitment to acquire, develop, and sharpen the most important outdoor skills. Part of my motivation was my admiration for accomplished mountaineers, but also, as a father of three growing sons, I wanted to be fully prepared for the serious responsibility of leading family wilderness adventures. Since time was my most precious resource, I wanted to be sure I invested it wisely. I started with a detailed search for the very best instruction in backcountry skills. I reviewed the wide selection of outdoor literature and personally talked to many of our country's most respected rock climbers, mountaineers, and outdoor guides and instructors, as well as park rangers and superintendents. A single answer very clearly emerged: "If it's personal skills you're after . . . if you really want to learn to do it yourself . . . if you want to be a mountaineer's mountaineer, then you should go to NOLS—the National Outdoor Leadership School in Lander, Wyoming." I took their advice, and my relationship with NOLS began.

After many years of participating in almost every NOLS experience offered, I would like to add my voice to those of so many others. If you want to learn how to live harmoniously and comfortably in the harshest environments, to develop and sharpen personal skills, to become a seasoned wilderness traveler, to strengthen your leadership abilities so that you are properly prepared to assume the responsibilities of expeditionary leadership while at the same time developing an understanding, love, and appreciation of the natural environment, then NOLS is the place for you.

NOLS enjoys the reputation as the nation's foremost outdoor skills school. NOLS instructors and former students are found on most major American expeditions and teach at virtually every outdoor school or adventure program in the country. I have watched with pride as NOLS instructors amazed internationally acclaimed Russian mountaineers by telemarking off of Europe's highest summit, and then, in what appeared to be an easy graceful ballet, gliding up a legendary Russian rock route never before attempted by Americans.

I have also watched with pride as a dedicated Board of Trustees has encouraged and supported the school's commitment to furthering its role as the preeminent source of outdoor skills and leadership training. Rather than diffusing its energy into marketing adventure travel or psychological experience, NOLS continues to maintain its clear focus on skills, leadership training, and the protection of our fragile wilderness environment. Today, at schools in Wyoming, Alaska, Washington State, Mexico, and Kenya, NOLS provides a unique curriculum with a wide selection of exciting training opportunities.

However, it is to the current and past instructors, to their accumulated knowledge, experience, and creativity, that NOLS owes its extraordinary achievements. From the experiences, successes, and failures of the very best outdoor leaders, the NOLS philosophy has evolved, and it is that philosophy which is at the heart of this guide. Peter Simer, Executive Director of NOLS, and John Sullivan have presented a wealth of outdoor lore in a thorough and enjoyable manner. Each and every sentence is based on actual wilderness experience. It is an exciting presentation and second only to being there, which leads to my final piece of advice. If you want to have your cake and eat it too, if you want to be an accomplished wilderness traveler, or a mountaineer's mountaineer, call the school, select your course, then come feel the rock and taste the cinnamon rolls.

> Homer L. Luther, Jr.
> Chairman of the Board of Trustees
> National Outdoor Leadership School

Introduction

THIS BOOK is a manual of three-season backcountry living techniques taught by the National Outdoor Leadership School. Regardless of your reason for entering wilderness areas—to fish, hike, bird-watch, climb, hunt, shoot a camera, or just relax—the skills taught at NOLS can make your overnight camp-out or weeks-long expedition safer and more enjoyable. For camping in the spring, summer, and fall, this book will help you select and care for equipment, dress effectively, cook tasty nutritious meals, and find your way through rugged terrain. We have designed the book so that you can read it from cover to cover, or use it as a resource for specific subjects such as "Fitting Boots," "How Stoves Work," or "The Effective Rest Break."

Throughout the book you will find a recurring theme: how you can safely accomplish your goals in the backcountry while leaving little or no trace of your presence. Since its founding by Paul Petzoldt, NOLS has been concerned with this question. Every NOLS instructor, from Paul on, has continually looked for ways to minimize his or her impact on the land. Even though the school teaches many specialized courses in mountaineering, fishing, climbing, cross-country skiing, winter camping, and other challenging outdoor pursuits, at the heart of every NOLS course are the lessons for responsible wilderness living which are contained in this book. (A description of courses offered by NOLS can be found in Appendix IV.)

Many people are laying claim to the future of the wilderness. Some insist on the development of natural resources; others demand access for recreational pursuits; still others desire the preservation of wild lands as an end in itself. While not diminishing the significance of this struggle for fair land-use policies, NOLS believes that ultimately the preservation of our natural inheritance will depend upon the sophistication and commitment of the individual wilderness user. Can an increasing number of Americans find personal renewal in the backcountry without destroying it? NOLS believes that the answer must be yes. And that is why we want to share the resources of this book with you.

Peter Simer
John Sullivan

Chapter One

Camping with New Sensibilities

It is the first day of a NOLS course in Wyoming's Absaroka Mountains. Sweat drips from NOLS instructor Doug Dalquist's red beard as he methodically places one foot in front of the other, using a "rest step" to work his way up the steep switchbacks of Two Cubs Pass. Taking a breath, he locks his left knee and swings his right foot forward. Exhaling, he locks his right knee and shifts his body weight from left to right. By locking the knee of his straight leg, Doug places all of his weight on his skeletal system, giving the muscles of that leg a moment of rest.

Doug first came to NOLS fifteen years ago as a student; he had just completed a degree in physics from Michigan State University. He became a NOLS instructor and was soon teaching three courses each summer. It took a few years before the NOLS outfitting operation could round up the 14EE ski boots he needed to lead winter courses, but eventually a custom pair was made, and Doug has since taught year-round.

A quarter-mile back, another NOLS instructor, Tony Cullen, has pulled off the trail with several students who are taking off their boots to look for hot spots. Tony, a deep-sea diver when he is not teaching at NOLS, points out an obvious but often overlooked fact: for backpacking, feet are essential equipment. New boots chafing tender ankles can be a threat, particularly early in a course when people are embarrassed to slow down an entire hiking group just to check their feet. "Inspect them regularly," Tony says. "If you can identify the problem and treat it while it is still

19

only a small red spot, rather than a full-grown blister, you may save your expedition several days of delay and yourself considerable discomfort."

NOLS instructor Louisa Willcox, a graduate student in forestry at Yale, hikes with a student who is having some doubts about carrying his pack for the next five weeks. "Remember, we are now at about 8,000 feet," she says. "Two days ago you were living at sea level." She assures him that drinking plenty of water, eating well, and hiking at his own speed will help him become acclimated and feel stronger.

"Look at that," Louisa points to a field shimmering with white and yellow wildflowers. "Those are alpine buttercups and spring beauties," she says. "They are a sign that the snow has just melted in this area." As they walk into the field to get a closer look at the spring growth which does not emerge in the high country until midsummer, the student's concern for the weight on his back seems to recede.

Most instruction on NOLS courses is practical—demonstrations of a skill which can immediately be put to use. Last night at dusk, the seventeen students and their three instructors arrived by bus at a remote roadhead just in time to have introductory lessons in how to set up a shelter, use a stove, and fix macaroni and cheese. Today on the trail, the students have learned several travel techniques: they hike in small groups so that their presence will not disturb wildlife or other people visiting the wilderness; they wear "earth" colors which blend in with the setting; on steep inclines they use the "rest step" to conserve energy and hike more efficiently. Although their packs are heavy and the hiking is tough, most of these students have already begun to sense that at NOLS they will learn to enjoy the wilderness in new ways.

In the late afternoon, the group assembles for a class within a stand of lodgepole pines. Packs finally off their backs, the students quietly relax among the shafts of shadow and light. Beyond the trees, a broad, green meadow is divided through its center by a clear, rushing stream. As Doug speaks, a breeze sweeps through the grove and his voice is accompanied by the slow creaking of the tall trees quivering against the sky.

"The first few days in the mountains can seem a bit uncomfortable," Doug says. "Everyone is figuring out their equipment, adjusting their clothes, worrying about their feet. With all those things on our mind, we often miss the beauty of the place. And because we don't really feel at home yet, we often overlook the hundreds of small ways we can scar this landscape."

For most of us, even those with considerable backcountry experience, virgin land, an area without the imprint of man, is so different from the environment of our daily lives, that we need a few days to adjust our sensibilities to it. Early in an outing, we may come upon a scene of particular beauty: a bed of wild violets intersected by a cold, clear stream; a moss-covered Engelmann spruce, fallen amidst delicate ferns; the view from the top of a high ridge where endless rows of ice-etched peaks stretch to an infinite horizon. We see it, and our first impression is often an unexplained feeling that we have "been here before."

Indeed we have. The bed of violets and the infinite rows of ice-etched peaks are handsomely bound in expensive books, attractive coffee-table centerpieces. The powerful spruce beneath the cool veil of green fern has been photographed and ceaselessly duplicated in four-color nature calendars. For most of us today, our first experience of wilderness is not a sensual hike through the backcountry; it is the framed, flat reproduction.

No wonder, then, that the primary impulse of some campers is to find reaffirmation of that illusion and to treat the wilderness like another commodity—they "consume" it. They hike up a rugged switchback, are rewarded by the spectacle of a perfect alpine meadow, and then come down to the very center of its lush environs, set up camp, and possess it.

"Minimum-impact camping, when it really works, is an instinct," says Doug. "At first it seems like a set of rules, but the rules are just to sensitize us to look closely at our surroundings. Once we develop confidence in our backcountry living techniques, once we cut through our preconceptions, we begin to see much more of the subtle beauty of nature. Then we desire to blend in with it and protect it."

This is the philosophy that sets the tone on a NOLS course.

FINDING A MINIMUM-IMPACT CAMPSITE

Minimum-impact camping is learning to protect the sights and sounds of the backcountry so that other people who may be in the same area will also have a good wilderness experience. At NOLS we try to camp at least two hundred yards from fragile environments or points of visual drama like meadow floors or the shores of a lake. The camping area which Doug, Louisa, and Tony have chosen is in the timber above a meadow. It is away from the trail and out of sight. The disturbance to the natural setting has been minimized. To another camper coming over the hill, the view of the meadow, with its lake and tributary stream, has been left undisturbed. The wildflowers, the water quality, the ambience of the fragile ecosystem have not been altered.

A group such as a NOLS course can potentially have a high impact on a wilderness area. Our students disperse that impact by breaking into cooking groups of four to six people to a fire. The instructors will direct each group to stay ten to thirty yards from another, and if the whole group is called together for a class or meeting, the location will be away from any group's cooking area, which is already receiving impact. Subsequent meetings will not be held in the same location.

This course will pack up and move on tomorrow. If they were to stay a second night in the same location, the impact of their presence on the land would significantly increase. Small plants bruised by initial traffic around sleeping and cooking sites would be killed by the fourth or fifth day. In general, it is best to avoid camping in one site for more than three days. Always move on before the impact is noticeable.

Even a large group can remain camouflaged amid dense timber, particularly if camping equipment blends into the natural setting. NOLS issues tents and backpacks in earth

MINIMUM-IMPACT CAMPSITE

tones of blue, brown, and green, rather than bright Day-Glo colors, to help ensure that we fade into the beauty and solitude which our students, instructors, and other backpackers are in the wilderness to enjoy.

Safety is a major element in campsite selection. Doug points out numerous potential dangers that exist on this peaceful, shaded hillside. There are dead standing trees, commonly called "widow makers," propped up among the live pines. Easily overlooked, they are a particular threat to safety when you are most vulnerable, asleep in your tent. Even a gentle wind can blow them over. Be alert to the presence of widow makers and always avoid camping under or near trees that appear dead or have dead limbs.

There are several game trails meandering through the area; they can also bring surprises and possible danger. "When a moose unexpectedly wanders into your campsite, you may be alarmed," Doug tells his students. "But the real danger is posed if the moose becomes startled; after all, the moose has probably been using this same trail all summer." Avoid camping on major game trails.

Make sure your camp is not located at the foot of a cliff or hill where rocks might tumble down. In the desert, avoid camping in dry riverbeds, which can turn into torrents in a flash flood.

Another important criterion for determining the suitability of a potential campsite is the ground cover in the area. Some NOLS courses explore the lush valleys of the Pacific Northwest. Some take place on barren stretches of coastal desert in Mexico. Others hike through the central plains of Kenya, or camp on the black pebbled beaches of Alaska's Prince William Sound. In each location, students and instructors must look at the variety of ground surfaces around them to find the least vulnerable place to camp. Areas with fragile plant cover, such as meadows or tundra, are the most easily damaged.

Sand and gravel make excellent campsites. Beaches are particularly good because it is so easy to restore the sand to its natural state. When camping on salt-water beaches, it is important to camp above the high-tide line. The sand of dry streambeds in the mountains and desert can also make excellent campsites. Here again, special caution should be taken: in desert areas particularly, flash flooding is always a threat.

A campsite in a timbered area is much better than the lush green grass of a meadow floor, which looks so inviting but may hide soggy damp earth beneath. In most timbered areas, the primary ground cover is duff, a layer of decaying vegetation such as leaves and needles; often litter, small twigs and undecayed leaves, is scattered on top. Duff is a relatively soft, spongy surface quite comfortable for sleeping and no worse for wear after human use.

During the summer in the high mountains you will often come across patches of snow, which may make fine campsites. Camping on snow, however, requires special considerations. Thicker sleeping pads and waterproof tent floors are necessary to protect you from cold and dampness.

If you do not need a shelter, or if you have a free-standing tent, large flat rock slabs make decent sleeping platforms. Clearly, no impact is left from your stay, and you are not bothered by protruding roots and rocks, which can disturb your sleep when camping on soil or duff.

When you find a campsite with a suitable surface, don't re-landscape the area; adjust your camp to the site's natural contours. Moving a log may seem like an innocent act of convenience, until you realize that within that log are interdependent communities of animals, insects, and decaying biological matter. Also, the scar left by a moved log will be apparent to anyone who comes across it.

Since sound carries less far among trees than across water or an open meadow, a campsite which is properly hidden visually will also be more able to contain the sounds of people enjoying the outdoors. With proper campsite placement and a little care, the natural atmosphere of sound can continue undisturbed. Radios and tape recorders turn the backcountry into a one-dimensional backdrop for a beer commercial. These sounds are foreign to a wilderness setting, and they interfere with the whistle of the wind, the creak of a tree, the silence, the startling whirr of a diving whippoorwill.

Doug points out that camping in the timbered area above

the meadow will help to mute the sound of voices, which would echo around the valley if the campsite were on the flat meadow floor or near the lake. Their campsite on the hill among the trees is not, however, a sacrifice to environmental responsibility or safety. It has some very practical attributes that will enhance the comfort of the campers. Among the trees they are more sheltered from the wind. There are usually fewer mosquitoes and flies on higher ground. And the campsite is located on a south-facing slope, which will get the warm early-morning sun hours before it reaches the meadow floor.

It is important to give yourself plenty of time to find a good campsite. "Rather than hiking till dusk, then camping at the first convenient clearing," Doug says, "on NOLS courses we try to reach our destination by late afternoon." He explains that by arriving early, you can take off your pack, restore your energy with a quick snack, and then, refreshed and alert, look for a safe, comfortable, minimum-impact campsite. Finding the right site takes a bit of effort; it is decidedly easier if you have plenty of daylight so that you can see what you are doing.

SETTING UP CAMP

While Doug has been talking to the students, Louisa and Tony have been busy setting up the three areas of a model minimum-impact campsite: a sleeping shelter, latrine, and kitchen. The most apparent impression of the camp which Louisa and Tony have set up is that it is handy, organized, and neat. The food and cooking equipment is in one area, and what is needed for sleep, dressing, and washing is in another. Near the tent, the backpacks are standing against a tree trunk with low branches sheltering them from possible inclement weather. Although Tony and Louisa have unpacked a considerable amount of gear, they have kept their individual pieces of equipment separate from those of their camping partner, and none of it is randomly scattered about. If an unexpected snowstorm were to hit, and cover the area with several inches of cold powder, each would know where to find his gear.

The Sleeping Area

Wilderness shelters are discussed extensively in Chapter Three, but it is interesting to consider them here from the perspective of minimum impact.

Since this is a summer trek in a dry climate, the students and instructors are carrying rain flies rather than tents. Rain flies are excellent minimum-impact shelters which provide fresh air, protection from sun and precipitation, and are more versatile and have less impact than a tent. To demonstrate this, Louisa and Tony have strung their rain fly between four trees; thus there are no stakes puncturing the ground. Since the fly is dark green, it blends in with the trees, and is only vaguely visible at thirty yards. Certainly, no one hiking along the trail in the meadow would be able to see it.

Another type of shelter, the bivouac sack, a waterproof nylon or Gore-Tex cocoon which fits over the sleeping bag and supplies protection from moisture, provides the most unobtrusive way to sleep in the wilderness. It allows you to sleep safely in the fresh air under the stars. Since a bivouac sack requires no permanent attachment to the ground and can be moved around each night, you can sleep without leaving a trace.

A tent requires a fairly large, flat area without protruding rocks or sticks which might puncture the waterproof floor. Natural anchors like trees can be used to attach tent lines if they can bear the tent's weight without bending, and if there is no possibility of damaging bark. Tent stakes, though often necessary, will puncture the ground and may injure intricate root systems.

Perhaps the most damaging camping practice is the habit of digging a trench around a tent. This leaves a permanent scar on the campsite, and is rarely effective in preventing flooding. Both conservation ethics and common sense dictate that tents should be pitched on higher ground, where they will be protected from runoff.

Camp Kitchens

Tony has set up a camp kitchen about twenty feet up a slight incline from the tent fly. It is particularly important when using a campfire to make sure that tents and backpacks are out of range of flying sparks. Even when using a stove, this distance is a good precaution. Spilled fuel is one quick way to permanently damage nylon equipment.

In recent years, the compressed-gas or liquid-fuel stoves have replaced the campfire as the most sensible and least harmful way to cook in the wilderness. There are many times when a trip simply cannot be made without a portable stove: on trips to arid desert regions, for example, or in the increasing number of mountainous areas where there is little or no firewood. While the proper use of stoves is discussed in detail in Chapter Three, it is important here to understand their practical and ethical advantages. Stoves are safer than open fires in areas of high fire hazard, and most backpackers now realize that stoves have become a necessity as the probability of finding adequate supplies of firewood diminishes annually.

Still, many of us have a store of pleasant memories created by the glow of a campfire. They can be warming, enjoyable, and romantic. Yet those same campfires have scarred more wilderness land than any other element of outdoor living. Governmental wilderness regulations often spell out what you can and cannot do regarding campfires. Some forest areas forbid the building of fires altogether. Others require permits, which must be carried at all times. You must find out the specific regulations for the area in which you plan to camp. Then you must decide if a campfire is really needed, if the ecosystem can tolerate it, and if it can be built in an environmentally responsible way.

At NOLS we always use stoves unless the following criteria for building a campfire can be met:

First, a campsite must have sufficient firewood—that is, deadfall, lying loosely on the ground—to sustain a fire. Limbs or twigs should never be broken off living or dead trees. If we are staying in an area for two or three nights, we collect firewood beyond the natural boundaries of the campsite. Wood should be collected for one fire at a time, and should not be broken into small pieces until just before placing on the fire. The last deadfall in an area should never be burned. If wood is that scarce, use a stove.

Second, we use fires only for cooking, if at all. Sitting around a booming fire all evening is a waste of a diminishing backcountry resource. Usually, after a hot meal by a cooking fire, it is time to bed down anyway.

Third, when camping with a large group, four to six people should use each fire. This limits the number of fires and the amount of wood consumed, and at the same time minimizes the damage which often results from heavy traffic in camp cooking areas.

If you do build a campfire it should be built in an untraveled area, not visible from a trail. The fire site should be relatively flat and open, without overhanging branches or combustible ground cover. It should be away from tents and other equipment, and should never be built next to a log or rock, which could be permanently scarred by the flame. On windy days or in very dry conditions, use a stove.

Fires should only be built in areas where there is access to mineral soil—sand or gravel, which is not combustible. Often mineral soil (soil without decomposed organic matter) can be found on the surface in sand or gravel areas such as streambeds. Or it may be just beneath the layer of duff which usually covers the ground in heavily forested regions.

For his class on firepit building, Tony first cuts with his shovel a circle of sod roughly one foot in diameter and eight inches deep. Eight inches should get you down into mineral soil (if it doesn't, restore the area and find another spot), yet it is not so deep that the pit will smother the fire. Tony carefully removes each piece of sod from the pit, keeping it as intact as possible. He places the sod in a cool place away from the traffic of the camp. Tomorrow morning, when Louisa gives her course on how to break camp and restore the area to its original state, these pieces of sod will be replaced. In the meantime, they will be given plenty of water to keep them moist and to nourish the few small plants growing in them.

Next, Tony scoops up mineral soil from the bottom of

the firepit and banks it around the pit's perimeter to avoid drying out any surrounding vegetation. This perimeter should also be kept moist.

Tony has collected only enough firewood for one fire; the largest pieces are no thicker than a silver dollar, the smallest are just twigs.

Tony tells the students that all wood used should be burned completely. Never put a "night log" on the fire that will remain half-burned in the morning; a charred log is a visible reminder that the area has been used as a camp.

Fires should be attended at all times, with a bucket of water nearby (NOLS uses large collapsible plastic jugs). Duff is flammable, and can smolder for days before emerging on the surface. The roots of trees can also burn, eventually emerging and igniting the tree. For this reason, firepits must not be dug in areas where the duff is over two or three inches deep. If you hit large roots, you must relocate. The sides of all firepits must be lined with mineral soil to minimize these risks.

To light the fire, Tony props the twigs against one another, building a small tepee in the middle of the firepit. He adds a bit of dry pine needles to make it more combustible, and then puts a match to it. As the small flame begins to take, he feeds the fire with more twigs, then gradually adds larger pieces of wood. As the fire burns brighter, Tony gives a few tips on building a fire in the rain.

"If your wood is damp, you can usually find dry twigs and pieces of bark at the base of large trees," he says. "If you can get a flame going, you can continue feeding it with twigs or pine cones and then add some of your damp wood, which is probably only damp on the surface."

In climates with a lot of precipitation, it can be more difficult. On Prince William Sound in Alaska, most of the firewood floats in on the tide and there are few dry twigs. Since the outer portion of the wood is wet, it is necessary to cut into the dry center of the wood, then whittle out small pieces, which will take the place of twigs. If you do find dry twigs in a very damp environment, it is a good idea to put some of them in a plastic bag and carry them with you to start your next fire.

The firepit is one of three types of fires NOLS builds, each type appropriate to specific settings.

When there is abundant mineral soil available without excavation (in sandy areas or old streambeds, for example) there is no need to disturb the topsoil by digging a firepit. Simply build your fire in the mineral soil.

Another good setting for a fire is on top of a flat rock. First spread a three-inch layer of mineral soil on top of the rock so that you will not scar the rock or harm the lichen, the colorful small plants often found growing on rocks. If you cannot find mineral soil on the surface of the ground (another place to look is at the base of uprooted trees), you can probably find it under the duff or sod. Be sure to use the minimum impact technique of cutting a small circle of sod, keeping the sod in one piece as you remove it from the hole, and watering the sod thoroughly, so it will not become dry.

During the fire-building demonstration, a student asks Tony what you should do if you come upon an old fire ring in the backcountry. The technique of ringing a fire with rocks is long outdated, because it leaves a significant scar on both the land and the rocks. Anyone who does much backpacking quite regularly runs into these reminders of a less sensitive time. If you come upon a fire ring, it may be best to use it rather than build another type of fire. This would concentrate your use into the pre-existing impact of the area. However, if a fire ring shows signs of recovery, such as plant recolonization, you should disassemble the fire ring and camouflage the area so that future camping in the area will be discouraged. If there is a stream or lake nearby, throw the blackened rocks in the water. If not, scatter them in various directions so that the impact will be diffused.

Safe cooking techniques which do not scar the land is the first requirement of a minimum-impact kitchen. A very close second is the need to keep a healthy kitchen. Begin by separating your cooking utensils into personal items and group items. Group items should be used only for cooking and serving, not for eating. Personal items should never be shared. This keeps bacteria from spreading to others. Your

FIREPITS

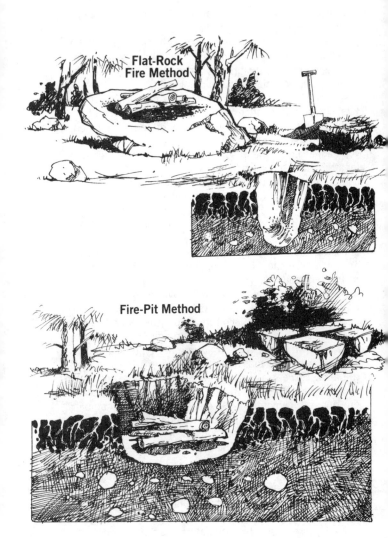

own germs probably won't make you sick, but they might make someone else sick.

Next, don't use any soap or detergent for dishwashing. This is not only environmentally sound, but also an important health precaution. It is hard to thoroughly rinse soap from utensils in the wilderness, and any residue which might be left can cause diarrhea. If you use hot water to clean your utensils regularly, a good standard of sanitation in the kitchen can be maintained without soap. We have found that a little grease left on a plate is far superior to the unpleasant aftereffects of soap.

Make sure you wash your dishes far away from streams or other water sources. After a meal, scrape and rinse utensils with hot water. If food is stuck to the bottom of a pot, fill the pot with water and let it stand overnight. By morning it will be much easier to clean. In bear country, however, it is wise to finish cleaning all of your dishes after each meal.

When an abrasive is needed, there are many good natural abrasives in the wilderness. Sand, gravel, pine cones, or pine branches on trees work fine, but be careful not to disturb the visual integrity of the campsite. These natural alternatives work as well as scouring pads, which often contain soap or chemicals, and which cannot be burned when you are through with them. Some people use unsoaped plastic scouring pads in the backcountry, but they need to be boiled frequently to kill any bacteria which might build up in the pad.

If after each meal you can get your cooking and eating utensils fairly clean, they will be in good condition to carry with you the next day. Then immediately before your next meal, sterilize your cooking gear in boiling water (bacteria can build up on dishes and utensils while you are carrying them in your backpack).

You need to plan your meals carefully to avoid having leftovers. Bite-sized scraps must be burned or carried out. They cannot be buried, since animals are likely to dig them up. Nor can they be left on the surface, where they would be unsightly and upset the natural food chain of the animals in the area.

Special care must be given to the disposal of crumbs, bits of food, and natural scouring pads. When you finish washing, pour the dirty dishwater—including bits of food and scouring debris—into the edge of your cooking fire. The water will seep back into the ground and any particles which remain can be burned to ash. Or you can dispose of this waste by spreading small amounts discreetly under numerous surrounding trees and bushes.

Catholes and Latrines

Louisa has built a latrine twenty-five yards beyond the tent in a level area of dense bush. The methods used to dispose of human waste in the backcountry are relatively simple, but proper disposal requires a thorough inventory of the local environment. The type of ground cover, amount of moisture in the area, size of one's group, local animal communities, and the level of human traffic in the immediate vicinity are all important factors. The goal is to use the methods most appropriate to your camping group and the environment around you.

The critical factors in the breakdown of human wastes are warmth, moisture, and bacterial action. In some ecosystems, the intensity of the interplay between these factors is greatest several inches below the ground. In other environments, the combination of moisture and sunlight on the surface yields the quickest decomposition. As with most backcountry skills, understanding the basic processes involved is more important than hard-and-fast rules.

During the summer, in the wet, remote backcountry of Prince William Sound, Alaska, NOLS's policy is for fecal matter to be left on the surface, where heat and moisture provide the action for rapid decomposition. In this way we avoid scarring the land; and since there are very few people in this area it is likely that the feces will decompose before another camper comes along.

In other remote areas, such as the desert of southern Utah, leaving fecal matter on the surface would be unthinkable. Here the hot sunlight and dry environment tend to preserve the feces rather than decompose it. Though this desert has few visitors, it is possible that a camper visiting the area would find the mummified remains of the excreta of a visitor who preceded him three or four years earlier.

When burying waste appears to be environmentally sound, you must choose between two methods: catholes and latrines. A cathole is dug by scooping out one shovel of dirt, probably no deeper than six inches. When you are finished, refill the hole with the dirt and camouflage the surface with needles, twigs, or other natural litter. Catholes should be dug out of sight of trails and well away from lakes, creeks, or other water sources.

Generally, the cathole method is used by individuals traveling alone or in small groups in areas of low use. Around a campsite, members of a small group should try to head off in different directions, so the impact of the catholes remains diffuse. An abundance of catholes in one locale is bound to catch the eye of later travelers.

For larger groups, especially in high-use areas, group latrines are the most environmentally sound disposal system. Latrines should be used for human wastes only. Toilet paper should be burned and materials that can't be reduced to ash, such as sanitary napkins (see "Women's Medical Concerns" in Chapter Seven), should be carried out in plastic bags.

To dig a latrine, find an area that is private and covered with a sturdy ground cover such as duff. Cut a circle of sod approximately one foot in diameter. Remove several pieces of sod intact and place them in a cool place away from traffic. The sod should be watered regularly so that any plants growing in it remain healthy. A latrine should be ten to twelve inches deep, which will ideally place the bottom on highly decayed vegetation or organic soil. If it is dug too deep, the feces will be deposited in mineral soil, slowing the bacterial action of decomposition. On the other hand, a shallow latrine is likely to be dug up by animals. Latrines should be elliptical in shape to make camouflaging easier, and used for only one day in order to prevent too high a concentration of waste. In selecting a latrine site for a second day, choose an area which does not require use of the same trail.

Latrines should be located close enough to camp for convenience and far enough away for privacy. Particular care must be taken to make sure the latrine is not located in a spot where it can drain into a water source.

Leave a spade at the latrine site, so that a small amount of dirt can be dropped on top of each deposit. This will help protect the area from flies, and also aid in the decomposition of the feces.

When the latrine is full to within three to four inches of the top, it should be filled in with dirt and the original

LATRINE

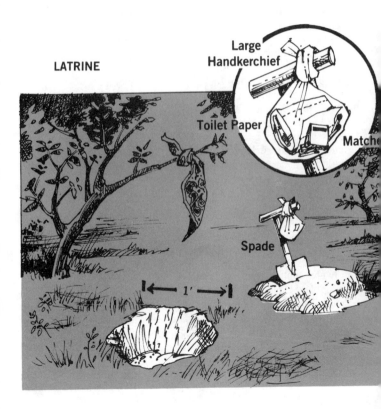

Large Handkerchief

Toilet Paper

Matches

Spade

1'

ground cover returned to the top of the hole. The area should be camouflaged so that no trace of human use is visible on the surface. Camouflaging techniques are described under "Breaking Camp," later in this chapter.

Whenever toilet paper is used at a latrine or cathole, it must be burned completely. In a septic tank toilet paper may break down into filaments, but in the mountains it is not biodegradable. Many people assume that toilet paper is a necessity; however, there are many adequate natural substitutes. Moss or leaves are excellent for this purpose, although most people don't believe it until they give it a try. Snow also works well. Using a natural substitute is a favor to the environment, but judgment must be used. In some areas, using toilet paper and burning it is preferable to depleting an area of moss. You must analyze the immediate needs and size of your group, and the capacity of the local ecosystem.

Disposing of waste in the backcountry in an environmentally sound way requires careful consideration. You must always remember the basic process of decomposition. Sometimes you must weigh basic health needs against potential damage to the land. You must also consider unsightly remnants that other hikers may come upon. One good way to lessen the impact of waste disposal around a campsite is to take care of this requirement as much as possible while traveling during the day. A simple cathole in a remote area off the trail will probably never be noticed by other backcountry travelers, and the feces will rapidly decompose.

GOOD WATER, GOOD HEALTH

"One of the most difficult concepts to get across," Doug says, "is the importance of protecting water sources in the wilderness. Everyone understands the concept in the abstract, but there is a strong tendency to camp too close to water." Why? Because it is convenient in the short run. But it is also very likely that the water will become polluted. There aren't many pure water sources left in the wilderness, and it will be very inconvenient in the future if we have to carry all of our water. To prevent contamination, where practical, NOLS camps at least 200 feet from any water source.

Lakes and streams are obvious sources of water, but don't overlook melted snow or the water left by a storm in the potholes of rocks. They can be adequate for both drinking and washing.

Livestock in an area may mean bad water. If you are camping near range land, you should scout for cattle or sheep droppings near the water source. If horses are using an area, make sure you camp on the upstream side of any trail.

When camping in the desert, remember that the few existing water sources tend to become highly concentrated centers for animal life. The presence of a campsite near a desert water source will disrupt a complex set of animal routines.

Once you have found a good water source, protect it from pollution. That means learning how to maintain a high standard of personal hygiene, which can contribute to the physical and psychological health of an expedition, while using very little soap. Even the best biodegradable soaps will pollute the water. They should never be used directly in a fresh water source.

In most cases, healthy standards can be maintained without using soap. The best way to wash clothing is simply to rinse the salt and dirt out and hang it in the wind and sun to dry. It is worth noting that when soap is used to wash clothing in cold, hard water, there is usually a residue which remains in the fabric that can cause skin irritation. To bathe in the outdoors, simply remove your clothing and walk into the water. This will remove sweat and dust and can be remarkably invigorating.

When you need a more thorough bath and soap is called for, be very careful to keep the soap away from the water source. Go down to the water, fill several large containers, then wet yourself in the lake or stream. Haul the containers of water about two hundred feet from shore—if possible, uphill—to an area where the soap will not harm the vegetation or percolate back into the water table. Lather up, then rinse thoroughly with the water from the containers. With all of the soap removed from your body, go back to your original water source for a final rinse.

A similar method should be used when washing face, hands, or feet with soap. By keeping the soap a long way

WASHING IN CAMP

from the water supply, it will degrade and dissipate before it can seep back into the water table.

Never wash your cooking utensils or your clothing directly in a water source. At NOLS we carry a collapsible plastic container so that an adequate supply of water for these purposes can be kept within the camping area.

After the students have received a thorough introduction to the techniques of minimum-impact camping, Doug divides them into cooking groups (four people to a group) and sends them out to find a good campsite. As they get up to go, Doug offers a suggestion: "Once you have found a spot that looks safe and comfortable, make a visual survey of the area before you begin unpacking your gear. You should get a general feel for how the space is divided, and for the textures and surfaces of the landscape. A strong image of the campsite as it existed when you arrived will be very helpful when you begin to break camp and restore the area to its natural condition."

He concludes the afternoon's class with some final advice on campsite selection: "After a fairly hard hike, it may seem like a lot of work to set up camp right. But if you work a little harder now, you will be a lot more comfortable being lazy later."

BREAKING CAMP

The next morning, the rays of the sun gleam above the horizon around six-thirty A.M. They illuminate the sheer cliffs at the far end of the valley; the massive rocks glow pink as if fired from some hidden source within. As the timbered hillside begins to warm, the silence is broken by a shrill sound from the middle of the meadow. A red-tailed hawk circles high above, her call a grating, slurring cry. Perhaps she has a nest in the trees. Perhaps she is angered by the presence of the backpackers near her meadow. With broad wings fully extended, she veers from updraft to updraft, angrily screaming at the world below.

For some in the camp, who are up and beginning to

collect firewood, the sound of the hawk enlivens their morning. For others, deep in their sleeping bags, it is an unwanted alarm.

Soon each campsite is experimenting with its own version of breakfast. For most it is granola with milk, and a cup of hot coffee. A few of the more experienced campers try their hands at pancakes. Over the next several days there will be a number of classes in baking, which will make hot cinnamon rolls and peach coffee cakes a real possibility for morning meals; but that is a story for another chapter.

Since this is the second morning out, the schedule is fairly loose, giving campers a chance to get used to their new cooking equipment. By nine, most have finished breakfast, and it is time for their major class of the morning, how to break camp.

Louisa has gathered the group at Doug's campsite to demonstrate the preparation for breaking camp which can begin the night before. After your evening meal organize three groups of gear: items you will need for that evening, the next morning, and on the trail. Then pack up all remaining gear. Next, pack the gear you will need on the trail the following day so that it is conveniently located in your pack and pockets. The other two piles of gear will be packed in the morning. Before you go to bed, soak your firepit and any surrounding duff with water. Then fill your container with the water you will need for breakfast. Taking these steps the previous night will save a considerable amount of time—time which you will need to camouflage your campsite to its original state and still begin hiking in the cool of the morning.

"On most mornings when we are planning to travel," Louisa says, "we will want to get on the trail by eight-thirty, so cooking will be done on stoves, even if you used a wood fire the night before." Using a fire in the morning can cause long delays while you wait for the coals to burn to ash. Fires also require constant attention, whereas a stove allows you to accomplish other tasks while keeping only an occasional watch.

In good weather, hang your sleeping bag and pad out to

air as soon as you get up. In bad weather, stuff them into their sacks immediately. A logical division of chores is for one person to cook breakfast while the other drops and packs the shelter. Once the cook has the stove lit and the water going, he can finish packing his own backpack. Getting all equipment packed and out of the way makes it much easier to do camouflage work on the campsite. Obviously, cooking items will be in use, but they are usually the last things packed anyway.

With all but a minimum of gear packed, you can relax, have a good breakfast, and finalize your planning for the day's hike.

After you have finished breakfast and cleaned and packed your cooking gear, it is time to begin restoration work on the campsite. There are four major areas of impact with which you must deal: the sleeping site, the fire site, the latrine site, and traffic lanes.

Even when using a fly, tent stakes are often necessary, and they can have a major impact on the sleeping area. Fill in the holes and replace any rocks or deadfall you may have moved. Look around for scuff marks and trampling and clean them up. A light coat of ground cover, taken discreetly from under a tree and scattered lightly over these areas, will help them to blend in. Remember that your goal is to leave the campsite in its natural condition.

Your cooking area has probably had the hardest wear of any part of the campsite. If you have used a fire, your camouflage work must be done with great care. All coals should be burned to ash or crushed. Make sure the ashes are out by feeling them with your bare hand. Then take the ashes into the woods and scatter them in all directions. You should not have collected more wood than you needed, but if you have, scatter it also. Diffusion is a major strategy of minimum-impact camping; ashes and extra wood should be spread lightly so that they will not be noticed, or cause a major change in the soil chemistry.

If you have been using a firepit, drown the ashes and coals, scatter all remaining ashes, and return most of the mineral soil you removed back to the hole. Water it well, then place the pieces of sod back in the hole exactly as they were. With the remaining soil, fill in any gaps and, using a trowel, crosscut all edges so that plant recolonization can occur between the pieces. Water the area well, particularly all the edges of the sod and adjacent duff, which may have become quite dry. Now look at the surrounding ground cover, and camouflage the top of the firepit to match. Use duff, aspen leaves, pine cones, whatever it takes to restore the surface to its natural state.

Always be careful not to over-camouflage. A big pile of duff is a sure giveaway that there is something underneath. Good camouflaging is an art that takes a subtle touch.

If you have built a flat rock fire, scatter the ashes and return the mineral soil to where you got it. If you had to dig up any squares of sod to find the mineral soil, replace them and, again, water thoroughly. Rinse the rock with water, wash off any remaining residue of soil, and landscape the entire area.

Latrines are restored in a manner similar to firepits, except that you should obviously not scatter the contents of the hole. Simply replace the missing sod, crosscut the edges, water well, and landscape.

The paths taken between the various areas of your campsite have undoubtedly experienced noticeable wear. Look for scuff marks and disturbed rocks, which need restoration or camouflage. There is little you can do about trampled grass; that is one reason camping in meadows should be avoided.

If you have camped on snow, remember that your imprints will be apparent to the next person who comes through the area. By reshoveling the snow around your sleeping and cooking areas, the large imprints will not be as noticeable.

After their class, the students return to their campsites and begin putting into practice their lessons in minimum-impact camping. A few will be tempted to take short cuts, but they will soon realize that their short cuts will be quite visible when they are through. Throughout a five-week course, it is not uncommon for instructors to take students to previous years' campsites. As students' awareness of their environment grows, they can spot the subtle signs of

impact even at a carefully restored campsite. Plants growing over a firepit affected by a dose of ash in the soil will
often return in a slightly different color than the surrounding vegetation. Well-camouflaged latrines will sometimes
sink slightly lower than the rest of the ground. Most people
can't tell the difference; they see the pristine wilderness.
But the educated eye can spot this reminder that "no impact" is a worthy but difficult goal.

When all of the campsites have been restored as closely
as possible to everyone's remembrance of the stand of
lodgepole pine they entered yesterday afternoon, they
move their packs down the hill, outside the camp area.
Then small groups of students join each instructor on a
tour of the site. The big tasks, restoring firepits and latrines, are usually done well the first time through, although over-camouflaging is often a problem.

What is usually missed are small pieces of debris, like
bits of monofilament or tea bag strings, which can be spotted quite easily once all equipment is removed from the
area. We have found that the most common type of trash
left in sleeping areas is the clear backings and strings from
Band-Aids, moleskin, and other first-aid items. If you have
used any of these, look around carefully, pick them up,
and place them in a small plastic trash bag which you
should carry in your pack. If you put small items of trash
in your pockets, they tend to fall out as you put your hands
in and out of your pockets throughout the day.

The question which everyone must ask as he tours a
former campsite is "Does it look the same?" Have you
minimized and camouflaged your impact so that in an
hour, if another person walks through this area, the raw
perfection of nature will be present?

As Doug and several students make a final walk around
the perimeter of a campsite, the sun is edging higher in
the sky and the meadow below is alive with soft breezes.
The harsh, steep cliffs across the valley contrast with the
delicate white bog orchids on the valley floor. The cold
stream rushes across its shallow pebbled bottom, then
turns and etches a placid arc through clumps of willow and
green fields graced by fireweed.

"It looks just like a picture postcard," one of the students says in awe.

"No," Doug responds. "I think that picture postcard must look just like this meadow."

Chapter **Two**

How to Dress for the Backcountry

THE HUNDREDS of students who each summer take a National Outdoor Leadership School course in the Rocky Mountains are dressed and equipped from their underwear out at the NOLS "Lumberyard," a collection of white-washed sheds and warehouses in Lander, Wyoming. At the center of this logistics operation is the NOLS issue room, a cavernous enclosure filled with more than 300,000 pieces of outdoor gear.

Hard-driving stereo rhythms quicken the pulse this warm July morning as students from two NOLS courses are is-sued clothing and equipment for their expeditions. Bright shafts of sunlight pour through small paned windows, re-vealing a room of bustling activity. In a far corner a student unzips a pair of wool pants and reaches for a larger size, having just learned that he needs to be able to comfortably tuck the tails of two wool shirts inside the waistband. In a brightly lit alcove off the main room, Don Webber, NOLS resident boot expert, looks for a size 12 boot as young students wait for a fitting. Behind Don rises an inventory of over 1,300 pairs of boots, their colorful boxes stacked floor to ceiling, a graphic wallpaper of well-known boot brands: Fabiano, Lowa, Trappeur, Asolo, Kastinger, Vasque. Against the issue room's back wall, wide wooden shelves hold layers of green and blue sleeping bags, stored unrolled, out of their sacks, so as not to damage the loft of their insulation. A woman climbs into one of the bags, pulling the drawstring tight above her head as her instruc-tor checks around her feet, making sure she has enough room to sleep comfortably. In the glare of an open doorway, Tod Schimelpfenig, NOLS equipment manager, inspects the fit of a student's backpack as another student asks him how to fit his gaiters.

"On days like this, loud music and coffee keep us going," laughs Tod. But the fast pace and constant beat do not diminish the care and thoroughness given to each answer, each inspection. For the next five weeks, these students will have to depend on the clothing and equipment issued today to satisfy basic needs: safety, comfort, shelter, and warmth.

Tod understands the requirements of wilderness living from the deserts of Baja to the glaciers of Alaska; he orders and maintains the gear issued in NOLS courses in Wyoming and at NOLS branch schools around the world. He knows that personal experience will answer many of the questions which come his way daily from students receiving their first lessons in dressing for the backcountry. With experience you discover how your body adjusts to the changing conditions of the wilderness. Do you require an additional layer of clothing when the sun goes behind a cloud? What type of hat is most comfortable when you are carrying a pack? What weight of boot should you buy?

Tod also knows that a competent outdoor person must rely on certain fundamental criteria if he or she is to understand the significant progress currently being made in the field of outdoor clothing, and distinguish that progress from increasingly sophisticated advertising hype. "First," says Tod, "you need to understand how your body functions, how it reacts to the ever-changing conditions you are likely to encounter in the backcountry. Then, you need an introduction to the basic qualities of fabrics used in outdoor clothing." With this understanding, you, like Tod, can select clothing for the arid plains of Kenya or a blizzard-swept Alaskan glacier. More important, you can walk into any backpacking or sporting goods store and make an educated purchase which will serve you well.

HEAT LOSS: HOW IT WORKS

The knowledgeable outdoor person understands that clothing does not provide warmth; clothing helps to regulate the loss of heat which the body produces. This heat, which is created by the metabolizing of the food we eat, leaves the body in five different ways: respiration, radiation, conduction, convection, and evaporation. A fundamental understanding of these five components of heat loss is more important than all the fancy outdoor clothing money can buy.

Respiration heat loss occurs when cool, incoming air is warmed in the lungs and exhaled. Avoid heavy, labored breathing to minimize this loss. You may have experimented with controlling respiration heat loss on a very cold day by breathing through a scarf or tunneled hood.

Radiative heat loss is caused by the escape of infrared radiation from our bodies. It is easily minimized for most of the body by wearing insulating fabrics or some of the new radiant heat barriers, aluminized fabrics that reflect the radiation back to the body.

Conductive heat loss, which occurs when contact is made between your body and a cooler surface, can be minimized by not standing or sitting on the cold ground when resting, especially on snow or rock. Placing an Ensolite pad, or even this book, under you can limit conductive loss.

Convection occurs when body heat warms the air adjacent to the body; that air then rises, and moves away from the body. An important element in dressing for the backcountry is trapping that air around the body.

Trapping air around the body is complicated by the fifth process of heat loss, evaporation. Evaporative heat loss occurs when you perspire. When the body is warm and sends blood rushing toward the surface to cool, the pores of the skin open, emitting water. When the water evaporates in the outside air, it cools the skin. The evaporation of this water from the body presents one of the most difficult problems in dressing for any type of strenuous outdoor activity. How do we trap the heat escaping from the body through conduction, convection, and radiation without trapping the moisture which our body is producing through perspiration?

The solution to this problem comes in two parts. First,

let's see how best to trap warm air around the body. Then we will explore methods to minimize the presence of moisture in that trapped air.

In warm-blooded animals, cold air causes the blood vessels near the skin to constrict, keeping the warm blood away from the chilled exterior in order to help retain the heat of the body's central core. In animals covered with hair, such as bears, constricting of the blood vessels triggers a muscular reaction which pulls their body hair, causing it to stand up; as the hair bristles, air is trapped within it. The natural heat radiating from the animal's body then warms this trapped air, transforming it into a layer of warm insulation.

Human beings do not have a natural layer of insulating hair. When cold air causes blood vessels near the surface of our skin to constrict, all we get are goose bumps. If warmth is not forthcoming, we begin to shiver, a reflex to get warm. To stay warm, we must supply artificial layers of insulation—clothing.

The outdoor clothing issued by Tod and his co-workers in the NOLS issue room is designed to complement the body's built-in thermostat. Rather than padding the body with heavy material, we dress in loose-fitting layers of clothing which create many insulating pockets of dead air around the body. These air pockets are then warmed by our own body heat.

Trapping and warming air around the body is only part of the process of dressing for the outdoors. Staying dry can also contribute to warmth and comfort, and that can be a bit more tricky. Moisture comes from two directions: from the outside, from cold rain and snow; and from the inside, from perspiration, which initially is at body temperature but can quickly cool and chill the skin. A coated waterproof garment is an easy solution to the first type of moisture. Its seal prevents the absorption of water, thus protecting you from snow or rain. However, if while wearing a coated waterproof garment you are hiking strenuously, the garment's seal will prevent your perspiration from escaping. The real danger develops when the exertion stops, when you sit down to rest and the dampness trapped on your skin's surface cools and begins to draw heat from your body's central core.

There are a number of ways to avoid this situation. First, you should make sure that any waterproof garment you wear is loose-fitting so that fresh air can ventilate around the body, helping to keep your skin dry. Second, in periods of heavy precipitation, you may choose to avoid strenuous exercise while wearing a waterproof garment. Third, you may choose to wear one of the new "breathable" waterproof fabrics (discussed later in this chapter), which prevent precipitation from getting in, but allow perspiration to escape. Or, fourth, if rain or snow is falling moderately and you need to continue hiking, it may be that the dampness from the precipitation will not get you as wet as the perspiration which would build up under a waterproof garment. As long as you are wearing fabrics which maintain their insulating value when wet, you may become damp, but not cold. These decisions, which are commonly required in the backcountry, must be based on a fundamental knowledge of the fabrics and insulators used in outdoor clothing.

FABRICS AND INSULATORS

A critical element in regulating heat loss from the body is the type of fabric you choose to wear. Will that fabric provide good insulation for warmth and good ventilation for dryness?

There are four conditions—hot, cold, wet, dry, and their various combinations—that are found in the natural environment we experience in the backcountry. The insulating and ventilating properties of a given fabric or fill material will determine how well we can moderate our own body temperature under these conditions. Some materials are more effective against cold or wind. Others are more comfortable to wear in the heat. Some fabrics absorb water, while others repel it. Loosely woven fabrics ventilate through their fibers; most tightly woven fabrics do not. In order to create a good layering system of insulation and ventilation around our body, we need to choose the correct fabrics and insulators for specific weather conditions.

An understanding of the materials used in the outdoors requires a familiarity with some textile terms. The term *warp* refers to the strands of thread which are held tightly on the weaving loom. The *fill* is the threads that are woven at a right angle to the warp. Many fabrics such as nylon and taffeta will be described with thread counts of their warp and fill. A 103 × 84 thread count simply means that there are 103 strands of thread per inch in the warp and 84 strands in the fill.

Another term you will often come across is *denier,* which refers to the weight of the thread. A denier of thread is equal to .05 gram per 450 meters. Most cloth used for outdoor clothing or equipment ranges from 20 to 600 denier. Seventy-denier thread is used in taffetas and ripstop nylon, 200-denier thread in oxford cloth, and 400-denier in pack cloth. The heavier the thread, the stronger the fabric and the fewer strands per inch in the weave.

We will consider three categories of fabrics and insulators: insulating fabrics, insulating fills, and shell fabrics.

Insulating Fabrics

Insulating layers, including the layer of material next to the skin, should first be judged on their breathability, their ability to "wick" moisture away from the body. Perspiration comes out of the body as water vapor. This vapor must be able to pass through the material into the outside air. All fabrics absorb, or soak up, at least some moisture. In a fabric suitable for an insulating layer, the fabric may absorb, but the *fibers* of the fabric should neither absorb nor adsorb (allow moisture to cling to them). If the fabric pulls the moisture toward it, and the water does not cling to it, then vapor pressure and heat, which are greater near the body than in the outside air, will "wick" the moisture through the fabric. If an insulating fabric cannot wick moisture away, then the body will quickly become clammy and wet during any type of physical exertion.

Wool is the most common insulating fabric used to outfit

NOLS students. The wool fiber, which is rough and uneven, traps air to provide insulation, yet the fabric remains
"breathable"—that is, ventilating air can pass in and out
between the fibers. Because raw wool fibers contain lanolin, a natural oil found in sheep's wool, they do not absorb
water; instead, any moisture on the skin is wicked away
from the body between the fibers of the fabric. This makes
possible one of wool's most advantageous qualities: it continues to provide warm insulation even when wet.

Several layers of lightweight wool will give you more flexibility than one layer of heavy wool. NOLS routinely issues
wool pants, shirts, socks, hats, and, in colder climates,
wool sweaters and underwear.

High-quality new wool is significantly warmer and absorbs far less water than old or reprocessed wool, in which
the lanolin has worn from the fiber. When buying a wool
garment, be sure to check the label: "virgin wool" is the
best.

A weakness of wool is that it is vulnerable to abrasion;
this makes it particularly unsuitable for rock climbing.
NOLS places patches made of a wool/synthetic blend at
vulnerable points on wool clothing, such as shirt elbows
and the seats of pants, to ensure a long life for the garment. The tighter the weave of the wool, the more abrasion-resistant it is.

Cotton, for many, is more comfortable against the body
than wool. It is also more abrasion-resistant. But when you
are headed into the backcountry where cold, damp weather
is expected, remember that cotton is quick to absorb
water, and when it does, you are in trouble. Unlike wool,
cotton fibers will absorb and retain moisture, leaving you
covered with water-soaked clothing with no insulating
value. Wearing cotton next to the body while exercising
strenuously probably ensures a perspiration-soaked inner
layer of clothing. In a cold climate or in high wind, this can
lead to chills and hypothermia, a severe lowering of the
body's temperature that can be fatal if not attended to
properly.

If you are wearing wet cotton in the backcountry and the
weather gets chilly, remove it immediately and replace it
with dry clothing, preferably made of wool.

Pile was developed about twenty years ago, and was first used as a wool substitute in Scandinavia among fishermen of the North Atlantic. Since pile fiber absorbs little moisture, it has proven to be ideal for cold, damp climates. When it becomes wet, pile maintains much of its insulating ability. As with wool, it can usually be dried by body heat alone.

Pile is created by blowing slivers of fibers at a right angle into the coarse knit pattern of a backing material. A variety of fibers, including polyester, acrylic, wool, nylon, and various blends, can be used in this knitting process.

A major advantage of pile for cold-weather camping is that it is lighter than wool or synthetic fill fabrics. Compared to wool, pile offers equivalent warmth at half the weight. As is often true in this type of equation, however, the heavier fabric, wool, is more durable.

Polypropylene is another synthetic fiber which is a good wool substitute. Polypropylene has the same ability as wool to wick water away from the body, and it is often used as a long-underwear fabric for cold-weather use. Lighter than wool, and similar to pile in appearance, polypropylene makes a particularly good undergarment for people who are allergic to wool.

Insulating Fills

A fill material is a loose insulator which is sandwiched between two layers of tightly woven fabric. There are two categories of insulating fills: *down,* or natural fills, and *synthetic fills.*

Down, the soft fluffy material from beneath the outer feathers of geese and ducks, has been keeping humans warm for years. Down particles adhere lightly to each other, forming many tiny air pockets. The trapped air is warmed by body heat, and since down is breathable, the body's moisture can escape.

Because it is extremely lightweight and naturally available, down has long been one of the most popular insulators for outdoor clothing. However, down has a major drawback: when it becomes wet, all of its insulating value is lost. It becomes heavy with retained water, and useless.

When there is a possibility of rain, snow, or heavy perspiration, it is dangerous to rely on down as a major layer of insulation.

As down has become increasingly expensive in recent years, the synthetic insulators, created in the laboratory, have become increasingly efficient in terms of their warmth-per-weight ratio, and attractive to the budget-conscious backpacker. The goal of laboratory technicians is to create a synthetic down. That goal, although not yet accomplished, seems to be on the horizon. The products they're producing now are seriously competing with down in the insulation marketplace.

A major advantage of the synthetics is that they are not absorbent and thus, unlike down, maintain their insulating abilities while wet. Their major drawback is that their thermal efficiency—that is, their insulating warmth-per-weight ratio—is lower than that of down.

Synthetic fill is manufactured in layers of matted material called batts. The fibers bond together in such a way as to create tiny air pockets within the batts which trap the body's warmth.

The synthetic fills are made from various forms of polyester. The most popular types currently on the market are DuPont's Hollofil II and Quallofil, Celanese's PolarGuard, and 3M's Thinsulate. Undoubtedly in coming months and years other synthetics will be introduced which will continue the progression toward a synthetic down.

Shell Fabrics

Shell or outer-layer fabrics have traditionally been divided into two categories: noncoated and coated. Noncoated shell fabrics are usually made from a tight-weave material and are designed to provide good wind resistance. Fabrics are coated to make them water-resistant. The most common coatings are urethane (cheaper and lighter) and neoprene (more expensive, more effective, but heavier). These coatings seal the material so that it cannot breathe; moisture cannot pass through the fabric from either direction.

Waterproof coatings must be administered with high heat by special machinery and are usually applied at the factory. However, most equipment manufacturers provide small seam-sealing kits with their products. The owner of a coated garment should periodically reseal the seams, which tend to lose their repellent properties more rapidly than the rest of the garment.

Nylon is the most versatile fabric for the outdoors, and the fabric which is most commonly coated for rain and snow protection. Nylon is particularly useful as an outer garment because it is lightweight and, if it is uncoated and gets wet, it dries quickly. It takes abrasion well, makes an excellent windbreaker, and is stronger than cotton for equivalent weight.

If cut, however, nylon will fray easily; should this happen, melt the frayed edge or use a nylon repair tape to stop the process. Ripstop is a special type of nylon in which a stronger thread which can stop a rip is integrated into the weave.

Synthetic blends are often found in shell fabrics because they combine the better traits of more than one fabric. The blends are created either at the spinning stage, mixing two types of fibers together to form a blended yarn, or during the weaving process, using one type of fiber for the warp and another type for the fill. The most common synthetic blend in outdoor clothing is 60/40 cloth. The weave of this fabric combines nylon and cotton threads, providing additional strength and wind resistance. Since 60/40 cloth is already a heavy fabric, it is seldom coated for waterproofing. The fabric is more water-repellent than cotton, but unless it is treated with a waterproofing compound, it should not be used as rain gear because it absorbs water, which in very cold weather will quickly freeze.

Stretch blends such as spandex are becoming increasingly popular in the ski-clothing industry because of their durability and fit. However, the skin-tight fit eliminates the insulating space needed to provide warmth; on extended wilderness trips your cold body will be a constant reminder of your vanity.

A recent development which has broken the traditional

division between coated and noncoated shell fabrics is the new waterproof and breathable fabrics such as Gore-Tex and Klimate. They are two of the biggest success stories of the new "miracle" synthetic outdoor fabrics introduced during the 1970s. Until their introduction waterproof gear, made of plastics, coated nylon, or rubberized cloth, did not breathe.

The key to Gore-Tex and Klimate is a porous film laminated between inner and outer layers of fabric. The microscopic pores (nine billion per square inch) discriminate between water as vapor (individual molecules of water) and water as liquid (hundreds of thousands of water molecules bonded together in each drop). Water in vapor form can pass through the pores, which are about 700 times larger than a single water molecule, but as liquid, in drops thousands of times larger than a pore of the fabric, water is filtered out.

Gore-Tex and Klimate protect from both wind and rain, so they may reduce the number of additional pieces of equipment needed for different weather conditions. Manufacturers are now using them for parkas, gaiters, sleeping bags, tents, and a wide variety of other outdoor products.

BACKCOUNTRY CLOTHING

It used to be that a few respected companies, which fully understood the requirements of backcountry travel, produced high-quality outdoor gear for sale to a specialized market. But that has changed radically. "The simple truth is," says Tod, "that in the last three or four years, outdoor clothing has become fashion."

He is quick to point out that many companies still make good backcountry apparel. However, now that the "outdoor look" has become fashionable, some companies that formerly catered to a specific audience of outdoor enthusiasts recognize that a lot more money can be made in the mass market, a market vulnerable to the whims of style. Tod, who attends three or four huge outdoor equipment shows a year, recalls one particularly bizarre incident at a winter sports gear show in Las Vegas.

"It is strange enough to go looking for wilderness gear at the Tropicana Hotel," Tod says. "You walk past the slot machines and plastic palm trees into a convention center with a large sign reading, 'Everything for the Outdoors.' " He was looking for the booth of a well-known manufacturer who has produced quality parkas for many years. NOLS has tested one of their parkas in the field and found it to be excellent. Tod finally spotted the parka, worn by a man dancing to disco music on a small stage. A nearby M.C. happily chattered, "This year on campus, the outdoor look is in, and what will make a bigger splash with the coeds than our waterproof, 60/40 cloth parka? Its sleek, no-pockets look is a classic for the 1980s, perfect outerwear for the boulevard or the backcountry."

"Well," Tod reflects, "I remember seeing that and thinking, 'With no pockets, where the hell do you put your compass and goggles?' It burned me up! The only reason they took those pockets off is so that they could create this year's fantasy, which has to be different from last year's fantasy. And that," he says, "is what fashion is doing to good, practical backpacking and mountaineering clothing."

You can find good gear to buy today; in fact, the development of a mass market has encouraged breakthroughs in material and design. But the hype tends to blur the real mission of dressing and equipping yourself safely and sensibly for the outdoors. Many seasoned buyers often feel confused.

Even with a basic understanding of the body's temperature control system and of the various properties of outdoor fabrics, if you are a beginning backpacker, NOLS recommends that you acquire your clothing as cheaply as possible. Remember, with a little experience you will have a much better idea of what is needed. Most of the clothing described in this chapter can probably be found in your closet. Or you can borrow it from a friend. And don't overlook the Goodwill, Salvation Army, or military surplus stores. They are excellent outlets for inexpensive wool clothing, a basic component of your first wilderness wardrobe. Of course, if you have the budget, you can easily translate each layer of clothing we describe into an expensive piece of quality apparel. There is nothing nicer than to treat yourself to well-crafted clothing that can last a lifetime. Just make sure you thoroughly understand what you need before you invest.

Now let us consider, from the skin out, the clothing which makes up each layer of protection.

Against the Skin

While every layer counts, the clothing that lies against your skin is a crucial, and often misunderstood, part of your backcountry clothing system. It is particularly important if you are planning to travel under severe weather conditions.

Cotton shorts and T-shirts are comfortable against the skin, easy to wash and dry out, and lightweight. But cotton is not the material of choice in cold and wet weather, when wool and synthetics provide better protection from the cold. For summer camping, particularly in dry areas, cotton may work fine as an inner layer.

Cotton undershorts can prevent chafing of the inner thighs, particularly when worn under woolen pants. Loose boxer-type shorts are recommended for both men and women because they do not hamper circulation. On extended trips, cotton shorts are also important for cleanliness, since they can be rinsed easily and dry quickly. Some people prefer cotton gym shorts worn as undershorts.

Those accustomed to wearing cotton undershirts make them a regular part of their backcountry wardrobe. They are light to pack and easy to wash; in a warm climate they can protect the shoulders from sunburn and provide a comfortable layer between the pack and the back. However, a lightweight, long-sleeved cotton shirt is a more useful piece of clothing. It can serve the same functions as a T-shirt, but its sleeves can be rolled up or down and its buttons can be adjusted to give you different degrees of ventilation as the temperature changes. Always remember that, before you get wet and cold, you should remove your inner layer of cotton.

If you find that you are often cold in the outdoors, you might consider including some type of long underwear in your layering system. But make that choice carefully; most long johns on the market are heavy to carry and not particularly functional for hiking. Always make sure that long johns fit loosely enough to provide unhindered body movement and plenty of circulation around the muscles. A common modification of long johns is to take only the bottoms and use a soft wool sweater as an inner layer on the upper body.

A union suit (one-piece, full-body underwear) gives you fewer layering options than separate pieces; it also is awkward to put on and take off. One alternative to a full union suit is to cut off and hem the sleeves and legs, thus providing warmth for the body's core while allowing free movement for your arms and legs.

Avoid long underwear with a high percentage of cotton. Presumably you take long underwear because you expect cold weather; under such conditions, a layer of wet, cold cotton next to the skin is an invitation to hypothermia. NOLS has found that polypropylene provides the best insulation for the least weight. Wool too will wick water to the outer surface and leave your body dry and warm.

Fishnet underwear is only useful and convenient in colder weather when it can be comfortably covered by another layer—it retains little heat when used alone.

Each person should experiment individually to see if long underwear is a practical solution for an inner layer of clothing. Since most long underwear is not comfortable for hiking or strenuous physical exertion, NOLS usually limits its use to winter, and to the late fall or early spring, when an extra layer of clothing is often required around camp in the early morning or late evening.

Middle-Layer Clothing

When you shop for clothes to wear around town, a variety of synthetic fabrics are available, offering permanent creases and other modern-day wonders. But when you dress for the backcountry, your middle layer of clothing is likely to alternate between two basic natural materials, wool and cotton, with synthetic blends making only an occasional appearance for reinforcement and special uses such as climbing. Your choice will depend on the outside temperature, the kind of activity you pursue, and your body's way of responding to these stimuli.

In warm weather, you will often want your legs to be bare. Short pants come in many styles, from everyday cutoffs to expensive mountaineering khakis with Velcro pocket flaps. If you have other camping clothes to protect you from inclement weather—wool for warmth and some type of wind and rain protection—then whatever shorts you have around the house, just so they are loose-fitting, should work fine. Recently, gym shorts and nylon running shorts have become popular. They are light to pack, comfortable to wear, and can double as underwear and swimsuit. Most people, however, prefer to have plenty of pockets. One problem with wearing shorts, particularly in the early summer, is the possibility of sunburning your exposed legs. Mosquitoes can also quickly encourage a return to long pants.

In hot, dry weather, or while hiking or climbing through thick brush, lightweight, full-length cotton pants may be comfortable and functional; they also provide protection from sun and mosquitoes. But if you are backpacking in an area that gets damp and cool, cotton pants could be just extra weight in your pack.

Jeans, the most popular cotton garment in the United States, are a poor choice for hiking and camping. Their tight fit usually prevents ease of movement, and anyone who has ever been caught in a storm wearing jeans knows that once they are wet, they dry very slowly and chill you through evaporative heat loss. In cold, wet weather, jeans are downright dangerous.

Wearing a pair of shorts with nylon wind pants as a backup in case you get into scratchy underbrush or cooler temperatures is a functional solution to protecting your lower torso in summer weather.

Wool pants are an important component of most backcountry wardrobes. They should be loose-fitting to guarantee freedom of movement and ventilation, and large enough at the waist so that two or three shirts can be tucked in comfortably.

Tightly woven military-surplus wool pants have been serving NOLS well for years. They are inexpensive and wear well. We reinforce the seat with a wool-and-synthetic patch to ensure longer wear. You can also add a drawstring at the bottom of the legs so that they can be tied up like knickers. Although not as stylish, our thrift-shop convertible models can provide the lower leg with the extra warmth which knickers lack.

Controlling the temperature of your torso, particularly as the external conditions change from hot to cold or from dry to wet, is essential to comfort and safety in the backcountry. On a warm day, a long-sleeved cotton shirt with a button front provides the ability to react to slight temperature variations as well as protection from sun and mosquitoes. If the weather suddenly changes to cool and damp, however, don't make the mistake of putting a wool shirt over a cotton shirt. For warmth and ventilation in wet weather, the wool insulator must be worn next to your skin.

A light- or medium-weight, long-sleeved wool shirt is basic clothing in most backcountry settings. Wool can keep you warm, even when wet, and can protect you from mild winds. If it gets hot, you can roll up the sleeves or unbutton the front. If it gets cold, you can put on an additional wool shirt over the first, providing another layer of insulating air space to maintain your natural warmth. Wool shirts should be roomy, to ensure ease of movement, and long enough so they don't easily pull out of your pants.

On any outdoor shirt, whether wool or cotton, pockets on the front will always come in handy. It is a good idea to have flaps with buttons, snaps, or Velcro on the top of the pocket to ensure safe storage of personal items.

Big wool sweaters are very fashionable, but ski fashion and backcountry comfort should not be confused. Wool shirts provide the same insulation as wool sweaters, and also allow you to regulate temperature by adjusting the openings of the cuffs and shirt front.

As a second layer of insulation, a loosely knit wool

sweater can be useful, particularly in weather that hovers in the 40s. The longer the sweater the better. NOLS often combines two sweaters, cutting off the bottom of one sweater and sewing it onto another. The additional length ensures that the sweater will not pull out of your pants, leaving part of your body unprotected.

Another popular means to control the temperature of the torso is to wear an insulated vest. The advantage of wearing a vest is that the upper torso can be well insulated while the arms remain unencumbered by bulky layers of material. This freedom for the arms can be beneficial in the midst of activity such as skiing or climbing. But if you wear a vest as an outer garment, it should not be relied on as a full layer of insulation, since the gaps under the armpits significantly lessen its insulating capacity. In order to serve as a full layer of insulation, the vest must be worn under a layer of clothing. A variety of insulating materials are used in vests, including down, Thinsulate, and pile. Although down is probably the most popular of the three, always keep in mind that, when wet, down loses all insulating value.

The Outer Shell

Outer layers of clothing serve several functions. They can protect from wind and rain and in some cases can keep you warmer. To be effective, exterior or shell clothing should always be large enough to fit easily over insulating layers. Wind and rain pants should go on easily over boots. Parkas should be large enough to fit comfortably over several layers of wool.

Wind threatens our comfort and safety in ways that are often misunderstood. The fact that wind may be cold is not the major problem. Wind causes discomfort when it penetrates our outer layers of insulation, thus excessively ventilating the air space next to the body, which must be *dead* air space to keep the body warm. Since wool and pile can, depending on the weave, be poor wind resisters, an additional outer layer is often needed to ensure that these materials continue to insulate the body during windy conditions.

WIND CHILL CHART

Temperature (°F)

Equivalent Chill Temperature

Wind Speed MPH	40	35	30	25	20	15	10	5	0	-5	-10	-15	-20	-25	-30	-35	-40	-45	-50	-55	-60
Calm	40	35	30	25	20	15	10	5	0	-5	-10	-15	-20	-25	-30	-35	-40	-45	-50	-55	-60
5	35	30	25	20	15	10	5	0	-5	-10	-15	-20	-25	-30	-35	-40	-45	-50	-55	-65	-70
10	30	20	15	10	5	0	-10	-15	-20	-25	-35	-40	-45	-50	-60	-65	-70	-75	-80	-90	-95
15	25	15	10	0	-5	-10	-20	-25	-30	-40	-45	-50	-60	-65	-70	-80	-85	-90	-100	-105	-110
20	20	10	5	0	-5	-10	-15	-25	-30	-35	-45	-50	-60	-65	-75	-80	-85	-95	-100	-110	-115
25	15	10	0	-5	-15	-20	-30	-35	-45	-50	-60	-65	-75	-80	-90	-95	-105	-110	-120	-125	-135
30	10	5	0	-10	-20	-25	-30	-40	-45	-55	-60	-70	-75	-85	-90	-100	-105	-115	-120	-130	-140
35	10	5	-5	-10	-20	-30	-35	-40	-45	-55	-60	-70	-75	-80	-90	-100	-105	-115	-120	-130	-145
40	10	0	-5	-15	-20	-30	-35	-45	-55	-60	-70	-75	-85	-95	-100	-110	-115	-125	-130	-140	-150

Little danger | Increasing danger | Great danger

SKOAL

COTTON
SHIRT

GAITERS

65°F
SUNNY
&
CALM

DRESSING PROPERLY IN ALL SEASONS

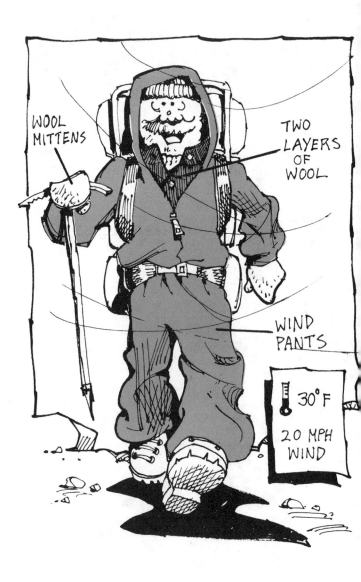

WOOL
MITTENS

TWO
LAYERS
OF
WOOL

WIND
PANTS

30° F

20 MPH
WIND

Wind pants, made of lightweight ripstop nylon, allow for ventilation while protecting the lower body from wind chill. Wind pants should fit fairly snugly over two layers of insulating clothing, so that they will not flap in the wind. Most have drawstrings around the waist, a considerable number of pockets, and zippers at the bottom so that they will go on easily over boots. Many people find that wind pants are a good replacement for cotton pants, and are comfortable to wear over shorts when protection from the sun or mosquitoes is required. The seat and knees should be reinforced to provide longer wear.

Wind shirts made of similar lightweight nylon come in pullover or zipper style. Once again, this outer garment should have plenty of pockets so you don't have to fumble through several layers of clothing to find your handkerchief or compass.

The primary difference between nylon wind gear and nylon rain gear is that the latter has been treated with a waterproofing agent. This treatment prevents moisture from the outside from penetrating the material, but it also makes it impossible for the sweat inside your clothing to evaporate. As described earlier, Gore-Tex and Klimate, fabrics which rain does not penetrate but which breathe (moisture from the inside can pass through them), are relatively new solutions to this problem. Gore-Tex and Klimate protect from both wind and rain.

Parkas, ponchos, cagoules, and rain pants are the traditional protection from wet weather. Most of these articles of clothing are now made in both coated nylon and Gore-Tex.

Parkas with a full-length front zipper are best for backpacking because they allow you to adjust ventilation and are easy to put on and take off. Keep in mind, however, that zippers tend to leak. A parka should fall to below the crotch without blocking your view of your feet; in bad weather, logs and boulder fields are more difficult to cross, and a good view of obstacles is essential for balance.

Though quite popular, ponchos are unsatisfactory as rain protection in the backcountry. They tend to flap in the wind, and rain often blows in. Their apparent advantage is that they can be put on over a pack. However, the gear in your pack can be more easily and effectively waterproofed by simply lining the inside of the pack with a large plastic garbage sack, or buying a waterproofed pack bag. And, contrary to popular belief, ponchos are not particularly effective as a makeshift tent fly.

A cagoule is longer than a parka and, unlike the poncho, has a solid front which is not disturbed by heavy wind. It protects the body down to the knees, and slits under the arms provide some ventilation while hiking. Its loose fit can also help counter the buildup of interior moisture. The lack of a front seam or zipper means that it is fairly leakproof; however, it also requires that the cagoule be put on over the head.

Rain pants are similar to wind pants, except that they are waterproof. Most people find rain pants to be impractical for hiking, since moisture builds up quickly around the lower torso during physical exertion. A cagoule is a good solution for providing rain protection for the legs while allowing for some ventilation. Rain pants or rain chaps come in handy, however, when walking through wet underbrush. When used for this purpose, the pants should not be too loose, since they will tend to snag on bushes.

All rain garments, including those made of nylon and Gore-Tex, will leak at the seams unless sealed. A number of seam sealers are available that can simply be painted on over the seam. To ensure protection, be prepared to repeat this process regularly, depending on how often you use the garment.

Head, Hands, and Feet

There is an old saying, "If your feet are cold, put on a hat." It works. With the brain receiving 20 percent of the body's blood supply, the conservation of heat in the head will mean that our bodies will have more blood available to heat our hands and feet.

Although many people think of the head as an extremity, there is one important difference: while the amount of blood in the hands or legs can be decreased in order to maintain the heat of the body's central core, the amount of blood in the head must remain constant and within a narrow range of temperature in order for the brain to function properly. This means that a great deal of body heat is constantly generated by the head, very near the surface of the skin. Because of this, over 50 percent of body heat lost through radiation or convection escapes through the head.

Of course, head gear is not used just to conserve heat. In hot climates it also protects you from the heat. A wide variety of head gear is suitable for outdoor use:

For cold weather, a *wool stocking cap* is the best. It can be adjusted to cover your ears when necessary, and retains heat while wicking moisture to the outside. At NOLS we sew a nylon shell around the outside of the stocking cap (Gore-Tex works even better) to provide wind protection and keep falling snow from sticking.

A *balaclava,* an adjustable hat which can cover the face and neck, is recommended for more extreme cold weather. It is commonly made from wool or pile, sometimes silk.

In the rain, a *brimmed hat* helps keep the water out of the face and from running down the back of the neck. A small brim of one or two inches works best while wearing a pack. A hat band which doubles as a chin strap is handy when the wind comes up.

A *baseball cap* works well in warm weather. It protects the top of the head from the sun and shields the eyes from glare.

A *handkerchief* tied around the head can provide sun protection; it can also be periodically dipped in cold water to provide additional coolness.

A *wool scarf* to keep the neck warm is a handy and lightweight form of temperature control. The scarf is easy to adjust from a loose drape to a tie, thus regulating heat at this important crossroads of the body.

NOLS issues both wool gloves and wool mittens for all summer courses. In the winter we add a heavy, insulated outer shell for the hands. Gloves are good for doing fine work with the fingers such as starting fires and tying knots. Mittens, on the other hand, are warmer than gloves because there is less surface area in contact with the outside and your fingers can warm each other. Both mittens and gloves should fit snugly but not tightly, and it is a bonus if they are long enough to be tucked into the sleeve.

You can find a number of pile mittens on the market today. They are warm and lightweight, and they dry faster than wool. The disadvantage of pile is that it wears out more quickly.

Cotton gloves are also issued for all NOLS courses. They come in very handy when handling hot pots and pans around a fire or stove.

Good wool socks will keep your feet warm by providing insulation, cushion them for a more comfortable hike, and protect them from abrasion and possible blisters by reducing friction. NOLS has found that two pairs of heavy wool socks provide the best protection and comfort for the type of backcountry experiences we offer. Of course, different circumstances create different needs. Some people prefer synthetic-and-wool blends in the mountains, while in the desert they find a cotton or silk liner cooler. Others wear a combination of wool liner and ragg sock, sometimes adding an insole for additional cushion. Finding what is most comfortable for you is important. If there is any chance that your feet will get wet, it is wise to stick with a sock fabric whose insulating abilities will not be destroyed by moisture; a fabric like wool.

You should carry one change of socks with you at all times. Since you will normally be wearing two pairs at a time, take a minimum of four pairs of socks on any trip. For summer courses at NOLS we issue a minimum of two pairs of short wool socks and two pairs of knee-high wool socks. When we anticipate a wet season, we often issue a third set of socks: one set to wear, one set to be drying, one set always dry.

Accessories

The best way to keep excess water and small objects out of a boot is to use a pair of gaiters. Gaiters are made of nylon or Gore-Tex, often with a waterproof material from the boot to the ankle and a breathable fabric above. Waterproofing above the ankle tends to trap too much moisture around the leg.

Short gaiters, which are five to six inches high, may be adequate in dry summer climates. If you are going to be crossing streams or walking across snow, long gaiters, sixteen to eighteen inches high and extending above the calf, are better.

The gaiter is hooked to the front of the boot lace to keep debris and small pebbles from riding up and entering the boot, and should be attached under the instep of the boot with a strap to hold the gaiters down. Better gaiters are zipped or snapped along the side or back. We recommend that gaiters have two methods of closing, such as a zipper and a flap that closes with snaps or Velcro. This takes the stress off the zipper and helps keep the zipper from freezing in snow. It also gives you a backup in case one closure fails. Be careful not to have your gaiters so tight that circulation is restricted.

A final accessory for a backcountry outfit, an important one to remember, provides a way to keep your pants up. There are several factors to keep in mind when selecting a belt.

Belts for the backcountry should be longer than those worn in town. They should be big enough so that several layers of wool shirts can be comfortably tucked into the pants. Leather tends to become heavy and crack when it gets wet, so a web or cloth belt is preferable. Keep the buckle small or it will rub against the pack's hip belt. A piece of tubular webbing, a nylon strap used in climbing, is a handy substitute for a traditional belt.

Many people have a difficult time wearing a knife on a belt at the same time they are wearing a pack. The pack will often chafe against the knife, creating discomfort. This situation differs with the shape of each body. If you have such a problem, it may be easier to keep your knife in your pack while hiking and wear it on your belt around camp.

The major problem with suspenders is the inconvenience in dropping your pants if the suspenders are not on the outer layer. Conversely, keeping the suspenders on the outside interferes with adding and subtracting layers; it is particularly difficult to put on an additional outer layer of pants. Once again, however, personal taste and experience should dictate how you hold up your pants.

Thus far, we have talked about how to dress from your bare body out and from your socks to your hat. We have left for last what is undoubtedly the most important piece of clothing in a backpacker's wardrobe, the boots.

CHOOSING, FITTING, AND CARING FOR BOOTS

Don Webber has probably fitted more people in backpacking and mountaineering boots than any person in the country. When novice backpackers come to the NOLS boot room for a fitting, it is Don's job to teach them the difference between the normal discomfort felt by most people when they step out of a pliable, form-fitting tennis shoe into a stiff, four-pound hiking boot and the real danger signals of a boot that does not fit.

The boot room is usually the first stop for NOLS students at the Lumberyard. That way they can wear their boots for a good part of the day before getting on the bus to head for the field.

"It takes time to get a good boot fit," Don says, watching a young man lace on a pair of Pivetta's. The man stands, his first time in a heavy mountaineering boot; he looks like one of those toy plastic clowns which are weighted on the bottom so they always pop back to an upright position. "Is the ball of the boot fitting the ball of your foot?" Don asks. "Okay. Walk around, see how it feels. Take your time."

Don points toward the back of the boot room. "Now," he says, "walk over to that concrete wall and kick it." If your toe hits the front of the boot the first time you kick a hard surface, he explains, it is likely that the toe will also hit the front of the boot when you walk down a steep grade. That means the boot is too short. "How's that feel?" Don asks. The man nods and says, "I think it's fine," somewhat hesitantly. "Walk around some more," Don says. "All new boots feel stiff and unnatural, so you need to put them through their paces to see if you have a good fit. Now kick the wall. Kick it again. Make sure it doesn't hurt."

The student is the last member of the two courses being issued today to be fitted with his boots. Some students, after walking around in new boots for an hour or two, will come back to the boot room to try another pair or perhaps have part of a boot slightly stretched. "If they are dissatisfied with their boots, we'd better find out now," Don says. "Once in the backcountry, if their boots don't fit well, all they can do is keep on walking."

The raucous rhythms of Bob Marley drift in from the issue room. After a busy afternoon, Don finally has a moment to gather empty boxes and straighten up.

"The whole boot scene began to change in the mid-1960s," Don says, "when there was a big upswing of interest in backpacking in this country. Since there wasn't a wide boot selection available in America at the time, people looked to Europe for good boots, particularly Switzerland and Germany. The problem with that was that most of the boots they were getting were heavy mountaineering boots, because that was the primary activity in Europe. By the mid-1970s we began to realize that most people in the U.S. weren't mountaineering, they were backpacking. They weren't climbing the Eiger, they were backpacking in the White Mountains. We didn't need such a heavy boot."

The weight of a boot makes a real difference in the amount of energy you expend on the trail. Assume your average day includes ten miles of hiking and you take 2,000 steps per mile. This amounts to 20,000 steps per day. If the boot you are wearing weighs three pounds, you are lifting 30,000 pounds per day per boot. With a one-pound boot, on the other hand, you would only be lifting 10,000 pounds per day per boot. For both boots, that is a 20-ton difference every day.

"You've got to be careful not to get a boot heavier than you really need," Don says. "In the middle of a long hike, you will be very grateful not to be carrying that extra weight."

Don points out that the boot market is beginning to swing radically in a new direction, toward super-lightweight boots. Recently, boot manufacturers have begun experimenting with a number of lightweight materials such as Gore-Tex, nylon, and canvas, joining them to new lightweight soles to produce boots which weigh about a pound each. At the same time, many running-shoe makers are approaching the market from the other end, strengthening and building up their products in order to create an ultra-light backpacking shoe.

The new lightweights can be divided into three categories. First, there are low-cut walking shoes for day trips carrying a day pack. Second, approach shoes, which are ankle-high boots which work well only on trails, can give you enough support to carry up to fifty pounds. The third lightweight is an off-trail boot which has a shank for reinforcement. A little experience is probably advisable before you buy the lightweight off-trail boot. If you have weak ankles or poor balance, you should avoid them altogether. All of the lightweights require a greater awareness of balance and where you put your feet. "They are definitely not for the klutz," says Don.

The basic goal of the consumer is to find a good balance between the weight of the boot, the support which the boot provides the foot and ankle, and boot cost. The major difference between a medium- and heavy-weight boot is the type of protection each gives the foot. Consider first where you will be hiking. If the land is fairly flat—on a trail, in the desert, on forest duff—a medium- or even lightweight boot may provide adequate support, and it will certainly be more comfortable. If you are going to be hiking the trails of the Adirondacks, you can use a much lighter boot than if you are planning an alpine ascent of British Columbia's Mount Robeson. Consider also the amount of weight you will be carrying in your pack. Greater weight requires the support of a heavier boot. If you are planning to carry fifty or sixty pounds off the trail across beds of scree and boulder, your foot will need added protection and support. It is, of course, often difficult to imagine all of the various terrains you might want to visit and the environments in which the boot will be tested. In the end, your boot selection will undoubtedly be a compromise between conflicting needs and your budget.

When you set out to buy your first pair of quality boots, try to locate a backpacking or mountaineering shop with a reputation for trustworthiness. You might want to do some reading in backpacking magazines, which often field-test various brands of boots. Salespeople will sometimes try to sell you whatever they have on the shelf; but a good store will be staffed by people seriously committed to backcountry adventure, and they can give you valuable advice.

The information in this section will give you a good start; you'll know the kinds of questions to ask, and what to look for. Remember, though, that your body is unlike any other, and you will have to put your foot in the boot to know whether it's right for you.

Because no two feet are the same, an argument can be made for custom-made boots tailored specifically to you. For the ardent backpacker who spends enough time in the field to wear out plenty of brand-name boots, this may be a sensible investment. But it's a big investment. It's usually, but not always, true that expensive boots cost more because of materials and workmanship. If you're a moderate backcountry traveler, or just getting started, stick to what's on the shelf, and select carefully. The price tag on the boot may still be high.

Parts of the Boot

Every boot on the market offers literature supporting its own particular design and style. An understanding of boot construction can help you sort out conflicting claims and select a boot which best serves your needs. But a decision to buy a boot should not be based solely on whether the leather of the uppers is facing in or out, or a claim that the tongue of a particular boot is constructed for maximum protection. After you have considered the intricacies of boot construction described below, don't forget the first rule: let your feet decide which boots are most comfortable.

Outsoles: Deep vs. Shallow Lugs

Among people concerned with minimum-impact camping, there is considerable controversy regarding the use of lug soles in the backcountry. Commonly made out of neoprene, a synthetic form of rubber, lug soles have a deep tread which can tear up the landscape, particularly in lush meadows, where damp soil easily catches in the crevices of the boot.

The Vibram brand currently has the dominant position in the sole market, although other brands such as Galibier, Pirelli, and St. Moritz also have good soles. Most brands offer five to ten grades of hardness and thickness as well as a choice of lug patterns. Mountaineering boots usually use the Montagna sole, which has a thick base and deep cleats. Lighter-weight boots usually use the thinner Roccia sole with more shallow cleats.

The treads on the bottom of the sole which can prove so harmful to the landscape also, of course, provide the sole's major advantage: by digging into the ground, the treads give the wearer added grip, balance, and leverage.

As a general rule, if you stay on well-traveled trails or hike in relatively flat areas such as deserts, you don't need a lug sole. Boots with smooth or ripple soles work fine in these areas, and they will probably be more comfortable.

BOOT CONSTRUCTION

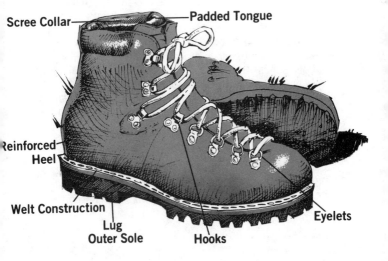

Scree Collar — Padded Tongue — Reinforced Heel — Welt Construction — Lug Outer Sole — Hooks — Eyelets

But if you are carrying a pack off-trail, hiking through scree or boulder fields, a lug sole is essential for safety and comfort.

If you wear a lug sole, you have an added responsibility to walk carefully. Place your foot in places where it will not erode the landscape. Avoid hiking through soft meadows; choose instead hardier terrain through rock, duff, or snow. The worst damage from lug soles is often found around campsites, where the high impact of camping is aggravated by heavy traffic. Be sure to pack a pair of camp shoes; tennis shoes work fine. A lightweight pair of camp shoes is a real comfort after a long day of wearing three- to five-pound boots, and they are essential for minimum-impact camping.

Midsoles and Insoles

The bottom of a good hiking shoe is something like a sandwich. We've just described the outsole, which makes direct contact with the ground. On the inside, making direct contact with your foot and sock, is the insole. Between the two, in the middle of the sandwich, is the midsole.

A really lightweight boot may skip the midsole altogether; but if you're hiking in the backcountry, the midsole is essential for comfort. It provides the cushion that allows you to be comfortable on a long or difficult hike. Without it, every pebble on the trail will leave a message on the bottom of your foot.

Midsoles can be made of leather, rubber, or synthetics. Rubber bonds well with the heavy outsole, but it is stiff and can get hot. Leather midsoles are soft and more flexible, and they breathe and absorb moisture, which will be plentiful in a heavy boot on a hot day. Some boots combine leather, rubber, and cork or foam filler for cushioning.

The inmost layer is the insole. It is often leather, but sometimes cellulose or foam rubber is used. The insole provides additional padding and more comfort when hiking. It should be well attached to the midsole; otherwise, the friction of your foot in the boot may pull it loose, making it bunch and causing discomfort.

Shanks

All heavy and most medium-weight boots have a shank, which fits between the insole and midsole. The shank is the backbone of the boot. Constructed most often of steel or fiberglass, sometimes of plastic or wood, the shank largely determines the boot's rigidity. In a medium-weight boot, the half shank will extend forward from mid-heel to just beyond the ball of the foot. Some heavier boots use a shank which extends through three-fourths of the full boot. Most people find this too stiff for hiking, but not stiff enough for climbing or cramponing. For technical mountaineering there are some boots made with a full shank.

Where the Sole Meets the Upper

The various components of a boot can be of high or low quality, but even high-quality materials won't do the job if they aren't put together well. What good is a heavy lug sole if midway through your trip it starts flapping free from the rest of your boot?

In less expensive boots, the sole is sometimes attached to the rest of the boot using glue or injection molding, a molten neoprene applied under heavy pressure. Although these methods are adequate for producing lightweight day-hiking boots, they are not suitable to bond the parts of sturdy, off-trail backpacking boots.

Good medium- and heavyweight boots are held together with a welt. The welt is the stitching between the sole and the upper. There are three common types.

Lightweight boots are often put together with a *Littleway welt.* The leather upper of the boot is folded inward where it meets the sole. The turned-in flap of the upper is inserted between the insole and the midsole, then stitched. This method tends to reduce the weight and size of the boot. With the Littleway welt you can trim the sole close to the boot. The Littleway is used on many climbing boots.

A stronger welt, found on most heavy hiking and climbing boots, is the *Norwegian welt.* This requires a large sole, with a rim extending outside the upper. The lower edge of the upper is turned outward, then attached to the midsole with a stitch slanted inward. The turned-out edge of the upper is then secured a second time to the midsole with a straight stitch.

The *Goodyear welt* is still found on some of the heaviest mountaineering boots. In recent years it has fallen from favor because, although it is less expensive, it is not as strong as the Norwegian welt. The bottom edge of the upper is turned inward and attached to the midsole from the inside with a stitch slanted outward. Then a "cap," a small piece of leather which goes completely around the outside edge of the boot where the sole meets the upper, is stitched to the midsole and the upper.

Leather

The upper of a boot can be made of various grades of leather. When cowhide is split, it becomes sheets of leather, which are categorized by type: top-grain, the leather from the outer side of the hide, where the hair had been; and split-grain, the interior cut of leather, which is suede on both sides.

Top-grain, or full-grain, leather is much more rugged, pliable, and water-resistant. It is also much more expensive. Most top-quality boots are made from top-grain leather.

Split-grain leather, from the inside of the hide, is not as strong. It can work well, however, in lightweight, less expensive boots for use in dry country. Split-grain also works fine for boot insoles and midsoles, and is used as reinforcement in lightweight boots around the toe, instep, and ankle.

Experts disagree on which side of top-grain leather should be used on the outside of a boot. Should it be the "smooth-out," which refers to the grain side, which was actually on the outside of the cow? Or should it be the "rough-out," with the suede, or flesh side, out?

The pores of the leather are shaped like cones with the largest holes on the rough side—actually the inside of the cow. The argument centers on where to put the point of the cone, the smooth side, which is the more water-resistant. If it is on the exterior of the boot, it stops water at outer surface. If it is on the interior of the boot, the point of the cone is protected from abrasion, thus the water-resistance may last longer. Usually, winter boots have the smooth side out and the summer boots have the rough side out.

Upper Reinforcing

Most medium and heavy boots have additional reinforcing in the heel and toe. This provides good protection from falling rocks and gives the foot better grounding. In the heel, a "heel counter" or "heel cup" made of reinforced leather or fiber may be sewn to the inside of the boot. Similarly, a heavy-duty fiber toe is part of the standard design for all heavy and most medium boots.

Single vs. Sectional Construction

Some boots are made with a single-piece upper: one piece of leather shaped to form the entire upper portion of the boot. The advantage of single-piece construction is that with only one seam, at the heel, the chances of leaking are minimized, and the boot will probably conform better to the foot. But to get a single large piece of leather from a hide, you have to discard parts of the leather, so single-piece boot construction is more expensive.

Sectional construction, usually using two pieces of leather to form the basic boot, can also provide a quality product. The leather in this type of construction is usually joined with a seam at the heel and at the instep. So long as these seams are well constructed so they do not rub on the inside of the boot, and well placed so they do not receive a lot of abrasion, this type of construction, the most common on today's boot market, can produce quality, comfortable boots. If more than two pieces of leather are used, make sure that the boot does not bend in uncomfortable or irregular ways. And make sure to waterproof the seams regularly. Over three pieces, beware!

All quality boots are stitched with synthetic threads,

either Dacron or nylon. Cotton thread rots, and is never used in a quality boot. The type of thread used on the boot will have a much greater impact on its quality than its single or sectional construction. When a salesman shows you a boot, first look at the thread. If it is cotton, ask to see another boot.

The Tongue

Good medium and heavy boots have one-piece tongues attached to both sides. This solid piece across the front of the foot helps to keep out snow, rain, and dirt. Often, it is padded for comfort. The tongue should not shift around when the boot is laced; movement can encourage thorns and small pebbles to work their way inside the boot.

Heavier boots may have a series of leather flaps which close over the tongue to provide additional protection.

The Collar

Many boots have a scree collar, or padded rim, around the top, designed to keep out snow and gravel. The collar doesn't really perform that function very well. But on a heavy boot, a padded collar protects the Achilles tendon from rubbing against a hard edge, preventing "squeak heel," a painful form of tendonitis (inflammation of a tendon) common to backpackers.

Lacing

Four types of lacing systems are used in boots: eyelets that are grommeted to the upper; swivel eyelets, which are small D-rings attached to clips riveted to the upper; speed lacing, small tubes through which the lace passes, allowing a single tug to tighten the laces from top to bottom; and open hooks, which are also attached to the boot with a riveted clip. Eyelets are the strongest and seldom break, because they do not have a lever arm. While hooks sometimes break or can be snagged on the underbrush, they are much easier to lace, particularly in cold weather. Many boots have a combination of lacing systems, with grommeted or swivel eyelets on the bottom and hooks on the top. The advantage of tube lacing is that you can tighten the boot with one tug of the laces; but if the laces escape from the tubes, they can be quite difficult to manage when your fingers are cold and stiff.

If any of the hardware in a lacing system breaks, it can be replaced by most shoemakers or at a mountaineering shop. However, if eyelets rip out early in the life of a boot, it is a sure sign of a poorly constructed boot!

Although some boots still come with leather laces, nylon braid is the most practical and popular boot lace available today. Rather than taking an extra pair of boot laces in your pack, plan to take an all-purpose nylon cord which can be used as tent cord or boot lace, or for emergency pack repairs.

Fitting Boots

Most French boots fit differently from American boots or Italian boots. Standard foot sizes vary from country to country. This diversity provides the marketplace with a large variety of well-made boots and the high possibility that you will find a good fit for your particular foot. But don't expect consistency in sizes from one country to another. Don is quick to remind students that their feet don't know their nationality. "You may be an American with a typically French foot," he says.

It is best to shop for a boot in the afternoon, since feet tend to swell during the day and boots should be fitted while your foot is largest.

Start by asking for a boot corresponding to your regular street-shoe size. If you are not sure of your exact size, have your foot measured. The variance in boot sizes is so great between American and European boots, and even between the various brands made in a particular country, that your street-shoe size is often just a starting point.

First put on the boot without a sock, or with a thin liner, which some salesmen will request. Slide the foot all the way forward in the boot and, while standing with knees slightly bent, see if you can put two fingers between the back of the boot and your foot. If not, the boot is too small.

Next, put on a pair of wool socks; there should be room for one finger between the boot and the heel. When you find a boot that passes both of these tests, then you should try the boot wearing the socks or sock combinations you plan to wear on the trail. NOLS has found that two pairs of heavy wool socks work best in rough backcountry. A thin liner sock covered by a thick outer sock is not an adequate combination for a serious expedition, though they may be quite adequate for most short backpacking trips. Make sure the socks are the right size. Bunched-up socks can distort the fit.

Wearing heavy wool socks with the boots laced comfortably, take a few steps. Concentrate on the heels of your feet. They should lift slightly off the bottom of the boot, a quarter of an inch or less, just barely losing contact with the boot. If there is no lift, the boot is too small. A lift of more than one-quarter inch indicates the boot is too large. Your toes should be flat, in contact with the boot all around, but not squeezed. The arch of the boot should follow the contour of the arch of your foot. You should be able to feel it, but without pressure.

The most important part of the fit is to make sure that the ball of the foot corresponds to the ball of the boot. If the ball of the foot is not in the right place, the boot will never conform to the foot's curvature.

Now walk around in the boot. If the store has stairs, walk up and down. Do you feel any wrinkles or unusual pressure points? If so, rearrange your sock or the tongue. If it still doesn't feel right, try a different boot. Take as much time as you need. This is a major purchase, and a good salesperson understands that it takes a little experimentation to find the right boot.

If it passes these tests, next kick the toe of each boot hard against a solid surface, the way students are told to do at the Lumberyard. If your toe hits the front of the boot, the boot may be too small. First try lacing the boot a little tighter, and kick the toe again. If it still hits the front, try a half-size larger.

Next, kick the hard surface with the same foot four or five times. If your toe moves progressively toward the front of the boot and then hits hard against the inside, you should try lacing tighter or try a half-size smaller boot. If your foot remains in a relatively constant position and does not bang the front, then the fit is good.

Many people have trouble because one foot is larger than the other. Generally speaking, right-handed people have larger left feet and left-handed people have larger right feet. Always fit the larger foot. If the smaller foot has too much room, try an extra sock or an insole.

If a boot fits well with the exception of one small pressure point, a stretching machine can slightly loosen the leather at any given point.

Subject each boot you try to the above tests. Eventually you will narrow the field and settle on the best fit.

Breaking In Boots

If you buy a new pair of medium- or heavyweight boots, it is best not to start out the next morning on a twenty-mile hike with a full pack. The boots will be stiff, and they need time to adjust to your feet. Wear them around the house for a few days or take a short day hike to give your feet a chance to get to know the boots. If, after wearing them indoors for a day, they still don't feel comfortable, take them back to the store and ask to try another pair. So long as the boots show no sign of wear, most stores will gladly exchange them.

Once you get outdoors and start walking on uneven surfaces, you might want to put a strip of adhesive tape or a patch of moleskin on your heel to protect that vulnerable point while your boots are breaking in.

Boots should be treated with some type of wax or sealer prior to use. In the NOLS boot room, Don uses a beeswax–silicone mix. Find out from the salesperson who sells you the boots if the leather was oil-tanned or chrome-tanned. Oil-tanned leathers are usually treated with boot wax or oil, chrome-tanned leathers with silicone wax.

Although some boot treatments are claimed to waterproof boots, this is not the primary purpose for the treatment. NOLS has found that giving a boot a good coat of shoe grease or snow sealer prolongs the life of the boot by nourishing the leather. If such treatment also provides waterproofing, the results are quite temporary. It is also good to remember that waterproof boots are waterproof in both directions, keeping water in as well as keeping it out. In other words, these boots will not allow the moisture from your feet to wick out through the boot.

Boot Care

According to Don, "Drying a wet boot improperly will age it faster than anything else." Getting a boot wet will not destroy it; the method used to dry a boot poses a far greater threat to its life.

Leather cells begin to rupture when heated to 140 degrees. Excessive heat will also crack the glue attaching the midsole and break down the seams. Attempting to dry out boots by placing them close to a campfire is the quickest way to destroy them. When you try to hasten the drying process, the different thicknesses of leather will dry at different rates, causing the leather to crack.

"Even direct sunlight can be damaging," Don says. If you are in camp and want to dry out your boots, simply wipe the excess water from the inside with a handkerchief and place them in the shade to dry. Direct sunlight shrinks the leather and curls the soles. On the trail always keep an extra pair of clean dry socks handy. If your boots get wet, wipe out the extra water and put on dry socks. The wool of the socks will wick moisture away from the foot, and the foot's natural heat will help dry the boots. With dry wool socks, wet boots are not a problem.

At night, in camp, open the top of your boots as far as possible. In the summer this will help to dry them out. In very cold weather, boots may freeze at night, and one way to help them thaw without cracking in the morning is to put them on and warm them up while wearing them. This is much easier to manage if the boot is wide open.

It is a better idea to take your boots inside your tent and tuck them in your sleeping bag at night to prevent them from freezing or becoming wet with dew. Boots also absorb some body salts from your sweating feet, and this makes them tempting snacks for small gnawing animals. One solution to the problem of bringing muddy or wet boots inside the tent is to turn your sleeping-bag stuff sack inside out and place your boots in it for the night. Another approach is to carry a small, stiff whisk broom and clean them before bringing them into your tent.

A common mistake people make with their boots is to leave them in the back of the car between outings. This can be very bad for boots, since the heat will dry them out and cause aging and cracking.

When you return from a backcountry trip, it is important to clean your boots before you store them. Leather boots should first be cleaned with a stiff-bristled brush, not a wire brush. Then clean with saddle soap, wipe off the residue, and put on a generous coating of waterproofing before you store the boots. The waterproofing also serves as a good preservative for the leather. Clean the inside of the boot and put a coating of mink or neat's-foot oil on the inside to keep the leather soft. Lightweight canvas boots should be cleaned with a wet cloth. Saddle soap should be used on the leather reinforcing. Good treatment at the end of a trip will add considerably to the life of your boots.

The best place to keep boots at home is in a cool, dry place. Shoe trees help maintain the shape of heavy mountaineering boots. If there is a possibility that a mouse or kitten may find the boot a comfortable place to set up housekeeping, store your boots in plastic bags.

Quality boots can be resoled. Ask your local outfitting or mountaineering store to recommend a good shoemaker. Competent shoemakers will stitch through old holes on the boot rather than weaken the leather by making new holes. When resoling, it is possible to change the style of your sole. If you have discovered that your boots are too light or too heavy for your use, this is a good time to correct this condition without purchasing a new boot.

Steel shanks, which are prone to rust, can also be replaced, but it can be an expensive operation. If rust is discovered, you should make sure the surrounding area of the boot is checked thoroughly for related damage. Sometimes rust will destroy the surrounding leather or rubber, making the boot unrepairable.

Specialized Boots

Heavy, snug-fitting mountaineering boots can be used for some types of climbing. With the right binding, you can wear hiking boots for cross-country skiing. But as you begin developing some competence in a particular outdoor activity, you will want to consider investing in a specialized boot.

For rock climbing you need an extra-light, tight-fitting boot which will give you maximum agility, leverage, and traction. Used only for rock climbing, these boots look similar to a high-top tennis shoe. They are quite fragile, and usually expensive; only for the devotee.

Some birders and hunters, who spend a lot of time walking in marsh, mud, or snow, swear by the shoe pac. These high waterproof boots, often made with rubber bottoms and leather tops, can keep feet warm and protected from outside moisture. As with most rubber boots, however, they cause your feet to sweat and are not recommended if you are planning much physical exertion, like carrying a pack.

For caving, a cheaper hiking boot is recommended. Nothing tears boots up faster than crawling around on your belly in narrow, damp caves.

Crepe-soled boots with breathable uppers work well for desert travel. It doesn't make sense to wear out an expensive lug sole on sandstone when softer rubber can give you good traction.

Winter mountaineering is a subject not treated in this book. Suffice it to say that boots made for three-season backcountry wear are not suitable for the heavy demands of the fourth season.

Boots by Mail Order

For some people, mail order is the only practical way to purchase good mountaineering boots. However, don't consider mail order buying unless the order form clearly spells out your right to return the unworn boots if they feel uncomfortable. Most reputable mail order houses will gladly exchange boots so long as they show no signs of wear.

By mail it is a bit more tricky, but not impossible, to get your foot matched up with the correct boot. When purchasing by mail, carefully follow the directions for ascertaining your boot size. Usually this involves having someone trace one or both feet onto a piece of cardboard, cutting along the outline, and sending the pattern in to the company. When making the tracing, be sure to wear the same type of sock you plan to wear with the boot.

When in college, Don purchased a pair of mountaineering boots by mail. Did it work out all right? "Sure," Don says. "It worked out fine. I had to return the boots they sent me twice before I got a good fit, but when the right boots finally arrived, they were perfect."

Don recommends that if you are ordering boots by mail, be sure to save everything that comes with the boot: boxes, tags, guarantees, even plastic wrappings. If you need to return the boots, they should go back exactly as they arrived. Also, be as specific as possible in describing what is wrong. This can be a real help to the person on the other end who is trying to fit you with the right boot.

The Foot Is the Important Equipment

There is nothing quite so foolish as the person who spends a great deal of time and money finding the right boots and then forgets to take care of his feet. It is not the boot which will move you down the trail at a good pace and ensure a solid grounding as you bound across a boulder field, it is your feet.

Good foot care requires that you change socks frequently. It is important to let socks dry out after a sweaty day on the trail, so a change at the end of a long day's hike is good practice. Socks will dry quickly in your sleeping bag, but not if you are wearing them. Some people sleep in the same socks they hike in; this not only prevents complete drying, it also does not allow air to circulate around their feet. This circulation is necessary if your feet are to toughen and become less prone to blisters.

Washing your feet every day is not only good hygiene, it can be very refreshing. Socks should also be washed regularly.

Recently, two schools of thought have developed regarding the use of foot powder. One school feels it helps to keep the feet dry. The other claims it provides a medium for bacteria growth and holds the moisture next to the skin. There may be truth to both statements, depending on personal chemistry.

The treatment of blisters is discussed in Chapter Six; it is a critical subject which every backpacker should understand. The word "backpacker" is an adequate description of the activity, but "footpacker" probably places the emphasis where it really belongs.

PUTTING THE PIECES TOGETHER

"When I first came to NOLS as a student," Tod recalls, "I thought that to be in the outdoors you always had to be cold and wet, that it was just part of the wilderness experience." Tod, who has now been a NOLS instructor for over ten years, quickly learned that it is possible to be comfortable in the outdoors even in revolting weather conditions; he learned to apply the simple rules of insulation and ventilation when selecting each piece of outdoor clothing, from his hat to his socks and boots. Once you understand the basics of this simple system, it is not long before it becomes second nature. Climbing a steep, narrow ridge at midday, you roll up a sleeve or unbutton a shirt to ventilate the body and stay dry. When the sun suddenly goes behind a cloud and a cold wind begins to blow, you close down the ventilation and perhaps add another layer of clothing insulation.

This manner of dressing may seen ingenuous, particularly when compared to advertisements promising that a garment will not only protect you from the harshest extremes of Mount Everest but will improve your sex life as well. The point to keep in mind is that no single piece of clothing offers a "solution." To live in the wild outdoors we need a good framework for selecting particular pieces of clothing for particular conditions. The layering system provides the flexibility to maintain a comfortable body temperature in the midst of all of nature's irregularities.

The best way to begin planning the clothing you will need for an expedition is to get specific information on the weather in the areas you hope to visit. What is the range of temperature you can expect? How much precipitation is likely? Remember to always prepare for the worst.

For excursions into alpine regions from the late spring to the early fall, our general rule at NOLS is that you need to carry one or two lower-body layers and two or three upper-body layers plus wind and rain protection. In tropical or desert areas, one lower-body layer and two upper-body layers should be sufficient. A list of clothing issued to NOLS students at the Lumberyard can be found in Appendix I. This list shows summer clothing requirements for the Rocky Mountain climatic region. You may find that your own body has different requirements, but the NOLS clothing list can give you a good, safe standard from which to start.

After your first or second trip into the backcountry, after you have tested some of the theories used by NOLS students and staff, and after you have determined the special needs of your own body, you can let yourself be tempted by more exotic items in the mountaineering catalogs and backpacking stores. You can begin to explore ways to make your backcountry clothing more lightweight, more durable, or more tailored to your own idiosyncrasies. With real backcountry experience, and perhaps a quick review of some of the more technical aspects of fabrics and insulators, you will have a fighting chance at distinguishing between state-of-the-art advances in wilderness gear and the seduction of this year's mountaineering fashion.

Chapter **Three**

Backcountry Equipment

WITH STEEP cliffs below and stark gray clouds above, an aging Indian truck jolted along the Kathmandu-to-Pokhara road. Through remote Himalayan villages and forests stripped of branches by fuel-hungry locals, the truck rumbled on, its canvas flaps slapping in the wet wind and occasionally revealing its cargo: 10,000 pounds of modern mountaineering gear.

The gear was for the American Women's Expedition to Dhaulagiri I. Nine climbers rode up ahead in a small bus, which, like all Nepalese buses, was painted a multicolored paisley. Three of the nine climbers were NOLS instructors: Shari Kearney, Cyndy Simer, and Lucy Smith.

It had been Lucy and Cyndy's job to assemble the five tons of equipment for the climb up the north face of the 26,820-foot peak. They had worked at it for over a year, but that did not ease the last-minute insecurity. First in the basement of the NOLS headquarters in Lander, and then in Kathmandu, they had checked and rechecked every piece of equipment. But as they bounced along in the bright little bus, umbrellas open above their heads as protection from the leaky roof, Cyndy found herself asking the same question she used to ask as a teenager before a weekend canoe trip: Haven't we forgotten something?

The year of planning had been a crash course in state-of-the-art outdoor equipment, most of which was donated to the expedition by American and European firms. In Lander the women inspected each seam and zipper, set up each new tent, assembled and lighted a multitude of stoves, and packed and repacked each backpack. They were following a basic tenet of practical outdoor planning: learn about your equipment at home, not in the field.

All three women had been active backcountry enthusiasts during a decade of rapid change in the equipment field. Lucy has worked for NOLS on the glaciers of Alaska and along the seacoast of Baja California, Mexico, spending thirty or forty weeks a year teaching in the backcountry. Cyndy has taught at NOLS Wyoming for a number of years, and ascended Mount McKinley the month before she left for Nepal. Shari caught the bug while working summers in Yellowstone National Park during college, then honed her skills climbing year-round on Mount Hood.

Their approach to backcountry equipment was a little less premeditated in earlier years. Shari remembers Yellowstone: "Most of us washed dishes all summer, so on our days off we outfitted our 'expeditions' from the hotel kitchen. We didn't have tents, so we used big plastic trash bags to cover our sleeping bags. My sleeping bag was one of those flannel numbers, with lions and cougars printed on the lining. I would wake up drenched inside my flannel bag and trash bag—I didn't know fabrics had to be breathable."

Finding they still needed a few minor equipment items, the climbers went searching in Kathmandu. It was a little like the old Yellowstone kitchen—you took what you could get. What they encountered in the narrow streets of the Nepalese capital were angry roosters, running rickshaw boys, chattering monkeys, red-robed lamas, and long, noisy bartering sessions with shopkeepers. It took them a week to finally check off the last missing items on their single-spaced, twelve-page equipment list.

Outfitting an expedition requires sober reflection and research. You have to know what kind of environment you'll be traveling in and what kind of activity you expect to pursue there. You have to think about how much money you want to spend. Shopping in your local equipment store may be less chaotic than looking for a tarp in Kathmandu, but it's by no means simple. The market for outdoor equipment has been growing exponentially, and while that means there is innovative, high-quality gear available, it also means you have to become an expert of sorts to find your way around in an outdoor equipment store. It's a far cry from picking a trash bag off the shelf in the Yellowstone kitchen.

SLEEPING BAGS

Today, there are hundreds of styles of sleeping bags on the market. There are bags for summer and for winter, bags for one season or three seasons, sleeping systems for year-round camping, bags cut for short men, short women, tall men, tall women, and children. There are bags which can be zipped together for double sleeping, and bags so light-weight they can fit into a day pack. How can you find the right sleeping bag, faced with so many choices?

The first question you need to ask is, how warm a bag do you need? Recognize that this is a personal question. Some people sleep hot, others cold. The "right" bag is one that matches your metabolism and the environment in which you will be camping.

Be realistic in assessing the environments in which you will probably be sleeping. Don't buy a bag for your dream climb of Mount McKinley if for the next year your primary stomping grounds will be the Santa Monica Mountains. The most common mistake that novices make is to buy a heavier, warmer bag than they need.

When considering the climate in which you will use your bag, don't focus on the coldest possible condition. Aim slightly under the mean nighttime temperature. You can buy a sleeping bag which will meet your needs in most areas of the country for three-season camping; the fourth season, of course, is winter, and that requires a different bag. A three-season sleeping bag may be a bit warm for summer and not warm enough in the fall. But with a slight modification in your sleeping arrangement, such as opening the zipper in the summer, or placing some of your clothing under you for additional insulation in the fall, a three-season bag will live up to its name.

Another environmental factor you need to consider when

selecting a bag is how much moisture is common to the areas in which you will be camping. One of the major insulators used in sleeping bags, down, loses all of its insulating abilities when wet, and takes a long time to dry. NOLS avoids down sleeping bags in most camping situations, but there are many who swear by down and would not use anything else. Still, if you are planning to camp in areas where there is significant rainfall, consider yourself warned: down is useless when wet. We favor synthetic insulators.

The construction of sleeping bags is another important consideration. Sleeping bags come in numerous styles and cuts. There are also important variations in internal construction. As always, the key remains finding a sleeping bag that fits the particular needs of your body, and gives you maximum quality for the lowest possible dollar and weight.

When purchasing a sleeping bag, you will probably have a choice of two sizes: regular, for people under six feet, and large. To "try on" a sleeping bag, open the bag on a flat surface, get in, zip up the zipper, and, if the bag has a hood, tighten it over your head. You should now be able to stretch your body from head to toe, without feeling constrained. If you have large feet, some bags come with a circular foot to give your feet room. Many people under six feet prefer the larger bag, and use the extra room for keeping clothing and boots warm inside the bag on cold nights.

The width of the bag is as important as the length. This is very much a matter of personal choice. A narrow bag minimizes the amount of air space in the bag, and will tend to turn with you when you change sleeping position. A wider bag gives more freedom of movement, allowing you to tuck your knees if you please. But a wider bag, because of the added air space, will tend to sleep cooler; not the ticket for someone with low metabolism.

Finally, keep in mind that your sleeping bag is not solely responsible for keeping you warm at night in the backcountry. The way you eat, your water consumption, and how you position your campsite will also affect your sleeping comfort. In Chapter Two we discussed how the body reacts to temperature changes. When we are cold, we get goose bumps and begin to shiver in order to warm up. When we are hot, we begin to perspire in order to cool down. A careful choice of sleeping bags can prevent both of these extremes so that the body can be truly at rest during the night.

Loft

Regardless of the type of bag you are considering, there is one standard of measurement that always comes up in discussing sleeping bags: loft. Loft, in its simplest definition, is the height of the bag when it is fluffed up and lying on a flat surface. This is primarily determined by the insulation within the bag. Traditionally, loft is measured by thoroughly shaking the bag out, laying it out on the floor, letting it settle for several minutes, then with a ruler measuring from the floor to the top of the bag. The measurement should be taken at the midsection of the bag, in the area where your lower chest would lie.

Sleeping bag loft can range from 1½ inches (in lightweight summer bags) to 8 inches (in expedition-type bags).

Recently a number of manufacturers have begun providing a separate measurement of the loft that covers your body when you're in the bag. This is a good idea, because when you are sleeping in a bag, the top half of the bag provides most of the insulation while the bottom half is being compressed under your body.

The Army Quartermaster Corps says that one inch of insulation, whether it is synthetic fiber or down, will give the average sleeping person 40 degrees of protection. However, modern industry statistics vary somewhat from the Army's; most manufacturers suggest around 25 degrees of protection per inch of insulation in a sleeping bag. Using these figures, and without considering other factors, with three inches of insulation on top of the bag, you can maintain a temperature in the bag of 98.6° in 23.6° weather.

But it is not quite that simple. There are other factors

that contribute to the effectiveness of the bag's insulation. If it has a hood to cover your head, you can figure an extra five degrees of protection. A sleeping pad underneath the bag (a must for anyone who has advanced beyond car camping on the beach) will also add some degrees, by minimizing the loss of heat through conduction. On the other hand, cold wind moving across the bag, or humidity, will lessen a sleeping bag's insulating capacity.

When comparing the loft of bags, keep in mind that the same amount of insulation will loft differently in bags of different shape and design. Some sales clerks will refer to the pounds of insulation in a bag; although this information is of value in terms of the weight you will be carrying on your back, it is not a good way to measure potential warmth. The amount of insulation provided by two pounds of filler can vary considerably depending on the filler, the shape, and internal construction of the bag.

Insulation of equal loft provides equal warmth, regardless of whether the insulation is synthetic or down. If lofts are equal, then criteria other than warmth can be applied in making your choice. The most obvious of these other criteria for sleeping bags are weight and the ability to maintain insulation when wet.

These two criteria lead us directly into the major controversy of the sleeping bag industry. Which insulator, synthetic or down, is best for backpack sleeping bags?

Insulators

On the Dhaulagiri expedition, both down and synthetic bags were used. Synthetics were the obvious choice for the long monsoon-season trek to the base camp. It rained almost every day, and that is reason enough to choose a bag with synthetic filler. Even when wet, synthetic bags will provide warmth. Most of the climbers used down bags high on the mountain where it is cold and dry. Down can provide more loft, hence more warmth, per pound of insulation, and thus is considered more efficient: more warmth, less weight.

Of course, Himalayan expedition conditions are something few of us will experience. But understanding and preparing for drastic weather is essential to good, safe backpacking. Most NOLS courses are three to five weeks in areas where sudden rainfall is common, and the school recognizes that unexpected spills in a stream or capsized kayaks should be anticipated. For this reason, NOLS issues only synthetic sleeping bags. The added weight is worth the certainty that the bag will always be able to provide warmth, even when wet. The NOLS rationale is not universally accepted, and the circumstances of shorter trips or different environments make alternatives worth considering. Down should not be ruled out absolutely.

Down comes from waterfowl, either geese or ducks. It is the soft, fluffy undercoating beneath the feathers of the fowl. The advantages of down as sleeping bag filler are that it is lightweight, compresses easily into a small area for packing, and is resilient, quickly springing back to its full loft.

When used as an insulator, down particles adhere to each other lightly, forming thousands of tiny air pockets. Our bodies heat up the trapped air in these pockets; in other words, we keep ourselves warm. The way in which the down particles adhere to each other allows down to breathe out the moisture that our bodies generate.

There has always been a controversy over which species of waterfowl provides the best down. Today that controversy is probably shaped more than most will admit by the fowl market itself: the down that is available is often dubbed "the best." The eider duck was long considered to be the best source of quality down. However, this poor fellow became an endangered species and attention turned toward the goose, who for a while reigned supreme. The jury is still out, but it appears now that the duck has reached a near peer level with the goose. Increasingly, however, because of shortages, costs, and various manufacturer preferences, much of the commercial down today is a mixture.

The down used in sleeping bags comes from fowl raised primarily for eating, not for keeping warm. The U.S. has a notoriously poor appetite for prime goose and duck, so most of the down in this country is imported. Fortunately, there are millions of Asians and Europeans who are more fond of goose and duck than Americans. But only about 10 percent of the value of a goose is his down, and it takes about seven good-sized geese to fill a sleeping bag. Fashion, which we have seen make considerable inroads into outdoor clothing, is placing great pressure on the down market. So down products, including sleeping bags, are expensive.

Most down is a mixture of varying grades, sometimes simply to reduce costs, sometimes because the down and feather merchants honestly believe that the mixture provides a better quality of insulation. The Federal Trade Commission requires that if the label on the sleeping bag names the species of down, say "goose down," that species must be the source of 90 percent of the down in the bag. While shopping for a down sleeping bag, beware of clever advertising phrases like "AAA Prime Northern" or "Super Down." These words mean nothing. A good way to check for quality down is to take hold of the sleeping bag with your fingers and feel the texture of the down through the material. Good down feels smooth, soft, and fluffy. If you can feel sharp quills or other hard objects, you are probably feeling chicken feathers.

Once the laughing stock of the backpacking world, synthetics now account for over 50 percent of the sleeping bag market. The reasons for the bad reputation of synthetics go back several years to bags, like the one Shari used in Yellowstone, that were made of coarse material and lined in flannel. (These bags still exist, often perched enticingly above the beef jerky in the grocery store.)

The goal of technologists in recent years has been to develop a synthetic down: an insulator which provides as much insulation as down, yet able to retain its insulating properties when wet and to dry quickly. Today, they have produced products which are increasingly lightweight, durable, and cheaper than down.

There are three primary types of synthetics on the market today: PolarGuard, Hollofil, and Quallofil.

PolarGuard is composed of continuous-filament, solid

polyester fibers. Each filament is covered lightly with a resin, which helps hold the filament together. Hollofil is a soft, springy fiber cut in about 2½-inch lengths. As its name implies, Hollofil has a hollow channel running through its center. Quallofil, the newest of the synthetic fibers, features four microscopic channels in each fiber, and traps more air and is also lighter. Excellent sleeping bags are made from all three of these synthetics. What may be even more important is that the evolution of a synthetic substitute for down is taking place so quickly that in the coming months and years innovative new products will be rapidly introduced.

Several years ago, on a high-altitude climb no one would think of using anything but down insulation in their sleeping bag. Lucy Smith, however, who did not mind the extra weight, stuck to a synthetic bag throughout her climb on Dhaulagiri. Her reasoning, shaped in part by many years teaching at NOLS, applies to more common settings than a 26,820-foot peak.

Lucy points out that rain, wet snow, or an unexpected spill in the water is not the only way a sleeping bag gets wet. "Suppose you are snowed in for five days. For most of that time you will stay in your bag in a tent. In a circumstance like that, your own body moisture, your perspiration, can soak your sleeping bag. Once that happens in a down bag, you've got nothing left."

Sleeping Bag Design

Sleeping bags come in two basic styles: square-cut and mummy. Square-cut bags do not cover the head, from which about 50 percent of your body heat escapes. Even when they have a hood, too much air circulates through the wide cut of the bag to make it effective for three-season camping. They may be adequate for summer camping, but not much else.

The mummy bag is preferred by NOLS and most experienced backpackers. A mummy bag is tapered around the body and allows less circulating air inside the bag. Circulating air keeps you cold, dead air keeps you warm.

The hood on the mummy bag keeps body warmth from escaping from your head. Better mummy bags have wider, round configurations around the feet, making sleeping more comfortable. In addition, because less body heat escapes through the head, mummy bags are warmer ounce-for-ounce than the square-cut.

Understanding the basic construction of a sleeping bag, and knowing how to identify quality work in a bag, is an important skill to take on any shopping expedition. Price is not the best standard to judge the merit of a bag. You need to be able to judge the caliber of each element of the bag in order to know if it all adds up to a superior product.

Shells

A sleeping bag has an inner shell, the fabric that lies against your body, and an outer shell, the outer covering of the bag. The insulation goes in between these two shells.

There are two types of shell cuts: differential cuts and contour cuts. In the contour cut, the inner and outer shells are the same size. This bag will slump around you, filling air spaces next to the body. However, if you lodge a knee or elbow hard against the material, you can displace the filler, leaving only two layers of fabric between you and the cold world.

In a differential-cut bag, the outer shell is cut significantly wider than the inner shell. This eliminates the possibility of displacing insulation.

The most widely used fabric for sleeping bag shells is ripstop nylon. The tightness of the weave is the variable between the cheaper and the more expensive ripstop. It is important that the fabric have a tight enough weave to hold the insulation. This means that the ends of the pieces of down or the ends of the synthetic material do not poke through the fabric. Because down is so fine, it requires a particularly tight weave as a covering fabric. The fabric must also "breathe." You can test this by stretching it over your mouth and blowing through. If you breathe easily, so does the material.

A second fabric used in sleeping bag shells is nylon taffeta. Army tests show that taffeta is actually stronger than ripstop, breathes better, and is more abrasion-resistant. However, once taffeta does tear, it doesn't stop at a convenient point, as ripstop does. In addition, ripstop is as much as one-third lighter than taffeta. Fill will loft easier if it isn't weighted down by heavy material.

For users of down bags, there are several new solutions to keeping the bags dry. Some bags are being made with Gore-Tex shells, which allow water vapor to pass through the fabric, but block water droplets from coming in. Moisture from the inside of the bag, yours, can get out, but rain from the outside cannot get in. A Gore-Tex shell also makes the bag more wind-resistant. However, Gore-Tex is more expensive and heavier than other shell materials.

Zippers

Big, thick nylon zippers are commonly found in good sleeping bags. Metal zippers conduct cold more than nylon and are eschewed by the purist and comfort-seeker alike. Metal zippers are also heavier to carry.

Zippers, even those made of plastic, often constitute a cold spot in the bag. A baffle, or draft flap, sewn on the inside of the bag the entire length of the zipper, can prevent heat from escaping through the zipper, eliminating the cold spot. Quality draft flaps will be slightly longer than the zipper and will be sewn to the upper inside of the bag. For maximum protection, the draft flap should cover not only the zipper but also the seam attaching the zipper to the bag. Be careful to note whether the draft flap's seam is sewn only to the inside of the shell and not all the way through the bag. Any seam which sews the inside and outside shells together, commonly referred to as "sewn-through construction," allows significant amounts of heat to escape.

Most backpackers prefer zippers that unzip at both ends of the bag. This allows ventilation at the foot of the bag on warm nights, and warmth when the zipper is fully closed when it is cold. At the upper end, zippers should have a

Velcro tab to hold the zipper in place so it doesn't come undone in the middle of a cold night.

Zippers come in two basic designs: those with interlocking teeth, and a coiled design. The coiled zipper is less vulnerable to damage and more airtight, and thus preferable.

Zippers used on sleeping bags should have tabs both inside and outside of the bag. A string added to the zipper tab will make opening and closing much easier with a gloved or mittened hand.

The best way to check a zipper is to get in the sleeping bag and zip it up. When you zip it from the inside, does the zipper get caught or snag? If the bag is designed to fit snugly, do you have enough room inside to operate the zipper? More than one person has carefully examined the quality of a bag from the outside, bought it, and then, after getting into the field, discovered that he didn't have room inside the bag to zip it up.

Bags with compatible zippers can be zipped together to form double bags. Some heat is lost around the shoulders and head this way, but you can minimize this heat loss by stuffing clothes in the open space, or make up for it by snuggling. If your partner has a high metabolism and you don't, you may have a net energy gain out of the arrangement.

Internal Construction

In order for the fill in a sleeping bag to provide adequate insulation, the fill, whether down or synthetic, must be distributed evenly throughout the bag and held in place so that it doesn't bunch too thickly in one place, leaving cold spots elsewhere in the bag.

This problem is much easier to solve in bags with synthetic insulation. PolarGuard, Hollofil, and Quallofil come in batts, solid sheets of insulation. There are a number of ways that this insulation can be attached inside the sleeping bag. The least expensive way is a sewn-through quilting construction, but this method greatly weakens the insulating ability of the batts. Better bags use a "double quilt sandwich" construction, in which separate batts are quilted to both the inside and outside shells of the bag, then a middle layer of batting is stabilized between them by sewing it to the edges of the bag. This method ensures that there is no seam which goes directly from the inside to the outside of the bag; thus, the cold spots of the sewn-through pattern are eliminated.

Down bags must also be constructed to prevent loose down from collecting in bunches or shifting too easily. Cheaper down bags use the unsatisfactory "sewn-through" method. The insulation material is stabilized by sewing through the inner and outer shells at intervals. As pointed out, this process is self-defeating, because where the outer and inner shells meet, no insulation is present, creating cold spots.

A better way of keeping down insulation in place is a series of baffles. Baffles are simply walls of fabric sewn at intervals between the inner and outer shells of the bag to prevent the material from shifting from one section of the bag to another.

There are three basic baffle patterns: box-wall, slant-wall, and V-tube.

SLEEPING BAG CONSTRUCTION

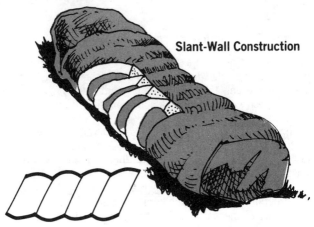

Slant-Wall Construction

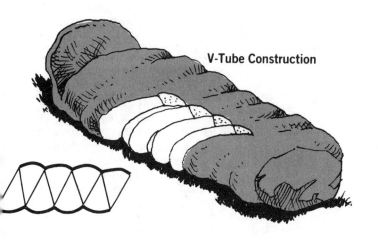

V-Tube Construction

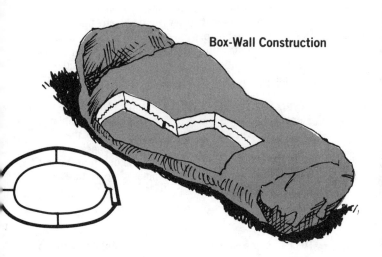

Box-Wall Construction

Box-wall construction is the simplest. The fabric is sewn into the material at right angles to the inner and outer shells. Of the three patterns, this allows the fullest loft of the material. However, the compartments must be filled with the proper amount of down, or the material will shift within the sewn area, causing cold spots.

Slant-wall, or slant-box, baffle construction is similar to box construction, except that the material is sewn in at an angle to the inner and outer shells. This method more successfully limits downward movement than the straight box, and still allows full expansion of the fill material. It requires a little more material and may be marginally heavier than box baffles. It may also be slightly more expensive, but it is currently the preferred type of baffling.

The third type, V-tube baffling, uses more material than the other two, costs more, and is heavier. However, it is generally considered to be the best system for eliminating downward shift. This type of bag does not allow as full a loft as the other types. Its use is generally limited to expedition-grade winter equipment.

In both synthetic and down bags, one area of great potential for heat loss is the sewn area where the top and bottom halves of the bag meet. If the two sections are simply sewn through, the bag has heat-loss problems along the seam. In addition, in down bags without a side-wall baffle, insulation from the top of the bag can shift to the bottom, losing much of its value to the sleeper.

Most good bags have a side-wall baffle. This baffle runs the length of the bag and is designed to prevent insulation in the upper half of the bag from traveling to the lower half, and vice versa. When buying a bag, check that the side-wall baffle is at least as wide as the depth of the loft. This can be checked simply by holding apart the inside and outside shells along the baffle.

Sleeping Pads

To provide insulation and comfort and minimize conductive heat loss to the ground, a foam pad is essential for backcountry campers. Your sleeping bag, whether synthetic or down, will compress under your body weight, losing most of its insulating power between your body and the ground. Synthetic bags don't compress as easily, but a pad is still needed.

The standard pad is made of polyurethane foam. The most common brand is Ensolite. Thicknesses vary from ¼-inch to ¾ of an inch. The thicker the pad, the more insulation on the ground, but also the more weight on your back. A little experimentation is the best way to determine what thickness is worth the weight. By all means, if you find yourself sleeping cold, first try a thicker pad rather than buy another sleeping bag.

Sleeping pads containing open-cell foam transmit water to the floor of the shelter and can freeze beneath you in the winter. Closed-cell foam holds the water, and dampens the bottom of the bag. The latter is not such a problem with synthetic fill, since it will keep you warm even though the bottom of the bag may be damp.

Another sleeping pad option on the market is an air mattress. Conventional air mattresses are primarily for cushioning. They keep you off the ground, away from moisture and the pull of conduction. But they provide very little insulation, because convection currents in the mattress carry heat from the bag to the ground. They also have an inconvenient habit of puncturing.

One of the more intriguing options now available is the Therm-A-Rest mattress, weighing about 1.5 pounds. Basically this is an air mattress filled with open-cell foam. The foam insulates, while the air mattress provides comfort. Some NOLS instructors balk at the added weight on a backpacking course, but if they are kayaking, the Therm-A-Rest is at the top of their equipment list.

New Waves

Recently a number of new innovations in sleeping bags have hit the market which are worth mentioning. These fresh ideas came from a number of different sources: from amateur experimentation that worked, from an old discarded concept which was given new interpretation, and from the laboratories, which continue to discover new fabrics for outdoor use.

Sleeping Systems

People who spend a considerable amount of time in the backcountry in all seasons of the year are faced with the problem of having to buy a number of expensive sleeping bags to meet all their needs: a lightweight bag for summer, a medium-weight bag for spring and fall, and a heavy bag for winter. Some people began experimenting by inserting their lightweight bag inside a medium-weight bag for winter use. The fit was often awkward, and it took a while to figure out all of the zippers, but enough people reported favorably that several major sleeping bag companies decided to design and market what is now known as a sleeping system.

The sleeping system applies the layering principle to sleeping bags. The most common system begins with a lightweight summer bag—often made with a sewn-through design and without a hood, side-wall baffles, or a draft tube—as a liner bag. The outer bag is usually a three-season mummy bag, which works well in everything but the hottest and coldest seasons. When the temperature drops toward zero, you put the liner bag into the three-season bag—the liner may attach with a zipper, loops, or Velcro tabs, or it may be free-floating—and you are ready for cold-weather camping.

Another type of sleeping system utilizes a layer of synthetic insulator designed to go over the mummy bag. This is a relatively inexpensive way to add ten to fifteen degrees of warmth to your sleeping bag.

Many of the sleeping systems sell by the piece, so that you can start by buying a three-season bag and, if you find you need more warmth, go on and buy other components of the system.

Keep in mind that sleeping systems often require lugging more weight around, if only because of the added layers of material. They can also be complex, with extra zippers that can go haywire, or duplicate hoods. But for the person who plans to be in the backcountry for a good part of the year and wants to minimize the expense of outfitting, a sleeping system is worth considering.

Vapor Barrier

The vapor barrier concept is a dramatic reversal of one of the basic premises of traditional backcountry safety and comfort. Rather than aiming for breathability in sleeping bags or clothing, it aims to surround the body with an impermeable layer, trapping all escaping body heat and body moisture. Usually this impermeable layer is a coated nylon shell.

The idea is based on the principle that the higher the humidity in the air, the less your body tends to perspire. Proponents of vapor barrier claim that the system is particularly useful in very cold weather, when it is important to minimize the amount of body heat lost. They maintain that once the water pressure in the air surrounding your body has stabilized, your perspiration tends to lessen.

Opponents claim that vapor barrier is uncomfortable, creating a slimy, clammy condition inside the bag.

Both sides have a point; vapor barrier is clearly a system which works for some individuals and situations and is a calamity for others. For the beginner, this is not the place to start. Even for the experienced backpacker, your first experimentation with vapor barrier should be on a modest weekend jaunt, not an extended expedition.

Radiant Heat Barrier

This is a variation on the vapor barrier system with one important distinction. Radiant heat barrier bags use a new fabric called Texolite, which looks a lot like a space blanket. A soft, aluminum foil-like material, Texolite is placed on the inside of an insulated bag in order to reflect the infrared heat which is radiated from the body. The fabric has small pinholes through which, it is claimed, the moisture of the body passes. Some people say it does, other people say it doesn't. Cautious personal experimentation is a good idea before you buy.

Radiant heat barrier bags are extremely lightweight, which makes their potential appeal considerable.

Sleeping Bag Care

Sleeping bags should not be stored in the small sacks in which they are usually sold. Both synthetic and down bags lose their loft when compressed for weeks or months. The best way to store a sleeping bag is open and fluffed up on a cool, dry shelf. Or you can put it in a large sack, to protect it from dust; but the sack should not compress the bag's insulation.

People often carry down bags in their backpack, but synthetic bags, which do not compress as much, are usually placed in a stuff sack which is tied under the main bag of the pack. The name "stuff sack" precisely describes how a bag is to be packed. Don't fold it or roll it, stuff it. Starting with the foot of the bag, take a handful and put it into the bottom of the stuff sack. Continue stuffing the bag, pushing down tightly with each handful to empty it of trapped air.

When you get into camp, always take your bag out and air it so that it can attain its full loft. Be sure to air it in the shade, since ultraviolet rays will deteriorate the shell of both down and synthetics over time. If there are any threatening clouds in the sky, set up your tent first and then air the bag inside.

Cleaning your sleeping bag should be done with extreme care. For the casual camper, who only goes out several times a year for short trips, it is unlikely the bag will need to be cleaned for many years, unless it is soiled by a spill. If the bag is in frequent use, cleaning once a year should be sufficient. Some experts contend that down bags lose 10 percent of their insulating power with each washing.

The safest way to wash a down or synthetic bag is in your bathtub, with loving care. Use a very mild soap; Ivory Flakes, Woolite, or Nu-Down all work well in lukewarm water. Since the bag is likely to be dirtiest on the inside, turn it inside out before washing. Knead the bag gently. Better yet, get in the tub with the bag and massage it softly. Never twist or wring it.

Some people recommend simply squeezing the air out of the bag in the tub after dissolving the mild soap in the water. Then let it soak for an hour or two. Drain the tub, refill it with clean water, and work out the soap solution. Either one of these systems works, but the essential point is to treat the bag like a baby: gently.

The most dangerous part of the process, particularly for a down bag, is removing the bag from the tub. The baffles which hold down in place are often very light; they can easily be torn by the pressure of heavy wet down. Gently squeeze the excess water out of the bag before you lift it, then remove the bag from the tub by supporting all the weight of the bag with your arms, hands, and other available appendages. If all of the bag's weight is not evenly distributed, the weight of the wet down is very likely to tear the baffles, leaving you with a useless sack. Although synthetic bags do not have baffles, and the polyester insulation does not absorb a great deal of water, it is still a good idea to proceed carefully with this step.

The best way to dry a down bag is to put it flat on the ground and leave it for three to five days, turning it every day. Synthetic bags, too, will dry more quickly in the fresh air. Never hang a wet down bag on a clothesline; this is a sure way to destroy the baffles.

Down bags can be dry-cleaned, but there are perils. Many dry cleaners don't have the same respect for your bag as you do and are not knowledgeable about handling down. Dry-cleaning solvents are toxic, and unless they are thoroughly removed, an innocent camper may awake with a terrible rash.

Synthetic bags should never be dry-cleaned. Temperatures of 140 degrees or more will fry the fill. The instructions on some synthetic bags indicate that they can be washed in a front-loading washing machine. If that is the case, make sure the machine is set on a delicate setting. The bag should be zipped, with the zipper pinned at both ends to ensure it remains zipped. Never put a synthetic bag in the dryer; the heat will destroy the insulation. Remember, the insulation is not heavily absorbent, so the bag will dry quickly in the open air.

STUFFING A SLEEPING BAG

Tips for Sleeping Warm

A warm, comfortable night's sleep often depends on more than your sleeping bag and pad. Above all, it requires that you know your own body and how to take care of it.

If you tend to sleep cold, anticipate the problem and make adjustments before you go to bed.

It is much easier to stay warm through the night if your body is well hydrated and if you have eaten foods high in fat and carbohydrates. A cup of hot chocolate with a spoonful of melted butter or margarine before bed can help accomplish both of these goals. Keep food and water handy in case you wake up cold. Eating and drinking pick up your metabolism and generate heat. You of course don't want to sleep on a full bladder, and there is nothing more frustrating, or more common, for a camper than lying awake in the middle of the night debating whether to get out in the cold to relieve himself. But with a little experience, you will come to know how much fluid you should take before sleep. You will also learn that as soon as you feel the need, it is best to get up, brave the cold, and then go back to sleep.

Try to be completely warm when you go to bed. It is your body heat that warms up the bag; if you go to bed cold, it will take a lot longer for you to warm the bag.

Another factor in sleeping warm is how you position your campsite. Try to protect yourself from winds and avoid valley floors where cold air settles. Sleeping in a tent will add considerably to your warmth.

If you do find yourself cold, the first piece of clothing you should add is a wool hat. The head is usually the one part of the body that is exposed, and it is the area of greatest heat loss. Many people sleep in the buff except for a wool hat. If you remain cold, try bringing your head down inside the bag.

When you are shivering, your first reaction is probably to put on clothes, but there are other ways to halt it. You might put a layer of clothing underneath you to add another layer of insulation between your body and the ground. Or use the clothes as a blanket on top of you.

Some people find that bunching good insulators like pile or wool around the hole at the top of the bag prevents a considerable amount of heat loss. Always make sure that you don't have damp clothing, particularly cotton, next to your body when you are attempting to sleep in a bag.

If suddenly you find yourself in cold, harsh weather and you are beginning to have serious problems staying warm, the best solution is to take off your clothes and get into a bag with another warm body, or zip your bags together. For serious cold problems such as hypothermia, placing the chilled person between two other bodies in a sleeping bag is the fastest way to restore warmth in the wilderness.

Shari has always had a problem staying warm in a sleeping bag. That is why she prefers a tight-fitting bag with a minimum of circulating air around the body. She has had particular problems keeping her feet warm; the traditional wool socks or down booties never seemed to work, particularly in cold high altitudes. The solution she found was to wrap her feet together in a wool sweater. The heat radiating from each foot helped the other stay warm. For someone who has trouble staying warm, and there are a lot of people in that category, Shari's type of experimentation is exactly what is needed to find your own personal system for sleeping comfortably in the outdoors.

BACKPACKS

On the 100-mile trek from Pokhara to the Dhaulagiri base camp, the porters used an ancestor of the backpack, the tump line, to carry their 66-pound loads. This simple device, a long strap usually made of hemp or bamboo fiber, goes across the forehead, down the back, under the lower end of the load, and back up to the forehead. The porter leans forward and the load then rests against the lower back, with the neck muscles used to balance the weight. This primitive design can carry a variety of shapes and sizes: some loads on the expedition were duffel bags roped together, others were waxed cardboard cartons taped shut. Mixed loads were often placed in woven bamboo-slat baskets, wide at the top and tapered to a fairly narrow bottom. Sacks of flour, salt, sugar, meal, dal, and rice were simply tied up securely and carried with the tump line to hold them in place.

After her return from Nepal, Lucy tried a tump line. She was teaching at NOLS Alaska for the summer, and the staff was moving into a new headquarters. When the truck full of boxed equipment arrived, the road to the headquarters was muddy and the truck could not make the last three hundred yards. "So we rigged up some tump lines and spent the afternoon lugging these large boxes Nepalese style," Lucy remembers. "They worked reasonably well, but the next day, when someone would call me from behind, I couldn't move my head an inch. My neck muscles just weren't conditioned to handle it."

The designers of the early backpacks cavalierly assumed that hikers' muscles would conform to their design. The standard pack was the rucksack, which placed all of the weight on the shoulders. Sometimes tump lines were attached to divide the burden between the shoulders and the neck. If your build or musculature did not match the standard rucksack, you simply had to endure the pain, or develop new muscles. As Lucy discovered, it would take many miles to develop a good strong Nepalese neck to carry a tump line.

Today, the process has been reversed. The market is filled with many good backpacking options, and when manufacturers get wind of a new need, they design to fit it. Lucy, who is six feet tall and has a different torso length than Cyndy, who is five feet four, uses a different size backpack. Men and women often have different requirements. Growing young bodies have different strengths and shapes than more mature bodies. Most manufacturers today make backpacks in a wide variety of sizes and styles. You should be able to find a model that is right for you.

While you are in the wilderness, your backpack will be your portable home, containing all your life support systems. When you are hungry, cold, wet, or beat, your pack must contain the solution to your problems—and let you get to that solution in a hurry. It will get rained on, accidentally dropped, and stained by leaky honey jars, but your pack must hold together and provide as much comfort as the weight you carry allows.

If your pack is not right, its weight will be oppressive. Like Lucy's experiment with the tump line, it will tell you for many days afterward that you have the wrong body for the job. Scenic hikes will turn into forced marches as you trudge along yanking on a strap here and a waistband there, hoping that constant adjustments will at least substitute new pains for old ones. Eventually, you will limp into your evening campsite and angrily seek relief by tossing the whole contraption on the ground. Troublesome backpacks at this point tend to crack and break.

Such horror stories are avoidable if you choose your pack with knowledge and care. You should never select a pack in haste, for half-formulated reasons. Beware of the seduction of an advertisement or the well-meaning tip of an acquaintance. Don't be won over by one sexy feature on a pack and lose your head. The romance will wear off under sixty pounds about an hour down the trail. If you choose carefully, on the other hand, your pack will boost your hiking ability and appreciation of backcountry travel.

What do you look for when buying a pack? How do you make a wise purchase?

First, make sure that the pack meets your needs. A pack that works well on a maintained trail can be a real bomb on a backwoods bushwhack. A common mistake, which applies to most outdoor equipment purchases, is the tendency to overbuy. Do you really need an extension tube? Or the ninety-pound bag capacity? Make a list of your activities which will require a pack—weekend hikes on trails, afternoon ski tours, ice or rock climbs. The more thought you give to the specific interests you will pursue in the wilderness, the more suitable your pack selection can be. If you spend a lot of time in the outdoors in diverse circumstances, face up to the fact that you may need more than one pack.

Second, make sure the pack is durable. Examine the workmanship—the stitching, the zippers, the welds, all the various attachments and rigging. "Bombproof" is the term NOLS applies to equipment able to hold up under months of continual backcountry use.

Third, make sure it fits. Comfort is essential to getting along with your pack. Have a knowledgeable salesperson, someone with backcountry experience, fit you. Try the pack on, load it down, and walk around the store. Better yet, before you go out to make a purchase, borrow or rent several types of packs. Put them through their paces in real situations in the field and compare their performance.

Keeping in mind the general principles of good workmanship, careful fitting, and attention to likely uses, there are some specific things to look for in buying a backpack. There will be more than one suitable choice for you in today's array of backpack lines, but with this guide you can narrow down the choices and then make your selection on the basis of cost and personal comfort. The first choice you will confront is whether to buy a softpack or an external frame pack.

The Softpack

The softpack is an updated version of the age-old rucksack. After World War II, a pack with an external aluminum frame was developed, making it possible to shift the weight of the pack from the shoulders to the lower trunk. The frame pack quickly replaced the rucksack as the backpacker's first choice. In the last decade, however, attention has again returned to the frameless pack, now called a softpack. It has undergone a dramatic metamorphosis since its G.I. heyday. The softpack of today is nothing like that old rucksack that dug into the shoulders and made hikers feel like suffering soldiers. The sophisticated internal design of the new softpack imitates one of the more beneficial features of the frame pack: it shifts most of the pack's weight from the shoulders to the hips.

When the modern softpack hit the market in the mid-1970s, it did not include any internal structure. Basically it was a large canvas bag with shoulder straps on top and a padded hip belt at the bottom, similar to those used in the frame pack. The restructuring of the weight in this new softpack was accomplished by carefully loading the bag with the heaviest weight toward the top. With the heaviest load on top, the weight of the bag is directed downward toward the hip belt, so that it can be carried primarily by the body's skeletal frame and muscles of the buttocks and thighs. The same principle of packing generally applies to arranging the load in a frame pack.

Today's model of the softpack depends increasingly on internal supports which are sewn into the canvas bag. These supports may not be visible, as in the frame pack, but they are important structurally. The two most common internal structures found in softpacks are vertical stays and X-stays. The stays slip into long sleeves; stays are often made of aluminum and can be bent to conform to the shape of the wearer's back. The stays help to transfer the weight of the pack to the hip belt and keep the loaded pack from settling onto the shoulders. With support flowing only along the stays, a certain rigidity is created, which reduces the ability of the pack to follow the body's movement, an original advantage of the softpack.

The market is now flooded with a boggling selection of softpacks that offer semirigid or flexible tubes, stays, and rods fabricated from fiberglass, aluminum, or steel. Some softpacks feature adjustable mechanical fittings. There are also convertible models, with detachable frames offering the attractive option of using the pack without the frame for short day trips or attaching the frame for extended expeditions.

A number of softpack companies now make a design especially for women, on the premise that most women have narrower shoulders and shorter torsos than men. Most of these packs are capable of holding less weight than those designed for men. For the casual female hiker this probably won't make any difference; for women interested in expeditioning, many of these specially designed packs will not be suitable.

Since the softpack is more flexible and rides closer to the body, it is more responsive to the subtle shifts and turns of the user. This feature frequently makes it the preferred choice of cross-country skiers, mountain climbers, and some hikers with back problems. It is also preferable in heavy brush or jungle, where the absence of a frame reduces snagging.

Shari, Cyndy, and Lucy used softpacks on the trek into the Dhaulagiri base camp, since the climbers were each carrying only their personal gear, which weighed fifty or sixty pounds. Softpacks were again used on the higher elevations of the mountain, when the loads were lighter than on the first weeks of the climb, and the climbing became more technical.

Tod Schimelpfenig, at the NOLS Lumberyard, estimates that about 30 percent of all NOLS instructors use soft-packs, and some students bring their own, particularly on courses like those in Utah's Canyonlands, where they are often walking on narrow rock ledges or using rope systems to travel up steep rock inclines.

Shari is one of the strongest advocates of the softpack on the NOLS staff. She made her first softpack herself, to use on a new route up Alaska's Mount Hunter. "I was carrying about seventy pounds on the ski into base camp," Shari recalls. "Then for eight days straight, we were climbing with sixty-pound packs. I was very pleased with the pack."

An important thing to look for when buying a softpack is the quality of the adjustment systems. "Some softpacks have a tendency to slip, particularly when you carry a heavy load," says Shari. "When you try on a softpack in a store, make sure you fill the bag with as much weight as you ever plan to carry. Then walk around and see how it does."

The shoulder straps on softpacks are adjusted by lift straps, which are pulled tight to put more pressure on the frame and to bring the load into snugger contact with the body. These packs frequently have a similar strap arrangement on the hip belt to adjust snugness on the lower part of the load.

If you are interested in a softpack, disregard the vociferous claim of a friend or expert and let experience be your guide. "You've really got to try it to know if it's right for your body," Lucy says. "Whenever I hear someone going on and on about how great their equipment is, I always wonder if they don't have so much money sunk into it that they are *determined* to believe it's perfect."

The External Frame Pack

The abundant supply of lightweight aluminum available after World War II was the major impetus for the remarkable evolution of the external frame pack. Several companies claim credit for the initial design of a new pack which refocused the weight off the shoulders and onto the lower torso. Regardless of its inception, many equipment manufacturers have improvised and improved on the original concept.

Frame packs are the only type issued by NOLS to students. Most backpackers carrying over sixty pounds of gear find that frame packs are easier to load and carry; while there are softpack models designed to accommodate the hefty loads required on extended expeditions, they demand a considerable amount of packing practice and skill to ensure proper balance.

If you are considering buying backpacks for use in an organized outdoor program, or for any large group, a frame pack makes it easier to move weight from a weak hiker to a stronger one or an instructor. The frame also makes it very easy to strap on an additional stuff sack. This is practically impossible with a softpack. And, as we shall discuss in Chapter Seven, frame packs can be used to make litters for evacuations. This is always a handy backup to have in the backcountry. Softpacks do not offer these options.

The original external pack frame was the H-ladder, constructed, as its name suggests, of straight vertical side tubes with three to five horizontal cross members. The H-ladder is still on the market and is considerably less expensive than other designs, but its straight up-and-down construction hardly conforms to the body's natural curves. With a straight ladder frame, the weight is carried away from the body, and the pack tends to pull you backward.

The development of the S-ladder frame was a major step

toward hiking comfort. Designed to follow the shape of the spine, this double-curved frame allows a closer fit between the body and the load. The advantages of such a fit are added balance, agility, and comfort.

A third popular frame, the U design, combines some aspects of the H-ladder and S-shaped frames. The outside vertical tubing is similar to the straight ladder frame except that it is continuous, forming either an inverted or upright U. The crossbars are curved to follow the horizontal curve of the back.

Another variation of the external frame is the hip wrap. The increasing use of the hip wrap frame has spawned some controversy. The hip wrap frame wraps the hips with padded extensions of the lower frame. These extensions, which are connected to a wide wrap around the waist belt, make an almost cagelike encasement for the lower torso. One benefit is obvious: excellent distribution of the pack's weight. Advocates say the hip wrap pack is amazingly comfortable. Women with small upper torsos and people with narrow backs or with back problems have said that without the hip wrap, they wouldn't consider backpacking.

The design of the hip wrap—partly encircling the hips —is also its most serious drawback. Torso movement is severely restricted, making it unsuitable for the off-trail hiking common to a NOLS course. When hiking on rocks, along ledges, in snowfields, or on anything but smooth trails, use of a hip wrap frame can be awkward.

If you hike on moderate trails only, and have had a problem finding a comfortable pack, you might be a candidate for the hip wrap frame. As always, the only way to find out is to borrow or rent one, give it a good workout, and see if it suits your needs.

In researching frames, you will hear and read about welded versus assembled construction. Basically, the welded frame is a rigid unit with cross members permanently attached to the side rails by welding. The assembled frame has adjustable cross members, which are attached to the side rails by various types of metal couplings.

The assembled frame, on which the crossbars can be adjusted to fit, is particularly appealing to anyone whose body is still growing. A twelve-year-old can outgrow a pack frame in a matter of months, and biannual replacement of pack frames is an expensive proposition. The assembled frames also offer considerable advantage to a family of four that wants to buy two pack frames for use by various members of the family. The adjustments of the cross members can provide a comfortable frame for a variety of body types.

Because of the huge variety of assembled frames, there is no one recommended method of examination. The best advice is to do a "hands on" test. Ask the outfitter to help you with the first adjustments and then run through them several times yourself. Learn the principle behind the coupling and see if it makes good sense, works simply, and will hold up to heavy wear. Since one of the disadvantages of an assembled frame is that you might lose some of the parts, find out as much as you can about part replacement. Will the pack be on the market for several years? Are replacements difficult to find or to deliver?

If your body has finished growing and your frame-size needs are fixed, and if you plan to carry heavy loads, you will probably find, as NOLS has, that a good welded frame will serve you better in the long haul. NOLS uses only welded frames because they are stronger and better able to withstand heavy, continual use. Just be sure you get a good fit. Few welded models allow for any adjustment of the frame itself.

In your search for a good welded frame, first look for strength. The welded frame is rigid by definition; the frame should not quiver under pressure. Then examine the weld; this is probably the most critical factor in a welded frame. What at a glance looks like a weld may actually be a braze, a process similar to soldering. In a weld the surfaces of two pieces of metal are melted down and joined, their alloys intermingling to form the bond; in a braze a third melted alloy joins the two separate pieces. A braze is simply not as strong as a good weld.

To distinguish a weld from a braze, look for tiny marks along the point of the weld. A braze has a more uniform collar with a smooth finish. No amount of grinding will remove a welder's marks. If the manufacturer's literature says you are looking at "heliarc welding," that is the best you can ask for. Even so, look for integrity at the weld point. Compare brand to brand and be certain that the workmanship is top-notch.

The best way to check a pack frame, whether new or used, is to lay it down on a flat surface so that the four corners of the frame are all resting on the ground. If all four points don't hit the ground, the frame is probably bent. If it is bent less than an inch, it is usable, but it probably has some cracks in the welds. If a frame is bent more than an inch, NOLS has found it is generally unrepairable.

If you spot a crack in one of your frame welds, it can be rewelded. Any reputable welding shop which does heliarc welds should be able to handle it. A small hairline crack in town can quickly become a break on a rough trail.

All NOLS pack frames are made out of strong aluminum tubing. We avoid the weaker rolled or welded magnesium tubing. The most common aluminum tubing used in good packs is identified by the number 6061-T6 in the literature attached to the pack. This is a solid alloy with a good track record for strength. Read the brochures which come with the pack. Make sure they identify the type of alloy used in the frame.

Packbags are connected to frames by many devices, most commonly by clevis pins. These are thick wire studs inserted through grommets in the bag, then through holes in the frame. They are often secured by a separate wire that runs lengthwise along the frame and is threaded through holes in the ends of the clevis pins. There should be a kink in the base of this wire to prevent it from working upward through the pins. Clevis pins are easy to lose, so it is a good idea to carry additional pins in your repair kit.

Examine the connection system carefully. If the bag has grommets, check to see that they are brass and that they are attached to all layers of the bag. Look at the grommets that receive the most stress. Be certain that they are properly reinforced. New methods of attaching bags to frames are constantly being introduced, but always look for quality and simplicity.

The Suspension System: Shoulder Strap, Hip Belt, and Backband

As with an automobile, a pack's suspension system determines the comfort of the ride. Substandard construction of the suspension system will cause your pack to jolt and sway like the old Nepalese bus hopping from pothole to pothole between Kathmandu and Pokhara. Discomfort is the least serious drawback to a faulty shoulder strap, hip belt, or backband; you could suffer injury or a condition such as pack palsy. Pack palsy, which is temporary damage to the brachial plexus nerve, results in a numb, weak arm. The condition can occur when shoulder straps are insufficiently padded or the top suspension points are incorrectly placed.

Ever since packs were redesigned to shift weight from the shoulders to the lower torso, the hip belt has been the most critical part of the pack suspension system. In a properly adjusted pack, the shoulder straps absorb only 10 to 20 percent of the load. With 80 to 90 percent of the weight centered in the hip belt, the belt must be exceptionally durable and well designed.

Twenty years ago, the standard hip belt equipment consisted of two narrow strips of webbing that buckled in front. No one today misses this Spartan approach. Now, most hikers rely on wider four- to five-inch belts with substantial padding.

Single-piece belts wrap around the hips and attach at the side of the frame. The load is not as well anchored as with the two-piece belt, and the weight feels suspended away from the body, a sensation many prefer.

Those who choose two-piece belts say that they keep the load centered and prevent it from bouncing around. Because two-piece belts are attached to the lower corners of the frame, there tends to be less sway as you hike. Critics say that two-piece belts are uncomfortable, that they push into your stomach, have less padding, and are especially cruel to tender hips carrying heavy loads. These small controversies lend some credence to our basic premise: every person's body is different.

When examining a hip belt, check for its ability to release quickly. The importance of having a quick-release buckle cannot be overemphasized. As a matter of course, on any NOLS expedition we unbuckle when traversing logs and crossing streams or potentially unstable snowslopes. You never know when you'll have to ditch your pack to save yourself.

If you find a frame that fits your body but does not have a quick-release attachment, or perhaps does not have adequate padding, it is usually relatively simple to replace either the existing buckle or the existing belt. Some pack companies make more than one size belt. Don't hesitate to try a small waist belt on a large pack frame, or a waist belt from a different model on another frame that you particularly like.

The purpose of backbands is to keep the pack from directly bearing down on your back. They add not only carrying comfort, but also improve ventilation.

Backbands, usually made of nylon mesh, need to be adjusted regularly, since nylon stretches. The lower backband should be positioned so that it fills the small of your back. Properly placed, it will keep most of the weight riding above the lower torso. If the band happens to slip below the small of the back, you will probably notice pulling on the shoulders and pressure on the lower buttocks.

In order to be effective, the backband needs to be tight. Check this periodically; your constant movement can loosen the turnbuckle or lacing system. Turnbuckles sometimes fall off completely, and are easily lost on the trail, so bring extra turnbuckles along in your repair kit.

Shoulder straps, though they have been relieved in modern packs of most of the packer's weight, still must act in tandem with the hip belt and backband to properly distribute the pack's load. Also, there are situations, such as stream crossings, when, for safety, the hip belt will be released and all the weight will be on the shoulder straps.

Like the hip belt, the shoulder straps should have ample padding covered with strong fabric, such as Cordura nylon. Make sure the stitching on the shoulder straps is double stitched and durable. Ideally, the straps should be tapered, with more padding on the top near the shoulder than on the bottom. This provides additional comfort to the sensitive shoulder areas and prevents padding from bunching up.

Most straps are two to three inches wide, padded with urethane foam or thick latex. When trying on a pack, watch to see if the straps rub against the tender skin of the underarms.

One or two sets of buckles are provided on straps for length adjustment. These should be durable and easily workable with the pack on your back, preferably with one hand.

There is an option called a "sternum strap" that now comes on many packs. It fastens over your chest, connecting the two shoulder straps horizontally. It can take some of the pressure off the hips and keep the shoulder straps in line. Some people with narrow shoulders like the way it pulls the shoulder straps inward, preventing rubbing on the shoulder joint. It may, however, constrict breathing.

The Bag

The basic choice in a bag design is between divided and undivided bags. An undivided bag offers more flexibility in packing and usually more room. Hikers who like to compartmentalize their gear like divided bags. Usually divided bags have a larger section on top and a smaller one on the bottom, but some are divided vertically. Some divided bags have a third storage compartment for a sleeping bag.

NOLS avoids divided bags because the compartments are often too small for the gear we need on our extended expeditions. Also, one NOLS objective is to give each student freedom to develop his or her personal packing style, and the undivided bag provides more flexibility. It is also possible that a special compartment designed for a sleeping bag may not give a proper fit to the bag you have or want. It will be more expensive and heavier, but you can buy a pack that has dividers that can be zipped in or out according to your needs.

Most packbags cover about two-thirds of the frame. The

two-thirds style bag allows for more than one bag position on the frame. This means you can move all the weight up or down as needed, a helpful option in some hiking situations. Expedition bags that take up the full frame are also available.

Keep in mind that you don't want to buy too much pack-bag. Be realistic and select just what you need. If you choose a larger bag and then find that your load is occasionally light, cinch it with straps or a lacing system to prevent it from jostling and to keep the heavy gear from sinking to the bottom. Some bags come with built-in compression straps which run horizontally around the bag or along the sides and which can be pulled to reduce volume. This feature saves you from having to carry an additional small day pack inside your bag for use on short excursions from a base camp.

There are two basic designs for loading the bag: top loaders and front loaders. Top loaders, the standard issue at NOLS, are easier to pack. They often have spread bars that keep the top open while you pack it. You can overload a top loader and, if the storm flap on the top of the bag is a decent length, you can pull the flap over the excess load and secure it with the cordlocks. Or you can lash a zip bag or stuff sack above the flap.

One of the problems with large top-loading bags is the frustration when something you need is packed, inevitably, at the bottom of the bag. This can be averted by thinking ahead about what you will need on a given hiking day. It also helps to organize the contents of your bag into stuff sacks, small nylon bags with drawstrings on the top, which come in a variety of sizes and colors for easy identification.

The major advantage of the front loaders, designed with one suitcase-like compartment or several horizontal compartments, is that once the zippers are open, everything is in sight. If you consider purchasing a pack with horizontal compartments, make sure it has a pass-through hole for items like fishing rods and tent poles.

Compartmental packs offer less volume for their weight, and there is a better chance they will break down. As Cyndy says, "A zipper on your packbag is just one more thing to be paranoid about." If that zipper breaks, a compartment-alized front loader is not much good. Be sure to check the zippers to make sure they are of high quality; they will be under considerable stress when the pack is fully loaded. For packs, NOLS has found toothed nylon zippers to be the best.

On any style pack, outside pockets, sometimes detach-able, are a great convenience. When you need your water bottle, compass, or map, it helps to know exactly where to find them. Extra pockets not only give you added flexibility, they can also save you money; by adding pockets, you can adapt a moderate-sized pack to carry a volume closer to that of a larger expedition bag.

Outside pockets do have limitations, however. Climbers tend to dislike them because of the danger of snagging on brush or jagged rock. For skiers, large side pockets can limit critical arm motion.

The most common bag material is either nylon pack cloth or Cordura, a more heavy-duty nylon. A bag of light-weight nylon is usually about 7.5 ounces; Cordura ranges from 9 to 12 ounces. You will also find bags made of lightweight nylon with the heavier Cordura used on the bottom. Though Cordura has its critics—some say it is unnecessarily heavy—NOLS has found it an extremely du-rable material for the kind of backcountry travel we do.

Before you purchase any bag, examine its stitching care-fully. The seams of a bag will tend to wear out first. The ideal number of stitches per inch is eight to ten; any less and the seam is weak, any more and the fabric is weak-ened. Look for double- and triple-stitching in places of greatest stress, especially the corners of pockets and the ends of zippers. Check the stitching inside the pack as well as the pack bottom and pocket seams. Good stitching is smooth, straight, and finished at the end of a row.

Many backpacks are available with waterproofing, or you can treat your bag with waterproof polyurethane paint. Waterproof backpacks are, however, somewhat of a mis-nomer. In a good rain or a spill in a river, the items in your bag are going to get wet despite waterproofing. One disad-vantage of waterproofing: if water gets into your pack, it can't get out. Many NOLS instructors do not waterproof their packs. Some people insert big plastic trash bags into their packs and sleeping-bag stuff sacks before they load them. For short trips, this is a good solution. Rain covers are available which fit over most packs.

If you keep your pack tightly closed on the trail and set it up under a large tree at night, it will stay fairly dry. You can protect your pack at night by tying your waterproof rain parka over the top of the pack.

How to Fit a Backpack

Unless you are convinced that you know quality merchandise and how to fit yourself with a pack, avoid discount houses. Chances are, the salesclerk will know less about packs than you. Go to a retailer who specializes in wilderness equipment.

Bona-fide backcountry outfitters should not rush you. Often backpackers themselves, they are interested in your safety, comfort, and enjoyment, and will be as selective as you are about getting the right pack and the right fit. Give yourself plenty of time. If you don't have the opportunity to borrow or rent packs, comparison shopping is the next best way to guarantee a good fit. Be particular and choose exactly what you want. If you feel rushed, remind the salesperson that you might be in the wrong store.

You and the salesperson should select a number of packs to try on. Put the waist belt on first and leave the shoulder straps loose. After you have tightened the belt, check where the shoulder straps attach to the pack frame, or to the softpack itself. In a good fit, the straps should attach at or slightly above shoulder level. It is important to check this when the pack is fully loaded, too: sixty pounds has an insidious way of pulling the strap attachments several inches below shoulder level, where they are sure to cause a stiff neck and shoulders.

The size of the frame is the single most critical factor in the search for a proper fit. Your height is irrelevant here; your torso length and shoulder width determine the frame size. The frame should be as wide as your shoulders, which you can check by looking into a mirror. With a properly fitted frame, nothing but the mesh backband, hip belt, and shoulder straps make body contact. The frame should never actually touch you.

When you have found a pack which appears to fit correctly, load it with as much weight as you will carry on a typical trip. Many wilderness shops have sand bags for this purpose, but be sure to put in some bulky items to test the overall balance of the bag. If you already have a sleeping bag, bring that along to see how it rides in the pack. With shoulder straps, hip belt, and backband adjusted, see how the pack responds as you twist and turn, climb stairs, bend over, and sit down. It should remain snug; it should not bounce or sway from side to side as you move.

Be sure to ask the salesperson to explain all of the possible adjustments on the pack. It is surprising how many people with extensive camping experience arrive at NOLS unaware of the variety of fitting adjustments on their own packs. These adjustments—on shoulder straps, backband, crossbar, and frames—are designed to provide a custom fit to your body. Use them.

A good salesperson will support you during this extensive dry run. When you leave the store, you should have no doubt that the pack you have purchased is as close to perfect for you as you will find.

Getting into a Heavy Pack

All along the well-traveled trails of Nepal one sees stone walls built to allow Sherpas and other hikers to set their loads down comfortably. You can back up to them, as to a loading dock, and settle your load without having to stoop or do a deep knee bend. It doesn't work very well if you're six feet tall, like Lucy, but for Cyndy it was perfect.

When you find a natural rock ledge in the backcountry like the manmade ones in Nepal, take advantage of it. It takes some practice to heft a loaded pack onto your back; if you can find a rock or a fallen log two to three feet off the ground, that's the way to go. Make sure the ledge is stable enough for the pack to be free-standing. If you can't

GETTING INTO A HEAVY PACK

find a suitable ledge, you will have to lift your pack and swing it onto your back, using the side of the frame on a frame pack or the shoulder strap on a softpack. If you need more lifting power, place one hand lower on the frame or on the crossbar. The first few times you're bound to stagger, but with practice you'll develop a certain grace.

The common method is to lift a pack with both arms from the ground to your right knee, extended at a right angle from your body. Put your right arm into the shoulder strap (it helps to loosen the right shoulder strap before you lift the pack), then swing the weight of the pack to the center of your back, leaning slightly forward. When the pack has swung around, against your back, push your left arm through the other shoulder strap. Adjust the straps to bring the weight close to your body and secure the hip belt.

Try the same technique on the left side. You may encounter situations on the trail that limit you to loading up on only one side.

Packing the Backpack

Every day in the wilderness is different. One day you are hiking through a field of boulders, the next through marshy meadow grass. The scene changes quickly as the sun comes out from behind a cloud, a mosquito lands on your arm, or a grazing moose inspires you to reach for your camera.

Your backpack needs to be organized for all these events. Place the items which you will always want handy —water bottle, maps, sunscreen, sunglasses, snacks, mosquito repellent, camera, perhaps a pad and pencil— in the pockets on the outside of your pack. Develop a personal system that remains unchanged from trip to trip. Then you will know instinctively where to find what you need, and you will recognize right away if you have left something behind.

Small but important items, such as pocketknife, matches, and compass, can be carried in your pants pockets rather than your pack. These are easy to lose, and they will be more secure if your pockets have buttons, snaps, Velcro, or zippers.

You will also want rain gear and an extra layer of clothing easily accessible. A convenient place to carry these on a frame pack is inside your sleeping-bag stuff sack.

Nylon stuff sacks are handy for organizing the inside of your packbag. Put underwear in one, socks in another. Stuff sacks come in various sizes. They can be color coded to help you retrieve items quickly. However, when using a softpack, you might find stuff sacks a hindrance to proper weight distribution. They prevent the load from packing solidly, which can lead to discomfort when the pack is on your back.

A major consideration in packing for the day is how to distribute the weight. For trail hiking over relatively flat ground, the weight of the pack should generally be high and close to the body. In a frame pack this means your clothing goes in the bottom of the bag and heavier items, such as food and cooking gear, go in the top of the main bag or strapped above it in a separate sack. In softpacks the lightweight sleeping bag is usually stuffed in the bottom of the bag, while in frame packs it is usually carried in a stuff sack attached to the lower crossbar of the frame. As we have seen, the design of most pack frames and new softpacks helps ensure that weight is carried high and close to the body.

This basic packing strategy changes when you hike on boulder fields or through heavy deadfall. Then you want to carry your weight lower to give you better balance for jumping and twisting. Packing your weight high creates a fulcrum at your waist that tends to pull you off balance as you hop across boulders or pick your way through blowdown. When the terrain is rough or steep, sacrifice comfort for safety. In all cases the horizontal distribution of the weight should be equalized so that the left side of the pack is in balance with the right side.

The best way to fill a pack is to stuff it; don't fold clothing or nylon gear. Folding takes up more room, and it tends to weaken the fabrics by bending the materials along the same lines each time they are folded. Push each piece of

THE PROPERLY PACKED BACKPACK

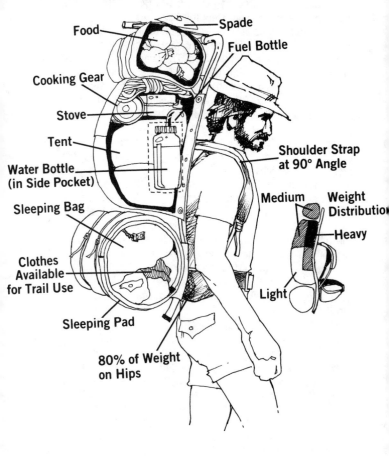

Food — Spade
Fuel Bottle
Cooking Gear
Stove
Tent
Water Bottle (in Side Pocket)
Sleeping Bag
Clothes Available for Trail Use
Sleeping Pad
80% of Weight on Hips

Shoulder Strap at 90° Angle
Medium   Weight Distribution
Heavy
Light

clothing down into the pack, filling up all the empty spaces; make it as tight and compact a load as possible.

Be sure to balance your load; if you load a water bottle on one side of the pack, balance it with a fuel bottle on the other side.

Avoid hanging things on the outside of your pack. There are many backpackers who resemble tinkers meandering down country trails, their pans, cups, and climbing boots all tied to the outside of their pack, thumping and clanging as they walk. The outside top of the pack is a handy place to tie a pair of socks that need drying, but they can easily catch on branches and be torn off and left behind. If you find yourself tying bulky items to the outside of the pack for space reasons, you need a larger packbag.

Finally, make sure your packed bag is tight and trim, with strap ends tied or tucked in. Protruding loops and cords invite mischievous tree branches to loosen stuff sacks and strew gear behind you.

Caring for Your Pack

Whatever style of pack you choose, its longevity and your own comfort can be increased by the way you take care of your pack. Like any piece of backcountry equipment, packs are not designed to take a lot of abuse. Even when you are tired, your pack should be taken off gently and placed on the ground, not dropped. A few good whacks on the corner of a pack frame can lead to a serious break.

When packing sharp objects, like climbing hardware or tent stakes, make sure they are positioned so their sharp edges don't rub against the bag. It takes a while to wear through and puncture heavy Cordura, but the constant rubbing will certainly weaken the fabric. Even a small bit of friction will destroy any waterproofing on the bag.

Be careful with the zippers, they can easily break. Overstressing a zipper is the quickest way to have a zipper breakdown, which can sabotage your trip. Try to keep zippers clean by keeping them out of the dirt. The proper place for a backpack in camp is upright, leaning against a tree or rock, not lying flat on the ground.

At the end of a long hike or during a midday break, many people impulsively use their packs as sitting cushions. The effects of such treatment will quickly show up in hairline cracks in the welds.

Packbags can be machine washed, but always on a delicate setting and using Woolite or other gentle soap. The bag should be taken wet from the machine and placed back on the frame so that if there is any shrinkage you will not have to struggle stretching it.

If you are new to backpacking, it will take a short time to develop your personal system for packing, wearing, and caring for a backpack. In the beginning you will find yourself adjusting shoulder straps, hip belt, and backband, and rearranging your weight. As with other wilderness skills, if you pay attention to what you are doing and take mental notes throughout the day on how you can fine-tune your techniques to make yourself more comfortable, your own style for living out of a pack will emerge. This style will become streamlined, and tasks will take less time and energy. If you start with a few basic principles and make adjustments as you go, the load on your shoulders may not lessen, but it will certainly become more comfortable.

SHELTERS

Tents are one of the great growth industries of the outfitting world, and the Dhaulagiri expedition got a good sampling of new wares. They could choose among geodesic domes, pyramids, fluted and I-pole, and many others. Lucy Smith enjoyed the newer, free-standing tents, because they offered more headroom; when she returned to an A-frame, she says, "I felt like I was caving. But," she adds, "a well-constructed A-frame must be given its due. When pitched correctly, you can have a lot of confidence in it." In the poor weather and avalanche conditions encountered on their expedition to Nepal, simplicity and dependability were what counted.

At NOLS we welcome the proliferation of tent styles, and buy a number of different kinds to meet the particular criteria of the various environments on our courses. In Wyoming, we camp primarily in forested areas where intermittent rain is common. The rainfall is usually intense, but brief. Here we need a tent with good waterproofing and sleeping space for two or three people. If a course is out at a time of year when the bugs are not, many instructors forget the tent and use only a strong rain fly.

At our Cascades branch, in the Pacific Northwest, rain is more frequent, and it often goes on and on. In this environment we need a roomier tent, so that equipment can be moved inside and more time can be spent there, comfortably. The rain fly needs to be larger to protect against blowing rain coming in along the bottom of the tent. The tent must have a "bathtub floor," with a waterproof piece of floor fabric that extends up the sides of the tent with no seams at ground level.

In NOLS Baja, we camp in a dry, desert climate, where adequate shade is a higher priority than rain protection. Bugs are not a problem there, so many NOLS instructors in Baja limit their shelter to a fly. When a tent is used, it is usually made primarily of mosquito netting, with a rain fly above, so that on warm nights the campers get the cooling breezes.

In Alaska, our wide variety of summer courses require several different types of tents. On Mount McKinley, and in other areas where we climb glaciers at high altitudes, we use an expeditionary mountain tent, which is larger and heavier, designed to provide maximum wind resistance. These tents have a storm tunnel entrance so that equipment can be brought inside for protection and convenience. On our kayaking courses on Prince William Sound, tents are exposed to heavy rainstorms, so we issue two flies per tent to provide double protection from the moisture. The weather on the Sound is often warm and humid, so good ventilation is needed between the flies and the tent to prevent a buildup of condensation inside the tent.

These kinds of practical environmental considerations should be kept in mind when selecting a tent; they give you a useful perspective on the many tent designs now on the market.

An entire book could be written about tents through the

A-FRAME STAKE TENT AND
FREE-STANDING DOME TENT

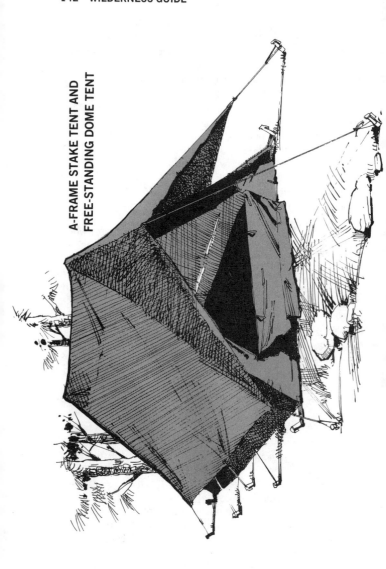

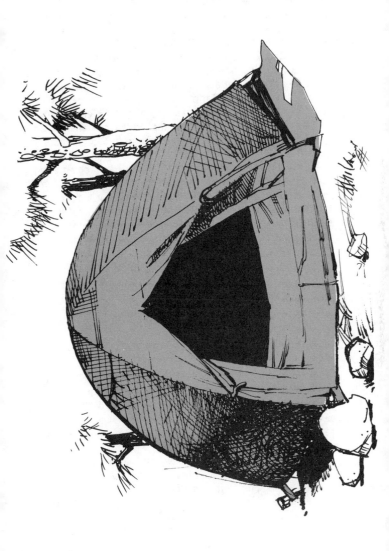

ages, from the tanned-hide shelters of the Mongols to the canvas A-frame of the Old West's mining camps. The recent upsurge in outdoor recreation has stimulated the current boom in tent design. Choices range from the simple A-frame and I-pole designs to semi-domes and domes, quonset huts and boxes, pyramids and multiple-chamber structures. The materials used in the construction of tents, once only ripstop and taffeta nylon, now vary widely. We see Gore-Tex, dacron, and dacron/polyester blends. Aluminum tent poles have been challenged by figerglass, graphite, titanium, and boron-fiber/aluminum combinations.

To make a choice among such wonders, we recommend four considerations. First, get inside a tent and see if it feels comfortable and useful. Second, look for simplicity: how complicated will it be setting up the tent in a driving storm? Third, examine the quality of the workmanship in the tent's construction. And fourth, think carefully about the environments where you plan to use the tent, and ask whether this is the right tent for such settings.

Buying a Tent: What to Look For

Most people don't set up a tent before they buy it. They will look at a number of different tents which are already erected in a display room, and choose one. This is a major mistake.

Setting up a tent is one of the major tests you should conduct before making a purchase. If the tent you are interested in is already set up in the store, ask the salesperson if you can take it apart and do it over again. This is really the only way that you can judge the simplicity and appropriateness of a particular tent.

Next, get in the tent. Lie down, flop around. Consider the available space. If it is billed as a three-person tent, what size persons is it sized for? Three like yourself, or three midgets? Your own height and weight will be the standard here.

Think about where you will be using the tent and how the specific design details will fit into those settings. Is there enough room for your equipment? What about conveniences such as pouches for glasses, books, and things? Is there adequate headroom? Will the height of the tent make it impractical in high-wind areas? Most tents for high-altitude or other windy environments must be close to the ground.

Once you are satisfied with the tent's interior, take a look at the ventilation system. A night in a poorly ventilated tent will teach you quite a bit about the metabolism of a sleeping body: a pint of water is lost during a night's sleep. If the tent doesn't vent this moisture it will condense, and you will awake in a rain forest, with all your equipment and clothing wet.

This is the chief weakness of tents with a single, waterproof wall. The common solution is the double-wall tent: an uncoated, breathable inner wall, usually made of nylon and cotton, and a separate waterproof fly erected above the tent, separated by an air space to keep the rain and snow away from the tent. Moisture escapes through the inner wall and is dissipated in the air space.

Recently, there have been several new designs that vary from this basic principle. The use of Gore-Tex in tent construction has eliminated the fly in some tent designs. The fabric, which is used on the sides and top of the tent, has minute pores which allow air and moisture from within to escape, but prevent water droplets from the outside from entering the tent. The great advantage of a Gore-Tex tent is that setting up is a one-step process; you don't need to erect a separate fly. The disadvantages, as we pointed out in our discussion of fabrics in Chapter Two are that Gore-Tex equipment is more expensive and requires extra care.

The other new variation in tent design is the vapor barrier tent. This is a single-piece tent made of coated, waterproof nylon. The vapor barrier theory, which we discussed in the sleeping bag section of this chapter, rejects the standard wisdom that breathable fabrics are required for backcountry safety and comfort. These tents allow moisture to accumulate within, which proponents claim keeps the temperature higher and checks excess perspiration among occupants by increasing humidity. If the theory interests you, try it out on a short trip before you make a major investment.

Good ventilation is still a major requirement of a comfortable tent, even if you are using a Gore-Tex or vapor barrier model. Vents, open to the fresh air and usually covered with mosquito netting, should be located at both ends of a rectangular-base tent. In a dome tent, vents should be well spaced to ensure good cross-ventilation. In a hot and humid climate, you may want an entire door, properly netted, to serve as a vent. Check the direction of the zippers on your tent entranceway. Zippers that run up the sides of the door and meet at the top will allow you to open them partially from the top. If the door zips across the bottom and up the middle, you have less control over how much outside weather you allow in when you try to boost ventilation. A good tent door will have middle, side, *and* bottom zippers, and be capable of zipping top to bottom or bottom to top, to give you the greatest variety of options.

Vents located in the lower part of the tent will create a chimney effect, with air moving in the lower vents and out the high vents even on windless days.

Next, you want to look carefully at the materials and construction of your prospective tent. Starting from the bottom up: The tent floor should be of tough, waterproof material and extend several inches up from the ground on all sides of the tent. The seams for the floor piece should be elevated inches off the floor to prevent wear, tear, and leakage. All seams should be tight, sealed and double. Even with a good tent floor, using a ground cloth under it will add considerably to the life of the floor.

The most common fabric used in tents is a three-ounce taffeta. A lighter-weight ripstop is also popular in tent construction—always limited to the walls of the tent, where less strength is needed. The type of fabric is a big factor in the total weight you must carry down the trail. Keep in mind when making your selection that lighter fabric may mean less weight, but it also usually means less durability. If you are just starting out, it probably makes better sense to buy a slightly heavier tent, which will survive a few early mistakes.

Tent poles are critical to the successful functioning of a tent. They should be strong, simple, and fit together snugly. Tent poles should not require a geometric genius to set up.

While setting up the tent in the store, notice how the poles fit together. The ferrules should slip snugly and easily into one another. If it takes a lot of jimmying to get this structure together, move on to another model. Once you have the tent assembled, examine all the poles to see if there are any unusual areas of stress. Poles are often the first thing to go under stress.

Most poles are thin-gauge metal tubing. The thicker the tubing wall, the stronger the tubing. Pole sections may be attached together with elasticized shock cord, which makes putting up a tent an easier exercise. Shock cords wear out, but they are easily replaced at most outdoor stores or by mail order. If your aluminum poles get bent, you can straighten them using a plumber's pipe-bending tool. Most plumbing stores will help you out. If the edges of a pole wear, use an emory cloth to sand them smooth.

It is not uncommon for some part of the pole structure to fail, even on quality tents. Tents can be placed under considerable pressure in the backcountry, and they are, after all, rather delicate structures. Parts can also be lost. If you don't stay alert to your equipment, stakes and poles can easily roll under a bush and get left behind. For this reason, it is wise to inquire about buying spare parts before you make your purchase. Ask if the manufacturer sells spare parts, how they are distributed, and whether this particular tent model might be taken off the market, which would make the purchase of replacements difficult or impossible. The longevity of the manufacturer whose brand you purchase may be the key factor in the availability of replacement parts.

Most tents come with metal stakes that are not big enough to function in a variety of environments, particularly in sand and snow. Replace them with nine- to twelve-inch stakes, made of either lightweight aluminum or tough plastic. Make sure, however, that the new stakes fit the loops of your tent.

Stakes should be carried in a separate bag to protect your tent from puncture. These bags are not usually provided with the tent, but can be purchased or made.

Tent stakes can tear up the ground considerably in a campsite. Whenever possible, attach your guy lines to trees. Long guy lines, extended with parachute cord, give you a lot more flexibility in setting up a tent.

Nylon guy lines often stretch, particularly when they get wet. Regularly adjust your lines to keep your tent taut. NOLS teaches a taut-line hitch which makes the process of tightening guy lines quite simple. The slippery taut-line hitch, a minor variation, is particularly good in cold weather. If the hitch is frozen, the small loop, when pulled, will break the ice and make untying easy.

Zippers are the bane of outdoor travelers, and in a tent they often succumb to fairly rough treatment. If there is any tension in a zipper when you try it at a store, it will have a tendency to fail later. A nylon coil zipper, either No. 5 or No. 7, is the common zipper used in tents. Any of the nylon zippers work better than metal zippers, which are much more likely to stick. When you have a problem with a zipper in the field, check it for encrusted snow, ice, or dirt. A small toothbrush and a little oil is your best hope for getting it working again. At times in advertising literature, you will see reference to a "self-repairing zipper." There is no such thing; it self-repairs until it breaks.

Make sure to check that the mosquito netting is reinforced in the places where it attaches to a zipper or hem. Particularly in entranceways, which will be zipped and unzipped regularly, the mosquito netting will tend to rip if it is not well constructed. Make sure mosquitoes can't sneak in where zippers meet: if there is a way in, the bugs will find it.

Tent flies, given regular use, wear out quickly from exposure to ultraviolet rays. They need to be strongly constructed to produce a good lifetime of use. Look for reinforced grommets and seams that are double-stitched with a flat-felled seam. Minimum-impact tents also require that tent flies, being the most visible part of the tent, should be a neutral color that will blend with the scenery.

To provide adequate protection in rough weather, the tent fly should fully cover the sides of the tent and extend well out beyond the entrance. A fly should fit tightly, or it

SLIPPERY TAUT-LINE HITCH

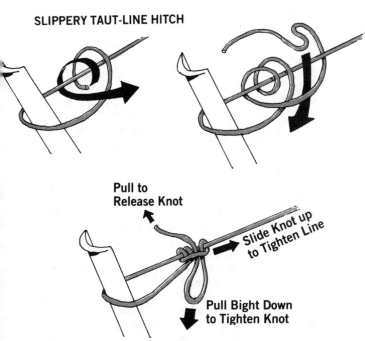

Pull to
Release Knot

Slide Knot up
to Tighten Line

Pull Bight Down
to Tighten Knot

may flap and tear just when you need it most, in harsh, windy weather.

Tents are one of the major investments you will make in camping equipment, so look for quality and buy the best one you can afford. If you have narrowed your choice down to two tents, both of which seem suitable, buy the one that is simpler.

Setting Up Your Tent

Having purchased a new tent, read the manufacturer's directions for assembly, then set it up and take it down five or six times before taking it into the backcountry. The first time out, you may have to set it up in bad weather under some stress. You don't want to have to be struggling with the instructions in a heavy rain.

When you pack the tent for a backcountry trip, double check to be sure you have all the parts.

Pitch your tent on smooth, even ground, away from rocks, twigs, or fallen branches which might puncture the floor. A hole in the ground underneath the tent can lead to a rip if you step on the tent floor directly over it. Situate away from fires and, if it is windy, out of the path of sparks. They are the most common cause of small holes in flies. Another thing to watch out for are "widow makers," dead trees that are still standing, which might be blown over by stiff wind.

Orient your tent to the wind, with the narrow end of a rectangular tent pointed into the wind. You don't want to take the wind broadside. Free-standing tents, which are not staked to the ground, are in jeopardy in high winds. Unless you have a considerable amount of equipment weight anchoring the tent, attach extra guy lines to make sure the tent stays in place. More than one group of campers have returned to a campsite to find their free-standing tent has blown away.

When your tent is erect, it should stand taut and stream-lined. This is not simply a matter of aesthetics. A loose or unevenly stretched tent will take a worse beating in wind and rain, placing additional stress on the material. A well-cut tent, properly erected, will spread the strain and last much longer.

Tent Care

Proper care of your tent, both in the field and at home, will give it a longer life.

In the field, make sure you clean off all twigs and small stones before you pack it for hiking. This small debris, when packed tightly, can result in holes and tears.

If possible, it is a good idea to let a wet tent dry before packing it. In the field, this is not always possible, and no damage will be done on a day's hike (although your pack will be heavier). At home, however, it is very important to dry your tent before storing it. If you don't, mildew will form. On nylon tents mildew will not cause any permanent damage, but it will stain the tent with a greenish blotch and give it an unpleasant smell.

There is generally little need to wash a tent if you take care of it properly. If the occasion does arise, the best method is to hang it on a clothesline, spray it with a hose, and let it air-dry.

Most tents eventually develop small leaks. These come from holes, usually caused by small sticks or flying embers, or from a faulty seam which has lost its waterproofing. There are many good seam sealers on the market, and some manufacturers include sealer with their tents. All seams should be sealed on a regular basis, depending on how often the tent is used. In the field, if you are not carrying seam sealer, rub cold wax from a candle into the seam. Remember, the wax should be cold, not heated. For small pinholes or minor tears, ripstop repair tape works wonderfully. Cut a circular patch for each side of the cloth and place them directly over the problem area.

Dome tents are much more difficult to repair, because the amount of stress inherent in the design can rapidly turn small tears into major tears. Generally, to repair a dome tent it is necessary to sew in a new section.

Don't wear your boots or shoes inside the tent. Hiking boots will quickly abrade the waterproofing of the floor material.

Lightweight Shelters

Tents are the most popular shelters in the outdoors, but there are two other types of protection, both of which offer significant minimum-impact advantages: bivouac sacks and rain flies used by themselves.

The bivouac sack slips over your sleeping bag, forming a simple shield from the elements. The sack is lightweight, takes up little room in your pack, and can be used in almost any climate or terrain. The object of the sack is to keep you and your bag dry, yet at the same time, it must breathe and pass moisture. A waterproof bottom is a must, and Gore-Tex is the preferred fabric for the top.

A bivouac sack has an attached flap to cover your head

BIVOUAC SACK

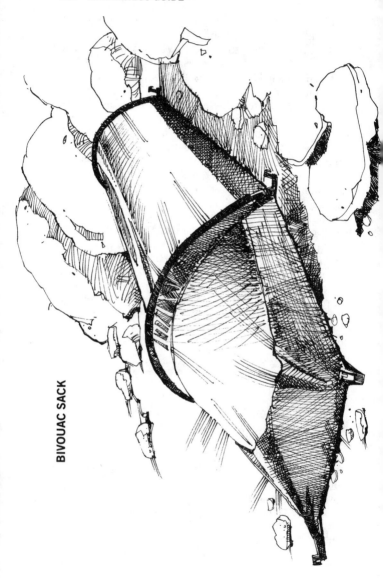

and face in extreme weather. Some sacks have small wands to keep the fabric away from the sleeping bag and to reduce claustrophobia. Mosquito netting is also available. For the solo outdoor person who wants to keep weight and bulk to a minimum, these units are handy.

The simplest form of shelter is the rain fly. This is preferred by many NOLS instructors, since it provides protection from rain and sun while offering an open, unencumbered area in which to sleep. Rain flies are inexpensive, lightweight, and versatile. They can be pitched in almost any configuration in almost any location. Most are made from 1.9- or 2.2-ounce coated ripstop or coated taffeta nylon, with reinforced pull tabs on the body of the fly. Easily packed, and quick to set up, they are available in sizes capable of protecting from one to four people. If you are using a rain fly, carry a ground sheet of tough, coated nylon to provide a waterproof floor. A rain fly won't keep the bugs out, but if the mosquitoes aren't really ferocious, a light, roomy, and airy fly is a functional and aesthetically pleasing form of shelter.

STOVES

Few items play a more important role in minimum-impact camping than stoves. Roaring campfires have an oldtime charm, but they are neither kind to the landscape nor, in many instances, practical. If you want to feed yourself efficiently and neatly, you should expect to carry that extra pound or two of a gas or liquid-fuel stove.

The newest generation of stoves is lightweight and compact, and should not add any considerable bulk or burden to your trip. This does not mean it is easy to make a choice: ask some of the top climbers and wilderness travelers and you will likely get a different favorite from each one. In addition, you must adjust your choice to the size of your backcountry group, your choice of meals, and the environment in which you plan to travel.

Stoves are potentially, but not inherently, dangerous. Used properly, they can be a convenience and a lifesaver. When accidents happen, they are usually the result of sloppy camping or misuse of equipment. Unfortunately, such accidents can be serious: no one laughs when a mountaineering expedition on Mount McKinley loses a tent because someone spilled a little fuel on the floor.

Experienced backcountry travelers talk about stoves with the mixture of irritation and obsession that most of us reserve for pets or loved ones. Everybody has a tale of the sputtering stove that shot flames three feet in the air, or the butane flame that flickered anemically while tired, parched climbers waited for ice to melt so they could have a drink. But for every tale of frustration, you should remember the warm soup on a rainy evening, or how quickly you can break camp in the morning after a stove-cooked breakfast.

The key to getting a good performance from your stove is familiarity and good upkeep. Read the directions all the way through. Try the stove out frequently before you take it on a long trip; if possible, try it at different temperatures and under varying wind conditions. Cook a few of the meals you are likely to cook in the backcountry. Different stoves are good at different things, and you should know the strengths of your own. This will also demonstrate the amount of fuel you need to take with you.

Take good care of your stove by cleaning it regularly, and carry a set of essential spare parts and the tools to install them if that proves necessary. If you use a liquid-fuel stove, you should bring along a funnel for pouring fuel into the tank.

Wind can be the greatest variable in stove performance. You will want to protect your stove from the wind, but you also need to be sure it gets properly ventilated and cooled. Don't be *too* efficient in protecting it. Digging a hole to completely guard it from the wind is not only bad minimum-impact practice, but the reflected heat in the hole will cause your fuel tank to overheat. An above ground pile of snow or rocks can provide adequate protection, and a regular hand-check will tell you whether the fuel tank is getting too hot. Remember, you should provide only a windbreak, not a complete cutoff of ventilation.

Consider packing gloves for handling your stove in the

RAIN FLY

backcountry. Pots and the stove itself will get extremely hot, and you could burn yourself badly and overturn your cooking setup if you are not cautious. Even if you have pot grips, gloves are a good idea—a blast of hot steam from a boiling pot could force you to drop the grips if your hand is not protected.

How Stoves Work

There are two basic types of stoves commonly used in the backcountry: stoves that burn liquid fuel, usually kerosene or "white gas," and gas-burning stoves, which commonly burn butane. Other liquid fuels, such as alcohol, have drawbacks related to weight, efficiency, or expense.

A liquid-fuel stove usually sits on or next to its own fuel tank. The tank has an opening into which you pour fuel, which must be capped with a safety valve, designed to relieve pressure when changes in temperature cause fuel tank pressure to rise too high. The opening should always be capped when the stove is in operation. Emerging from the side of the fuel tank is a line leading to a generator, a narrow chamber where heat turns the liquid fuel into vapor. On top of that is the burner, where combustion takes place.

To keep the fuel flowing from the tank up to the generator and out the burner, smaller stoves use a wick, while larger stoves use a hand pump, which pressurizes the fuel tank.

Most stoves must be primed to get them started. Into a "spirit cup," a small pan located just below the generator, you pour a small amount of fuel, using an eyedropper if you want to be neat, which you do, for safety reasons. When this fuel is ignited, it heats the generator, which will vaporize the fuel. A valve is located just above the generator to adjust the flow of fuel from the tank to the burner: keep it closed until the generator is properly warmed, then open the valve slightly and hold a flame next to the burner to light the fuel as it mixes with oxygen from the atmosphere.

The tank of a liquid-fuel stove should be topped to three-quarters full before each meal. If it isn't, you may have to interrupt meal preparation to refill, a dangerous task when a stove is hot. Your half-cooked meal, in the meantime, gets cold.

Always try to fill the fuel tank away from your cooking area, so that any spilled fuel will not be ignited when you light the stove. You should wipe any spilled or excess fuel off the stove itself, or allow it to evaporate. Similarly, when you put fuel in the spirit cup, don't get carried away: fuel that drips down the side of the tank will ignite, causing high-pressure problems and risking a much larger fire than you want.

Once you have the stove going, use the pressure or control valve to raise and lower the heat. If the stove "spits," sending droplets of fuel, often burning, flying into the air, shut it down and prime it again.

Most liquid-fuel stoves direct the flame at a plate burner, a small circular piece of metal that, when surrounded by flame from the burner, will turn bright orange and spread the heat under your pot. A stove working properly will have a blue flame. At low settings, though, a plate burner is inefficient, and at any setting it is noisy, like a miniature lawnmower.

White gas, which is actually naphtha, is volatile and burns very hot, so be careful using it. It is available only in North America. Kerosene is cheap, and readily available around the world; smoky, it is also often smelly (odorless kerosene is available), and leaves grime all over. Kerosene can be more difficult to light than white gas. Stoves that burn kerosene have hand pumps, which you use to increase the heat output; when you want to reduce heat you open an air bleed valve on the fuel tank. The better kerosene stoves use a pump and a control valve, which provides finer control.

At NOLS we prefer liquid-fuel stoves to gas stoves. The problem with gas stoves is that you have to carry in, and carry out, several gas cartridges. The longer you go in for, the more you have to carry, both ways.

There are two kinds of gas used in portable stoves: butane and propane. Don't bother with propane when you're

COMPRESSED-GAS STOVE

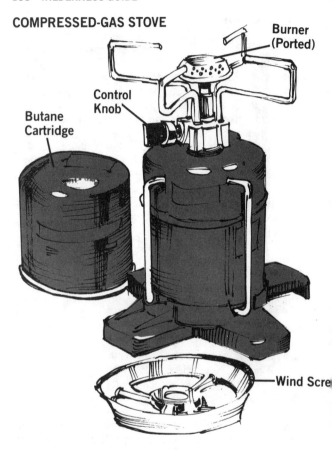

Burner
(Ported)

Control
Knob

Butane
Cartridge

Wind Scre

backpacking: it requires heavy-duty, and *heavy,* containers, under high pressure.

Butane stoves are uncomplicated. They consist of a fuel cartridge, a burner, a connecting device between them, and a control valve. The stoves can be either vapor- or liquid-feed.

In a vapor-feed butane stove, an upright cartridge is attached to the stove, and when the valve is opened the

LIQUID-FUEL STOVE

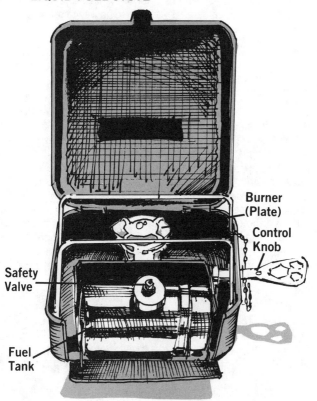

Burner (Plate)

Control Knob

Safety Valve

Fuel Tank

gas simply rises to a burner, which is ported to allow air to enter, mix with the gas, and ignite before it reaches the cooking surface. A liquid-feed stove is not much different: a wick draws the fuel up, it vaporizes, and ignites in a ported burner. Ignition is easy, and the valves allow good temperature control, so that you can lower your heat output for simmering more reliably than you can with a liquid-fuel stove. In addition, ported burners are quiet, unlike their burner-plate counterparts.

On the negative side, vapor-feed butane burners work

poorly under cold conditions—you may have to use body heat to warm the canister. There is also no way to tell when the fuel in a canister is getting low, so you may run out in the middle of a meal.

The Burning Issues

At NOLS we tout stoves as the minimum-impact way to cook in the wilderness. But we are also well aware of the dangers when stoves are handled improperly.

The first important caution is to avoid, as much as possible, using a stove inside a tent or near equipment or materials that could burn or be damaged. Even an experienced camper runs the risk of a small fuel spill inside a tent that could ignite and destroy it. Regardless of whether they ignite, petroleum distillates can damage nylon and other synthetic fabrics. In addition, a stove gives off carbon monoxide, which in an enclosed space can be fatal.

Cyndy points out that people often choose to cook inside their tent at exactly the point when they should get outside, even if the weather is uninviting. "If you have been holed up for several days in a tent because rain or snow makes travel difficult, it does not necessarily follow that you can't cook outside. Not only should you always try to avoid cooking in a tent because of the danger, it is also very important in times like this to get exercise. Keep your body attuned to physical activity. Get out in the snow or rain and cook. It is probably just what you need."

There may be times, however, when you have no choice but to cook in your tent, particularly in horrid weather when natural shelter is not available at your campsite. If you have a tent with an extended fly, cook under the overhang, so that your stove does not rest on the tent floor and fresh air is available. If you *must* cook inside your tent, place the stove at the point with the highest clearance overhead, which will often be on the center line, toward one end of the tent. Put your Ensolite pad underneath the stove; this will keep it level, insulate it against the ground temperature, and guard against melting the tent floor. Keep the stove near an open door, so you can throw it outside if something goes wrong.

A NOLS semester course camps on Alaska's Matanuska Glacier where tents are placed close together after probing the area for crevasses.
(Will Waterman)

Stream crossings, whether over the water or through it, should be done with great care. Here, one student "spots" for another as they cross a slick log in Washington's Pasayten Wilderness. (Will Waterman)

NOLS Instructor Phil Barnett prepares several loaves of bread for a cooking class in Wyoming's Absaroka Mountains. (David Kallgren)

A student learns to tie a double fisherman's knot on an Alaska mountaineering course. (Joel Rogers)

A knowledge of the flora and fauna of a region is one of the most satisfying parts of backcountry travel. At NOLS Mexico, some of the most interesting habitats are underwater. (Charles Fiala)

Instructor Lannie Hamilton (right) examines a student's gear at the NOLS Lumberyard in Lander, Wyoming.
(Heinz Kluetmeier/ Sports Illustrated)

The last step in camouflaging a fire pit is to spread natural litter over the surface.
(Will Waterman)

Using a compass to shoot an azimuth helps a student find his bearings in the North Cascades. (Joel Rogers)

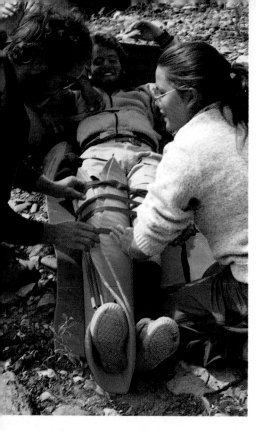

Early on every NOLS
course, the basics of first
aid are taught, including
improvised techniques for
splinting a leg.
(Joel Rogers)

Illustrating a bowline is one way NOLS students learn to tie the knot.
(Joel Rogers)

A student on Mt. Kenya examines "Icy Mike," the remains of an elephant at 15,000 feet. (Leslie Van Barselaar and David Kallgren)

Amid the spectacular rocks of Canyonlands National Park, students on a NOLS semester in the Rockies learn navigation. (Will Waterman)

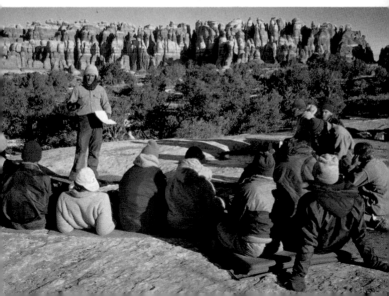

NOLS instructor Jon Salisbury oversees the construction of a packframe litter during a first aid class. (Joel Rogers)

Inspiration Glacier in Washington's North Cascades provides a spectacular background for a NOLS climbing class taught by Tony Jewell. (Joel Rogers)

We also recommend putting an Ensolite pad underneath the stove when cooking outside, both to insulate the bottom of the fuel tank, particularly if you are cooking on snow, and to provide a level surface.

In Chapter One, we described how to choose a cooking area as part of setting up your campsite. Once you have selected a cooking spot, don't refill or handle your fuel right there; take the stove away from the cooking site and your other camping equipment before you open the tank or add fuel. It is important to avoid having a flame in an area in which fuel may have been spilled. Never open the fuel tank while the stove is running. Let the burner cool off first, even if your half-cooked meal is freezing. Just because you are away from combustible fabrics and open flame does not give you license to be sloppy: your fuel will kill any plant life you drop it on.

To function well, a stove needs to be sheltered from the wind and placed on a stable, level surface, away from the camp's traffic lanes. A wobbly stove can tip, spilling fuel and hot food or water.

Careless handling of fuel, either when filling the fuel tank or priming the spirit cup, can cause a flare-up that will singe the ground or envelop the fuel tank in flames. This will cause great pressure in the tank, which will be released through the pressure relief valve. But the fuel from the valve can ignite too, so this situation is to be avoided. Fuel tanks can also overheat when you try to cook with a pot too large for the stove.

If you have practiced using your stove, you should know how much priming it needs and how to properly light and adjust it. If you are less familiar with your equipment, you run a greater risk of a flaring flame or sputtering gas when you first turn it on. Be especially careful of these dangers if you are using your stove inside your tent: start the stove and get it running smoothly outside the tent.

Gas cartridges hold some of the same risks as liquid-fuel stoves. They can puncture or malfunction, or you can cause problems yourself, such as forcing a cartridge onto the wrong stove or tossing one that doesn't work into an open fire, where it will explode.

Gasoline freezes at $-70°F$, so be careful handling fuel

bottles left exposed to the cold. If you grab a fuel bottle with a bare hand or you spill supercooled fuel on your skin, you can suffer contact frostbite.

A stove can also sabotage your trip while it's not in use. If not carefully packed, fuel can spill and spoil other items in your pack. And the delicate parts of a stove can be damaged if they are not put away properly.

To avoid fuel spills in your pack, stow your stove and fuel canisters upright in an outside pocket, if possible. Keep them as far away from food as possible—noodles soaked in white gas are no treat. Put fuel canisters and stoves in separate stuff sacks or plastic bags. Be sure that the caps are properly secured, and in the case of a liquid-fuel stove, release the container's pressure before you pack it, to keep it from forcing fuel out.

LET EXPERIENCE GUIDE YOU

The sight of Nepalese porters, dressed only in cotton shirts and pants, often barefooted or in thongs, carrying sixty to seventy pounds by their tump lines, leaves a strong impression on most Westerners. The Nepalese men and women, ranging from thirteen to fifty years of age, hike all day up steep, muddy trails with a cheerful countenance, making brief stops to drink tea and snack on dalbaht, a simple rice and lentil dish. They carry a blanket for cold weather, and sleep in it at night.

Westerners look at the Nepalese, and then at their own $100 backpack, their heavy-duty hiking boots, and their fiberfill sleeping bags, and they wonder what in the world they are doing.

That moment of self-doubt is important, because it signifies the next step in your relationship with the outdoor equipment world: once you have made your first careful selection of gear, there is still plenty of learning to do. You will look at the simple methods of the Nepalese, or read some of the "minimalist" literature now in vogue, and then wonder if you shouldn't move in that direction.

You should . . . but cautiously. The women who

climbed Dhaulagiri were experts, with years of experience in the backcountry. That experience taught them to survey the field of new and old equipment and take the best. They were experienced enough to know they were still learning.

"We took all the gear we thought we might need to get the job done," said Lucy, "and I'm not sorry. I would rather have a little too much than less than enough." That is your first goal in choosing equipment: take what you think you need to get the job done. Once you're more familiar with your equipment, the environment you're traveling in, and your own needs, then you can consider shedding gear that you found you didn't use, or switching to different designs. You won't know that until you're in the field. And for as long as you take your adventure in the backcountry, you'll be learning more about yourself and your equipment.

Bad weather and avalanche problems forced the American Women's Expedition to Dhaulagiri to turn back at 23,500 feet. A year later, while Cyndy stayed in Lander to have her first child, Shari and Lucy made their second climb in Nepal: to 22,494-foot Ama Dablam. Shari and Lucy became the first women to reach that summit. They had learned from the Dhaulagiri expedition, and were able to outfit themselves more precisely on the second trip. "It wasn't just equipment—we had learned about a lot of things," said Shari, "from weather, to expedition size, to our physical limitations. But we knew the environment firsthand, so we could trim our equipment list."

The rapid evolution of backcountry equipment provides new opportunities to lighten loads. New fabrics, new alloys, and new designs entice you to cut pounds off your load. Just be sure that you don't trade a few pounds at the cost of essential durability; try to see that weight, comfort, safety, and durability all go into the decision-making equation.

Appendix I contains sample clothing and equipment lists used by NOLS. If you have not backpacked before, or if you are thinking of hiking in a new environment, use these lists to see if you have forgotten anything essential.

Make your own list, keeping in mind the special features of the area in which you are traveling and any particular activity you plan. Look the list over to see if there is any way you can double up: Can one pan also serve as an eating utensil? Can an Ensolite pad serve as a ground cloth beneath a rain fly?

NOLS trains people to make good decisions in the backcountry—but those decisions begin before you actually step onto the trail. Pitching tents and crossing streams require careful thought and decision-making; so does a shopping trip to the local mountaineering shop.

Chapter **Four**

Cooking for Nutrition and Pleasure

THE FIRST NOLS students to reach the foggy shore noticed the smell as they unloaded their kayaks and hauled them from the chilly water of Alaska's Prince William Sound. It was an unusual smell, contrasting with the heavy presence of decaying duff, salt air, and the damp mustiness of wool clothing. This smell was sweet, even rich; then it was gone in a slight wind, a passing distraction at the end of a fatiguing day.

Early that morning, they had broken camp on Bainbridge Island and, setting out separately from the instructors, paddled their two-person kayaks into a thick mist. They traveled down the narrow, conifer-lined channel, huddled together on the rocks of Sober Point for a quick lunch of cheese and nuts, then headed into the icy waters of Whale Bay. The choppy sea encouraged them to hug the coastline, adding three hours of stiff paddling to their route. As they turned to round Duel Point, a strong gust brought the roar of Chenega Glacier's huge ice slabs, frozen for two million years, finally reaching the outer face and plunging with a sharp crack into the frigid waters. The last kayaks approached the black rock beach of the NOLS encampment around 4 P.M.

They emptied their kayaks, then hauled the boats over rows of seaweed, out of reach of the rising tide. As the students stood there in a moment of idle relaxation, a few caught a whiff of that remarkably savory aroma. It was warm and sweet and civilized—the smell of fresh-baked bread.

Randy Cerf, one of their NOLS instructors, had decided

165

that this was the day to educate his students to the potentials of outdoor cooking. During the first week of the course, each student had learned the basics of cooking over a campfire and stove; now Randy was intent on shaking off the doldrums of this gray day by encouraging real culinary creativity.

Randy first came to NOLS at age thirteen, and for twelve years moved through the instructor ranks, becoming one of the school's most seasoned outdoor leaders and proficient rock climbers. He has led several routes up Yosemite's El Capitan, pioneered first ascents in the Wind Rivers, and recently completed a 55-hour, nearly continuous climb up the west face of Mount Jeffers in Alaska's Kichatna Spires. While an undergraduate at Harvard, Randy often complained that his education was interfering with his climbing.

For his cooking class, Randy has prepared a meal assembled from his food bag and the natural larder of Prince William Sound. As an appetizer, mussels steamed in sea water, served in melted butter flavored gently with garlic salt. Next, a full-flavored seafood chowder, pieces of fresh rock bass and ocean perch in a creamy broth. As a main course, salmon quiche, a blend of flaked, fresh, pink salmon, cheese, and herbs baked in a light pastry shell. The bread that had caught everyone's attention was made with oatmeal and sunflower seeds and braided in a circle. Finally, blueberry cobbler made with the fresh plump berries which grow wild throughout these islands. The cobbler is seasoned with a hint of cinnamon, and baked under a crunchy, oatmeal crust. And, to top it off, a cup of hot coffee.

It was not what the students had expected when they pulled their boats out of the water and began to set up camp. Now, with blissful indecision, they confronted the choice of which tasty dish to sample first. They quickly forgot the choppy waters of Whale Bay and the dampness of the wool cuffs against their wrists. As Randy passed each dish around for a quick taste, he hoped that with this inspiration, and the cooking class which would follow, the meals prepared at each cooking site that night would reach honorable heights.

"The most useful ingredient for any backcountry meal," Randy began, "is appetite. And out here you are always hungry, whether you realize it or not." He paused a moment as his students licked the last of the blueberry cobbler off their fingers, then continued. "I say that because some people in the backcountry, this group obviously excluded, don't realize that they are hungry. They're in a new setting, they're uptight, they're worried about things like rain and mosquitoes, and they forget to drink a lot of water and eat regularly. As a backcountry cook, your first responsibility is to make sure people eat. Tempt them with something wonderful."

Not every NOLS instructor approaches the subject with Randy's zeal, but they all recognize the significance of good cooking to an expedition. It is important for three reasons: nutritionally, since the alternative—prepackaged meals—is usually low in nutritive elements; psychologically, since good, exciting cooking can boost the energy and morale of an expedition; and economically, since designing your own menu and buying staples available at any grocery store can be a lot cheaper than purchasing specialized, prepackaged freeze-dried food. After an exhausting day of kayaking, hiking, or climbing, a sudden whiff of rich, creamy Stroganoff or the sweet smell of apricot upside-down cake makes all seem right with the world. Energy and spirit return for even the most depleted. In addition a balanced meal will ensure your body's nutritional needs. Particularly on long wilderness trips, your health will depend on it.

FOOD FOR ENERGY

Staying healthy, building up muscles, remaining alert, warm, and cheerful, and maintaining high energy are essential for enjoyable backcountry travel. To make your trip successful you have to give your body the calories and nutrients it needs.

Whether you are edging your way up a steep rock ledge or lying perfectly still in a sleeping bag, your body is expending energy. The energy intake supplied by food is measured in units of heat energy called *calories.* A pound of cheese, for instance, contains an estimated 1,800 calories; a pound of margarine, 3,300 calories. An individual performing the heavy exercise common to outdoor adventure requires 3,200 to 4,500 calories per day. In cold weather, more calories are needed to keep the body warm. At NOLS we design our rations to provide an average of 3,700 calories a day in the summer and 4,250 calories in the winter.

Calories, however, measure only the heat energy in food. It would not be adequate, or appetizing, for a backpacker in winter to consume the required 4,250 calories by eating a pound of margarine and half a pound of cheese. In order to put together a ration plan which will encourage the body's efficiency, we must also consider the *type* of calorie we're consuming.

Most of the calories you need in the backcountry can be provided by *carbohydrates,* the starches and sugars which should make up about half of your daily ration. Pasta, flour, rice, potatoes, dried fruit, cocoa, pudding, fruit crystals, dried milk, powdered eggs, nuts, honey, and brown sugar are excellent sources of carbohydrates, and are the backbone of a backcountry ration.

While some carbohydrates, such as pure sugars, assimilate into the body within fifteen minutes of ingestion, which is ideal for an instant pick-me-up on the trail, others, such as the starch in pasta, take up to four hours to assimilate. That's fine: the extra time allows you to produce energy to warm you through the night or fuel a long morning hike. It should be noted that the nutritive quality of carbohydrates can be seriously affected by processing and refining. Whenever possible, include whole-grain and unprocessed foodstuffs in your rations.

Fats are a more concentrated form of energy and a more complex food than carbohydrates, so it usually takes the body from two to nine hours to metabolize them. One gram of fat produces nine calories of heat energy. While fats do not provide the instant vigor that carbohydrates can, they are a good long-term energy source to keep you hiking all day and warm all night. Fats will be providing energy to your body after carbohydrates eaten at the same time have been used up.

Twenty-five percent of your daily caloric intake in the backcountry should be fats. During the winter a higher intake, closer to 40 percent, is recommended, since fats play such an important role in making your body less sensitive to the cold. If you have a tendency to get cold in the middle of the night, one solution is to put a spoonful of margarine, a vegetable fat, in your cocoa before going to bed. Other good sources of fats are cheese, nuts, coconut, bacon, and salami.

The word *protein* is derived from a Greek term meaning "prime substance of life." It is the raw material which most of the body's cells require to keep on living. Skin, muscles, fingernails, and hair are primarily composed of protein. The protein within our bodies is made up of twenty-two chemical substances called amino acids. These amino acids can be arranged in a great number of formations, and each structure forms a different protein that serves the body in a different manner. In one form amino acids may provide the regenerative ability for hair, while in another form they travel in the blood carrying immunity to disease. Of the twenty-two amino acids, all but eight are produced in the body. The amino acids which the body cannot manufacture are called "essential amino acids," and must be obtained through the protein in food we eat.

When we eat a protein food, our body digests the protein by breaking it down into its basic amino acids. These ingested amino acids then combine with the fourteen amino acids already produced in the body. They can combine in numerous patterns and structures, but for each protein to work it must contain all eight of the essential amino acids. Some foods, such as meats, poultry, fish, eggs, and milk products, furnish all eight amino acids and are called "complete proteins." Other foods, such as beans, peas, lentils, peanuts, cereals, vegetables, and fruit, contain some but not all of the eight essential amino acids. These are called "incomplete proteins." Most of the complete protein foods are not very handy for backpacking because of weight or spoilage, so learning the proper combination of incomplete proteins is an important part of backcountry nutrition.

When considering how to combine incomplete proteins to create complete proteins, try to include foods from at least two of the following food groups, either in a single meal or over the course of a day: whole grains (rice, flour, pasta), dairy products (milk, cheese), legumes (beans, peanuts, lentils), and seeds (sesame, sunflower, pumpkin). The most complementary protein relationships are between milk products and grains; grains and legumes; and legumes and seeds. Tortillas with beans and rice with nuts are both examples of combining incomplete proteins to create complete proteins. So is the crunchy crust of Randy's blueberry cobbler, which mixes milk with oatmeal.

Percentage (by weight) of total rations in each major food group for a summer ration*

Meat or meat substitutes	11%
Dried meats, eggs, soy products (3%)	
Nuts, seeds, legumes (8%)	
Dairy products	18%
Powdered milk and milk-based drinks (10%)	
Cheese (8%)	
Fruit and vegetables	13%
Dried vegetables, potatoes (7%)	
Dried fruit (6%)	
Grains and grain products	33%
Flour, biscuit mix, cake mix (11%)	
Cereals, wheat germ, granola (11%)	
Pasta, rice, barley, etc. (11%)	
Margarine and oils	8%
Sweets	17%
Sugar and honey (8%)	
Instant fruit drinks, Jell-O, puddings (9%)	

* Non-nutritive food items such as coffee, tea, salt, and spices not included in total weight.

Even foods having complete proteins can be nutritionally enhanced through combination. If the protein in one food is relatively low in an essential amino acid, it can be combined with a food that is particularly high in that amino acid. In this way, essential amino acids present in the diet will be in closer proportion to the body's requirements for them, thus increasing the usability of the proteins you eat. Fish combined with rice, a diet which feeds much of the world's population, is an example of this process.

If your outdoor diet contains a balanced variety of carbohydrates, proteins, and fats, you will probably ingest an adequate supply of *vitamins and minerals* for short trips. On longer trips you might consider supplementing your diet with vitamins, particularly vitamin C. If supplemental vitamins are a regular part of your diet regime at home, it is probably best to continue the practice in the backcountry.

Drinking an adequate amount of *water* aids in the digestion of foods, keeps cells healthy, regulates body temperature, and helps carry wastes out of the body. Strenuous activity and high altitude usually increase the amount of water lost from the body through sweating. In cold weather, you can also lose about two quarts of liquid per day through respiration. Dehydration can make you susceptible to hypothermia, frostbite, mountain sickness, heat stroke, and many other problems.

In the summer you should drink a minimum of two or three quarts of water per day. In the winter three or four quarts are essential. The easiest way to ensure you get enough is to drink liquids at all meals and drink water whenever you are thirsty. Even if you are not thirsty, it is important to drink at all rest stops throughout the day. In areas where drinkable water is in short supply, plan ahead and carry an adequate amount with you on the trail.

Keeping track of your urine output is a good way to make sure you are getting enough water. You should be urinating at least two or three times a day. The urine should be clear and light unless there is a specific reason for color change, such as taking vitamin B supplements, which can turn the urine a darker yellow.

Many people have a tendency to drink their morning coffee and then hit the trail. Keep in mind that coffee and tea are diuretics and can cause dehydration. Drink a full cup of water after your coffee to get yourself off to a good start in the morning.

Good nutrition is the first criterion for rationing a back-country trip. A nutritionally balanced diet will begin with a good selection of whole grains, dairy products, legumes, and seeds. It may also include some meat or meat substitutes, fruits and vegetables, and sweets. The following chart provides a guideline for a nutritionally balanced ration.

RATION PLANNING

At NOLS, ration planning begins with the idea that in the backcountry you should eat whenever you are hungry throughout the day. Snack foods that you can munch on the trail, such as nuts, granola, and cheese, should be a part of a hiker's ration. These foods provide a handy source of quick energy when you are hiking and are also a quick solution for cold or hunger in the middle of the night.

Rather than planning rigid menus for each meal, we include in a ration a wide variety of ingredients which provide good nutrition and allow for choice at each meal. Basic foodstuffs combined with a little creativity are the ingredients for good eating.

For a weekend in the mountains, rations can be informal. You should include a good supply of food that yields a high amount of energy, like cheese or macaroni, which you can probably find in your refrigerator or pantry. For longer trips, particularly with groups of four or more, rationing can require considerable planning. Like most outdoor skills, it may seem painstaking and time-consuming the first time, but after you have done it once and begin to understand your needs, the process will become quite easy.

Here are six important criteria which when combined with an understanding of good nutrition can help you determine the right food to take on a backcountry trip.

1. *Purpose of the trip.* The major activities you anticipate on your trip should influence your choice of foods. If
you are going to do a lot of mountaineering and cover a lot
of miles, you want foods that can be prepared quickly.
Energy content will be important, so pack snack foods to
give yourself extra energy for long days. If you plan to fish,
consider this a potential protein supplement of your diet.
But never depend on the fish biting.

2. *Weight.* Food is a major part of the weight of your
pack. NOLS rations come out to approximately 1.5 to 2.2
pounds per person per day in the summer and 2.25 to 2.5
pounds in the winter. Eight to ten days' supply of food is
about as much as you can carry comfortably.

Freeze-dried foods, in which only 2 percent of the moisture remains, are lighter than dried foods, which often
contain a full 25 percent of their original moisture. Keep
in mind, however, that the freeze-drying process often removes some of the nutritional value of the food. Freeze-
dried foods are also more expensive.

Never use glass bottles, cans, or foil in packing your
food; these materials are heavy and must be carried out.
Glass is also unsafe. At NOLS we place all dried foods in
plastic bags and tie them with a simple, loose knot on top.
Freezer bags or poultry bags are stronger than sandwich
bags. Items like spaghetti can puncture a bag and liquid
containers can spring leaks, so pack a few extra plastic
bags. Spices and liquids belong in reusable plastic bottles.
Peanut butter and honey are carried in wide-mouthed plastic jars or plastic squeeze tubes.

3. *Spoilage.* Because of the risk of spoilage, most
meats and fresh food are excluded from summer rations.
If you carry all dried goods, it is nice to throw in a couple
of onions or potatoes, which will keep for three or four
days. Margarine must replace butter on longer summer
trips. Freeze-dried jerky or hard salami is the only practical
form for carrying meat for more than a day.

4. *Availability and expense.* The best way to ensure
good, nutritious meals and keep your expenses down is to
avoid freeze-dried foods and buy ingredients for cooking
from scratch. The more box dinners, commercially-mixed

drinks, sauces, and store-bought granola you take, the higher your food bill and the lower the nutritional value in the food.

If you are rationing for large groups, buy directly from granaries, dairies, or wholesale stores. When including freeze-dried foods in the rations, try to buy in bulk directly from an outlet rather than from retail distributors (if you are just rationing for yourself and friends, any excess freeze-dried foods can be safely stored for future use).

Investing in a food dryer is a good way to cut down the costs of dried vegetables and fruit.

Most of the rations suggested in this chapter can be purchased directly from a large supermarket. As you will see on the NOLS ration lists later in this chapter, most of the items we use are common staples and easy to find.

5. *Variety.* However rustic the surroundings, people remain finicky about what they eat. The more you know about your group's normal eating habits, the better you can plan their backcountry rations. Include various types of food: trail foods, baking goods, spices for flavoring sauces, and instant foods for rushed dinners. Also take along a few special ingredients and surprise your companions. If you are taking children, popping popcorn or making pan biscuits is a good campsite activity, and also nutritionally valuable.

6. *Preparations.* When planning rations, consider the circumstances under which you will cook. What cooking tools are you taking? Will you be using a stove or an open fire?

If you will be cooking entirely on a compressed-gas or liquid-fuel stove, your meals will most likely be cooked in only one pot, and baking will be very limited. On a more relaxed trip, you may want to experiment with fancier meals. In cold weather, avoid foods that need to cook a long time or require a lot of pot handling or intricate use of knives or fingers. You will probably be wearing mittens.

The following is a sample NOLS summer ration for two people for ten days. In the recipes which appear in Appendix II, you will see how these basic foodstuffs, most of them available at your local supermarket, can provide a remarkably varied, enjoyable menu.

Sample Ration for Two People for Ten Days at 2 pounds of Food per Person per Day

Tea, 10 bags; or coffee, ½ lb.
Margarine, 3 lbs.
Powdered milk, 2 lbs.
Powdered eggs, 1 lb.
Cocoa, 2 lbs.
Raisins, 1 lb.
Dried figs, 1 lb.
Dried coconut, ½ lb.
Dried peaches, ½ lb.
Shelled peanuts, 1 lb.
Toasted soybeans, ½ lb.
Roasted almonds, 1 lb.
Sesame seeds, ¼ lb.
Sunflower seeds, 1 lb.
Cheddar cheese, 3 lbs.
Monterey jack cheese, 3 lbs.
Gingerbread mix, ½ lb.
Grapenuts, 2 lbs.
Oatmeal, ½ lb.
Wheat cereal, ½ lb.
Granola, 1 lb.

Instant hash browns, 2 lbs.
Instant fruit drink, 1 lb.
Brown sugar, 1 lb.
Macaroni, 1 lb.
Spaghetti, 1 lb.
White rice, 1 lb.
Brown rice, ½ lb.
Instant potatoes, ½ lb.
Pinto beans, 1 lb.
Barley, ½ lb.
Tortillas, 1 lb.
Flour, 2½ lbs.
Cornmeal, ½ lb.
Soup mixes, ¾ lb.
Dried vegetables, ½ lb.
Popcorn, ¼ lb.
Baking powder, ¼ lb.
Yeast, ¼ lb.
Matches, ⅓ box stick type or 10 books
Soap and toilet paper, as desired

Seasonings: Tabasco, pepper, salt, cayenne, oregano, garlic salt, dry mustard, nutmeg, cinnamon, onion salt, curry powder, chili powder, flavoring extracts

Total weight: 40.75 lbs., or 20.37 lbs. per person

You can substitute other dried fruit—dates, prunes, apples, bananas, etc.—and other nuts, cake mixes, and legumes, or lentils, peas, etc.

The more you backpack, the more you learn about the types and qualities of food you need in the backcountry. Experienced backpackers already know the ins and outs of preparing rations. For those new to the experience, here are a few tips about buying, packing, and using various foods on the NOLS ration list.

Meats. On long backpacking trips, meat, because of its cost and weight, is usually a luxury used only for flavoring. For short trips, however, there are a variety of meat products suitable for backpacking, including compressed meat bars, freeze-dried meats, and sausages (the kind that do not require refrigeration). If you are on a tight budget, homemade meat jerky is relatively inexpensive and simple to make.

Soybean products. The protein in soybeans is fairly similar to that found in meat. In addition to roasted soybeans, which make good trail food and provide interesting texture for many cooked meals, you can buy soy flour for baking and soy-derivative products such as "ham" bits and "bacon" bits which can spice up a green salad or add flavor to omelets or quiches.

Dried eggs. Powdered eggs are available as whole eggs, or whites and yolks can be bought separately. Quality varies considerably from brand to brand, so it is wise to experiment at home before relying on them in the field.

Nuts and seeds. Shelled nuts are much more convenient for backcountry cooking, and preclude the need to carry out empty shells. Nuts make good trail food and add taste and texture to baked goods. To save money, buy unroasted nuts and roast them yourself.

Legumes. Dried legumes (split peas, lentils, beans, etc.) when combined with brown rice or other grains make a complete protein, and can add variety to a meal. They generally take a long time to cook unless you use a pressure cooker.

Milk. Several types of powdered milk are available: instant whole milk, instant nonfat milk, regular whole milk, and buttermilk. Whole milk has more calories and vitamins than nonfat milk, and is a better additive for baked goods. Instant powders dissolve more easily in cold water. A wide variety of breakfast drinks with milk bases are also easy to find in most grocery stores.

Cocoa. It is easier to use cocoa that has already been combined with powdered milk so that in the field all you have to do is add water. Cocoa is also handy for baking and candy making.

Cheese. Cheddar seems to be the cheese with the most versatile flavor for backcountry cooking. It also keeps better than most other cheeses. Powdered cheeses (the kind contained in most boxed macaroni-and-cheese dinners) are also available, but they are of limited use.

Margarine. Butter spoils rapidly on summer trips, so margarine is more commonly used. Buy pure vegetable margarine, and after removing all wrappers, pack it in a screw-top plastic jar.

Freeze-dried vegetables. Vegetables can add that special touch of color which makes a meal more appetizing. They also add vitamins and minerals to your diet.

Potatoes. Potatoes come in flake or powdered form and can be used as a separate dish, an additive, or a thickener. Though potato flakes or powders lose much of their vitamin C when processed, they are a versatile food for backcountry cooking.

Sprouts. Many backpackers on extended trips are beginning to carry sprouting colonies of soy, mung, alfalfa, and lentil beans, in small plastic bottles with a wide mouth for sprouting. Place a few beans in water and soak them for eight hours. Drain and rinse them often on the trail and you will have a regular harvest of fresh vegetables which can be used in salads, soups, or main dishes. Be careful not to let them freeze.

Dried fruits. Dried fruit, such as prunes, raisins, apricots, and peaches, retain approximately 25 percent of their moisture, and are thus heavier to carry than freeze-dried fruit, which have less than 3 percent moisture content. Freeze-dried fruit, however, are considerably more expensive. Sulfur-dried fruit, which must be soaked before using, contain more vitamins and minerals than other dried fruit.

Self-rising baking mixes. For simplicity and weight, it is important to buy mixes which do not require the addition of eggs and shortening. Remember that biscuit mixes can also be used to make cakes and pancakes. A few special mixes, such as gingerbread, cake mixes, or special flours, are a nice change of pace on an extended trip.

Wheat germ. Wheat germ is used primarily as a nutritional supplement for cooking. Roasted wheat germ will keep for up to a month without refrigeration.

Cereals. While uncooked cereals are the most versatile, and can be used for hot cereal, granola, and baking, the instant cereals are much easier to cook, usually taking less than a third of the time. Oat and wheat cereals are nutritionally superior to rice and barley cereals.

Pasta. Pasta is likely to form a major part of your backcountry diet, so take a variety of shapes and sizes. Wholegrain pastas (whole wheat, spinach) are nutritionally superior, but if you are not used to them try them at home first.

Rice, barley, buckwheat, grits. These are handy staples for many good dishes, from cereals to main courses. The instant forms are less nutritious but, unless you are carrying a pressure cooker, they are much easier to cook.

Sweeteners. Brown sugar is more versatile to use and easier to pack than white. Honey and jam should be packed in plastic containers with a tight-fitting lid; for extra protection, pack these jars inside a plastic bag.

Fruit drinks. Instant fruit drinks and gelatin desserts are good to drink either hot or cold. Be sure to get mixes which have vitamin C and sugar already added.

Candy. If you choose to eat candy, make it an addition to an already nutritious diet. Fruit candies are more practical and offer a greater variety than chocolates. Nut candies are nutritionally superior. Leave the candy wrappers at home or they will inevitably end up as litter.

Spices. A good spice kit can make the difference between superb cuisine and bland, monotonous meals in the back-country. A good basic selection includes salt, pepper, cinnamon, nutmeg, dill, curry, oregano, chili powder, and garlic. Tabasco, salsa, soy, and Worcestershire sauce can also add a dash of interest to a simple meal. Spices are best carried in small plastic bottles.

Soup bases. In addition to making a quick cup of soup, powdered bases and bouillon are also useful as flavorings for many dishes. When using them, remember that most bases contain a considerable amount of salt; use them cautiously. Many vegetarians prefer to take miso, a soybean paste, in their food bags.

RATIONING FOR HIGH ALTITUDE AND COLD WEATHER

Rations have to be readjusted for high-altitude and cold-weather expeditions. The higher the altitude, the less oxygen is available to metabolize food; complex molecules such as proteins and fats may be harder to digest under these conditions. Fats can still be a very important source of concentrated, long-lasting energy at high altitudes, and some people are not bothered at all by digestive problems. But take it easy the first time out. If they give you no problem, then keep high-energy fats in your diet.

High altitude can easily double your cooking time. At 15,000 feet water boils at 184°F and will not get hotter without a pressure cooker. A meal that takes thirty minutes to cook at sea level is not practical at high altitudes.

Extra soup and drink mixes should be added to your rations for cold weather or high altitude. Taking additional liquids will increase your blood volume, which helps to prevent frostbite and hypothermia. Coffee and other diuretics should be used in moderation because they prevent the body from absorbing water and dehydration may result.

An adequate supply of water is top priority in cold weather or at high altitudes, even though it may be more difficult to find. Snow must be melted slowly over a low flame, otherwise it will taste scorched and be undrinkable. If you have to melt solid snow, place a bit of water on the bottom of the pail and stir constantly. After each meal, melt an extra pot of water and fill water bottles. A warm water bottle wrapped in a mitten or bootie comes in very handy to keep your feet warm. Have both water and food available at night; thirst and hunger are the major reasons people sleep cold.

On snowy peaks during the summer, you can use the sun to melt drinking water. If you are spending a day in camp, put a dark-colored tarp or rain parka in a hollow in the snow. Then place a small amount of snow in the tarp and continue adding snow as it melts. The sun's energy absorbed by the dark color will melt large amounts of water fairly quickly.

THE OUTDOOR KITCHEN

How you equip your outdoor kitchen depends largely on personal taste and experience. After you have become comfortable at cooking in the backcountry, you will undoubtedly discover there are certain items which you cannot do without. Randy insists that a small flat cheese grater and a wire whisk are essential. Others may wince at the thought of the extra weight.

The type of cooking equipment you take into the wilderness will depend in part on your rationing plan. If you are going to eat freeze-dried meals, you can probably get by with one aluminum pot, in which you boil water, prepare an individual meal, and eat. You will also need a spoon and a container for water. For a couple of days this approach is fine, but for an extended trip of a week or more it will get pretty boring, and the nutritional deficiencies of the diet may begin to affect performance.

On a more extended trip, with a more varied diet, you need equipment for both individual eating and group cooking. At NOLS, for individual equipment we issue each person an enameled metal bowl, a metal spoon, and an enameled metal cup. The bowl is large enough to double as a mixing bowl for food preparation. Using both a bowl and a cup, rather than a combination such as the Sierra Cup, allows you to eat and drink at the same time. A culinary whiz will carry a drinking cup which can double as a measuring cup.

NOLS issues a group cooking set to every two or three people. Our equipment receives heavy use from many people, so we have selected it for durability as well as low cost, versatility, and minimum weight. This equipment is issued for courses ranging in length from two weeks to three and a half months. It provides all you need for both quick, one-pot meals and culinary extravaganzas:

—One large Teflon pan with lid. Teflon and Silverstone are a real boon to the campfire cook. Food does not stick to the pan. They minimize burning, are easy to clean, and work for both frying and baking.
—Two pots. These are good for everything from boiling water to preparing stews or other one-pot meals.
—Pot grips or pliers. These allow you to take pans on and off the fire without burning your hands. They are essential for campfire safety.
—One wooden spoon and a plastic or metal spatula. These should give you all the versatility you need.
—Cotton gloves. If you are cooking around a campfire, we strongly recommend a pair of cotton gloves as a safety precaution. In the backcountry the pain and inconvenience of a burn can ruin a trip.
—Collapsible water jug. We have found that a 2½-gallon collapsible jug is very handy in the backcountry. You can get a meal's worth of water in one trip to the water source. These jugs are lightweight and, when col-

lapsed, they don't take up much room in your pack. We also issue a 1-quart plastic bottle, preferably with a wide mouth. This can be used as a canteen, for soaking rice and lentils, and for mixing sauces or other ingredients.

As you experience more backcountry cooking, your own style and needs will become apparent. You will discover a few optional pieces of equipment particularly suited to your cooking style. The weight of your pack is the only limitation. One item that has become popular around NOLS is a lightweight aluminum pressure cooker. It cuts the cooking time of beans and brown rice in half.

Organizing your outdoor kitchen is the first step to a great meal. Establish two distinct areas, a food preparation area and a cooking area. In the food preparation area keep your utensils in order. When you use something put it back. "Have you seen the salt?" or "I can't find the spatula" are plaints heard in a disorganized kitchen. Allow yourself 360 degrees of uncluttered space around the fire or stove. If your way around is blocked, you will be tempted to reach across the fire for a needed ingredient or utensil. With a campfire, you will want to move around to avoid the smoke as the wind changes. The best way to avoid tripping is to make sure the area is clear. A simple rule is to have a five-foot clear area around a fire. In a cooking area you are particularly prone to accidents; you can easily trip around a fire or stove and spill scalding water or a pot of perfectly seasoned fish chowder. At the least, a meal is ruined; at worst, you have seriously burned yourself or damaged equipment. It is also easy to lose small utensils at a campsite; if you don't set them down carefully they are likely to disappear.

Wear shoes around the fire and use pot grips or cotton gloves for picking up hot pots. Remove a pot from the fire when you add a new ingredient; this protects your hands and makes it less likely you'll spill or waste food.

Remember that sparks from a fire can seriously damage nylon clothes or tent flies; make sure your sleeping area and backpack are a good distance from your cooking area.

THE OUTDOOR KITCHEN

Small
Wood Pile
10' or More
from Fire

Be careful when drying clothes around the fire, and do not dry boots in that fashion. It is easy to damage essential personal gear. If a spot near the fire is too hot to hold your hand there indefinitely, it is too hot for any item of clothing.

The inventory of spoons, bowls, spatulas, and pot grips that have been lost in the backcountry would stock many a big kitchen. Once they are gone, you can't just run out to the store to buy a replacement; you have to make do for the rest of the trip, knowing, too, that you have left litter somewhere behind that will never decompose. As you set up your kitchen area remember to organize for safety, convenience, and conservation.

PUTTING THE POT ON THE FIRE

If using a stove, you should cook over a low to moderate flame. If you cook over a fire, the coals should be hot but the fire controlled. Since a fire provides a larger cooking area, it also gives you more flexibility. You can arrange the fire so that one area is used for baking and another for cooking, or you can cook a main dish and make coffee at the same time.

In Appendix II, you will find a large collection of NOLS recipes with step-by-step cooking instructions. If you are new to cooking, start with the simple recipes and find out how easy and satisfying outdoor cooking can be. Soon you will be starting your day with perfect pancakes and finishing your dinner with Randy's cobbler.

Randy's first rule for backcountry culinary success is: Avoid disaster. There are four likely disasters that a new outdoor cook should watch out for.

The first is *burning*. Always cook on low heat, whether on a stove or over an open fire. Make sure that you have sufficient water in the pot, and check often to see if more is needed. As your sauces begin to thicken, stir often. Always cook in a clean pot which has no old food stuck to the bottom.

When baking, carefully regulating your heat source is

particularly important. At NOLS we bake by creating a Dutch oven using a frying pan and a lid. The pan is placed on a flat bed of coals; often a special baking shelf is built at the side of a firepit and coals from the center of the pit are scooped up and spread evenly on the shelf. A layer of coals and twigs are also placed on top of the lid so that heat will evenly surround the pan.

To prevent burning, it is important to check the temperature of the coals before placing a pan on them. Baked foods are more likely to burn on the bottom than on the top. Hold your hand about six inches above the coals; it should be hot, but you should be able to keep your hand over the coals for eight seconds. The coals and twigs you place on top of the lid should feel hotter and should cover the entire lid.

While baking, check the food and the coal temperature from time to time. If you are baking something prone to "falling," don't look in during the first five to ten minutes unless you smell something burning. Otherwise, when you check, remove the hot coals from the lid and look in quickly, trying to keep the cold air out. When you are finished checking, place hot coals back on the lid again. Replace coals as they cool off, both under the pan and over the lid.

Don't let a stove discourage you from baking. Use a low flame under the pan and build a small twig fire on top of the lid. Maintain constant temperatures under and over the pan, and you've got an oven environment for your favorite baked delicacy.

Whether baking a pie or brewing a chowder, you can avoid burning your food by paying constant attention to the amount of heat being generated by your fire or stove.

The second disaster Randy warns of is *overspicing*. NOLS issues spice kits to students to encourage cooking creativity. But spices should be experimented with cautiously, a little at a time. Add, stir, then taste. Let the flavor settle in fully before you decide to add a little more. Never add the spice directly from the bottle to the pot. Shake it into your hand first. An unexpected loose cap can turn a "hint" of spice into the main course. Be aware of the saltiness of flavor bases before adding salt. If you are cooking with a bouillon cube, remember you already have a good amount of salt in the dish.

The third disaster is *lumpy food*. Powders like flour or dried milk should be mixed with liquid before adding them to a dish or sprinkled a little at a time with constant stirring. With freeze-dried foods, let them boil for ten to fifteen minutes before adding other ingredients.

The final disaster is *overdone food*. This is, Randy concedes, a more subtle disaster, but it can be avoided. Thickeners such as milk or cheese should always be added last. Keep tasting as you are cooking, and remember, even after you pull the pot from the fire, it will continue to cook. It is always better to err on the side of undercooking, which is easily correctable.

To be a good outdoor cook takes the right attitude—a combination of caution and boldness. Caution in thoroughly understanding the nutritional needs of your party, and carefully planning a well-thought-out ration. Caution also in following new recipes step by step and using spices artfully, with moderation. Your confidence as an outdoor cook will grow quickly with a few successes because appetite is always working for you. Food tastes great after a day in the backcountry. Once you are past the disaster-prevention stage, pat yourself on the back. You have come a long way. "Now," says Randy, "you can carry on with élan."

Chapter Five

Maps and Compass

MAPS ARE a most wonderful invention, a language for translating the three-dimensional to the two-dimensional. There are a variety of cartographers' dialects which can demonstrate almost anything: the migration of elk, the spread of a religion, the solar exposure in different neighborhoods.

But to the backcountry traveler there is no map quite so wonderful as a topographic map. To a novice it may look like a two-year-old has scribbled all over a perfectly good map that showed roads, peaks, and lakes, and spilled green ink on it in splotches as well. It takes a little time with a topo map—as it does with any truly interesting map —to understand what is going on, and it takes even more time in the field to learn how to put a topo to work.

One of the real skills of map reading is to be able to foresee the kind of terrain you will encounter. A bald spot on a map at the base of a steep slope in the Cascades may mean the tangled debris of an avalanche chute now overgrown with alders and willows, impossible travel conditions. In Wyoming's Wind River Range, a similar bald spot may mean a boulder field. Or a meadow. Experience in similar environments will give you the knowledge and intuition you need to envision what lies ahead. When you can take out your topo map you will be able to see the mountains, lakes, and valleys it portrays.

There was a time, not that long ago, when finding a route through untraveled country was more an art than a science. It took a keen memory and powers of observation to become a noted route finder. Today with maps and compass in hand, anyone can become a dependable guide.

There are plenty of maps available for backcountry trav-

TOPOGRAPHICAL MAP

elers. They are published by the Forest Service, the Bureau of Land Management, and state agencies. Some hikers have been known to carry only a road map from a state highway department that shows in rough approximation that there are mountain ranges here and there. The maps you need for safe and enjoyable backcountry travel, though, are those published by the U.S. Geological Survey. Read correctly, these maps will tell you much more than just the distance between one campsite and another. They will tell you where you have to climb and descend and how steeply, and they will tell you where the terrain is forested or barren.

Certain standards apply to all topo maps. The top of the map is always north, the bottom south, the left west, and the right—well, you guess. The layout of the map corresponds to the longitude and latitude lines that we imagine encircling the globe (also referred to, respectively, as meridian and parallel lines). Lines of longitude run north and south; lines of latitude run east and west, parallel to the equator. On a globe these lines form a crisscross grid system, which is faithfully reproduced on maps.

We measure latitude and longitude by degrees, describing, for instance, the angle formed by a line from the center of the earth to the equator and by a line from the center of the earth to the North Pole as 90°. The longitudinal 0° line runs through Greenwich, England, and the numbers rise westwardly to 180° and easterly to 180°. The latitudinal 0° line is at the equator; degrees of latitude are numbered north from the equator to 90° in the Northern Hemisphere, and south from the equator to 90° in the Southern Hemisphere. Any topographic map of a part of the United States will be labeled on its outer margins to represent number of degrees north (latitude) and number of degrees west (longitude).

Topo maps come in different sizes and scales. One standard topo map size shows an area representing a full 1 degree of latitude by 2 degrees of longitude; it has a scale of 1 inch on the map to 250,000 inches in the real world, or 1:250,000. The scale of these USGS maps can be found at the bottom—1 inch represents about 4 field miles. This size map covers a total area of 4,580 to 8,669 square miles.

The reason for this variance in size is the globe itself. USGS topographic maps are quadrangles, not rectangles (they are often referred to as "quads"). The north and south borders of quads are not the same size, simply because the distance between longitudinal lines narrows as you move north toward the pole. As a result, while a quad near the equator may be nearly a perfect rectangle, in the northern reaches of Alaska quads are more triangular in shape.

Maps scaled 1:250,000 are helpful for planning trips and they make nice wall hangings, but they aren't detailed enough for pathfinding. The USGS offers more detailed maps, on a scale of 1:62,500 and finer. A 1- by 2-degree map (a scale of 1:250,000) might also be called a 60- by 120-minute map since there are 60 minutes to a degree. The USGS offers a 15-minute map on which the detail is 16 times as great as on the 1-degree map, and also a 7.5-minute map. The 15-minute map, covering between 197 and 282 square miles, is useful for pathfinding; the 7.5-minute map is the map we prefer to use at NOLS. It enlarges one-fourth the area of a 15-minute map, and each inch equals 2,000 feet of real ground.

On each map the northerly latitude is noted along the top edge in degrees, minutes, and seconds; for example: 44° 22′ 30″. Longitude is noted at each end of the vertical map edges. Latitude is written at the end of the horizontal map edges.

If you're handy with Scotch tape and had an enormous wall to use, you could put together a mosaic of topo maps to form an entire mountain range. Each topo has a name, and each lists the names of the eight other topos that abut its sides and corners in the grid. The name of each topo corresponds to some prominent feature in the particular quadrangle—a town, a mountain, a body of water.

The margins of a topo contain a lot of information in addition to what we've mentioned above. Along the lower edge of the map there is a much smaller outline map showing where the quadrangle is located in its particular state.

There are arrows at the bottom indicating the relation of true north to magnetic north (which we will discuss below, in the section on using a compass). When a road or trail leaves the map you will often find a note indicating how far it goes to the next significant junction.

But the map itself is the true wonder. None of the information, none of its color or fine line work, is just for show.

Take, for instance, the colors on a topo map. The color green denotes woodland, with trees thick enough so that a platoon—twenty-seven men—can hide from aerial observation in one acre. The color white denotes all non-forested areas, including boulder fields, grassy meadows, and above-timberline country. Blue indicates water—streams, lakes, rivers, or snow and ice. A solid blue line indicates perennial water either by encircling a blue-shaded lake or by itself denoting a year-round stream. An interrupted blue line with a sequence of three dots and a dash means that the stream or creek does not flow year-round. A dashed blue line enclosing a blue-shaded area indicates an intermittent body of water; when a dashed blue line encloses white space it means a permanent snowfield or glacier. Black features on a map indicate manmade things: trails, settlements, railroad tracks, roads, buildings, and so on. The borders of public lands and civic boundaries are also inked in black. More prominent manmade marks and divisions—such as major roads, fence lines, land grants, and the lines of townships, ranges, and sections—are indicated in red. Revisions made on a USGS map since the original survey are superimposed in purple—they are updates made from aerial photographs that have not yet been field-checked.

Contour lines, inked in brown, are the most important part of a topo map; they connect points of equal elevation. By reading contour lines you can find your elevation above sea level and the shape of the land around you. Of course, you won't find topo lines on the ground, like a river or a trail; they are abstractions, a way of making the three-dimensional world show on a flat piece of paper.

Contour lines crowd together in some parts of a map like the lines on an old man's face; in other places the map is as clear and unmarked as a baby's bottom. This means, simply, that there are great elevation changes in one area (where the lines crowd together) and fairly flat terrain in the other.

Contour lines are separated by contour intervals. The interval represents a change in altitude and is consistent throughout any one topo map. At the bottom of the map, the USGS tells you what the interval is on this particular map: on most 7.5-minute maps the interval is between 10 and 40 feet.

Every fifth line on a contour map is heavier than the others. This line is called an "index" contour line—if you follow it you will eventually find a number written across it. That number is the feet above sea level for this particular line, and it serves as a reference point for adjacent lines: if the contour interval is 10 feet, you know the line next to this one is 10 feet higher or lower than its neighbor.

Imagine an island rising out of the ocean to a height of 1,000 feet. One side inclines gradually to the top—an easy hike. The other rises abruptly from the ocean to the peak. If you could hold a huge knife level with the horizon and slice through the island every 10 feet, you would have 100 slices. If you then looked at the island from above and projected the border of each slice onto the flat plane below, you would have a contour map. On the gently sloping side the lines would be widely separated; on the steep side they would be jammed together. If you were familiar with topo maps and saw this projection, you would know to hike up to the peak from the side of the island where the contour lines were spaced widely. The closer the contour lines, the steeper the grade.

With experience you will begin to recognize landforms on the topo map. When contour lines break their normal flow to form a series of V-shaped indentations pointing toward higher altitudes, you know they indicate either a drainage or a valley. Pointing away from high elevations, the V's indicate a ridge.

Contour lines with cross-hatching marks on them pointing toward a common center or lower contour interval indicate a depression in the landscape.

Once you master the symbols on topo maps, a more important task ensues: learning to translate what you see on the map into what you see when you look around you. This is mostly a matter of experience, but it helps to be aware of a common misperception. The biggest mistake made by map readers is looking at the map assuming they are in a certain place and then looking around for landmarks that will confirm they are in that location. We call this "fitting the terrain to the map," and it's going about things backward.

To avoid this pitfall, don't open your map right away. Begin by checking your location: Are you in a place where you can see the terrain in several directions? Move a little way off your route if necessary; get away from trees and nearby obstacles that obscure vision. Then look around at the mountains, the streams, the ridges, and get a sense of how they relate to each other—the distances between them, the way one drainage feeds into another. Leave yourself out of the picture at first. Only after you have a good sense of how these features fit together should you locate yourself and your approximate distances from landmarks. Once you know the terrain well, open up the map: you can then fit the map to the terrain, and not the other way around.

This is not just a play on words. If you look at the map first, you establish certain features you intend to locate on the terrain, and with that preconceived notion, you'll probably find things that fit and overlook more important features that don't.

Once you think you've located yourself, play the devil's advocate. Ignore for a moment the landmarks that confirmed your location and find some new ones. Are they on the map? Then check the map to see if the contours indicate landforms that you haven't spotted—in other words, reverse the process. By the time you've done this you should have no doubt about your location.

The other important tool for backcountry navigation is the compass. Using an "orienteering" compass, a backcountry traveler can orient a topographic map in line with true north, find the way to a destination, follow a particular direction or route to a destination, and find the way back to the starting point.

Instruction in the use of a compass will *sound* complex. Once you get used to using a compass, however, it becomes simple—you no longer have to think through the process each time you orient. As with so many other backcountry skills, practice makes the difference. The time you spend fiddling with your compass on the hill behind your home will pay off in the backcountry.

An orienteering compass has a circular housing mounted on a rectangular base. The base has a fixed arrow on it, usually labeled "direction of travel," parallel to its longest edge and bisecting the shorter edge. The circular housing has a plastic or glass face and markings on the outer ring indicating the four cardinal points (north, south, east, west) and degree lines numbered clockwise starting at North. The bottom of the housing has an etched arrow pointing toward the North marking on the ring. The entire housing can be rotated on the base. Beneath the glass is the compass needle, which floats free; one end, usually colored, points to magnetic north.

The magnetic north pole of the earth is just above Hudson's Bay, about 1,400 miles south of the true North Pole. The magnetic needle can be misled by large iron or steel objects, but usually if you stay clear of iron or steel gear like ice axes or cast-iron frying pans, you will get an accurate reading.

At the bottom of most USGS topographic maps there is a diagram showing the amount of deviation at that location between magnetic north and true north. This deviation is referred to as declination. An arrow labeled "MN" indicates magnetic north; a second line, with a star at the end, is true north. To orient your map, place the compass over the map diagram and line up the direction-of-travel arrow with true north. This aligns the edge of the compass base with the edges of the map. Then rotate only the housing until the etched arrow matches the magnetic north line on the topo map. You then hold the map level and turn it until the floating magnetic needle in your compass is lined up with the arrow on the housing. This arrow is wider than the magnetic needle and will completely surround it when they are in line; this is called "boxing" the magnetic needle. With the map properly oriented, you can more accurately pick out terrain features and locate yourself.

You will sometimes find it helpful to "triangulate" using map and compass. Once the map is correctly oriented, pick a feature in the surrounding landscape and point the direction-of-travel arrow at it, holding the compass level. Then turn the compass housing until it boxes the magnetic needle. Where the direction-of-travel arrow first intersects the compass housing, you can read off the magnetic bearing of the object. Then lay one of the long edges of the compass base on top of the feature on your topo map and pivot the whole compass, including the base, around that feature until the magnetic needle is boxed by the arrow etched on the housing. Mark a line on the map along the long edge of the compass base. Your location is somewhere along that line. To fix your spot exactly, repeat the procedure using two different landmarks—your location is within the tiny triangle formed by the three intersecting lines. If this point disagrees with where you think you are, either you read the map incorrectly, used the compass incorrectly, or both. Try the procedure again.

Sometimes you won't be able to eyeball your surroundings, look at the map, and figure out where you are. You may be in a deep, narrow valley or enveloped by fog or surrounded by trees. In this case you use your compass and map to determine a bearing (the number of degrees from straight north), or direction, that will lead you toward your objective. You can follow a true bearing (based on true north) or a magnetic bearing (based on magnetic north), just so you are consistent; at NOLS we recommend a magnetic bearing because it requires less calculation.

The place you want to get to may lie at 45° west of magnetic north—but rarely will the terrain allow you to travel in a straight line over long distances, and if visibility is poor you may have to find a closer object. Determine your bearing, then pick an object you can see that is in the right direction and focus on it—even if it is only a few

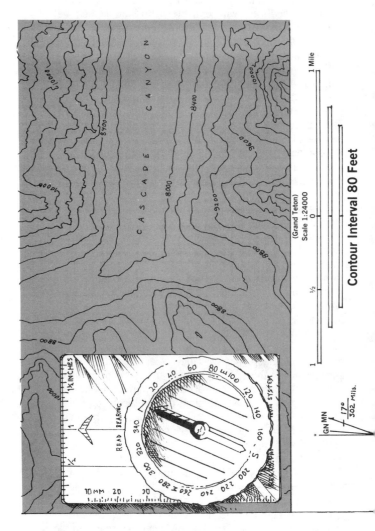

ORIENTING A TOPOGRAPHICAL MAP WITH A COMPASS

hundred yards away. When you reach this object, find another beyond it that is on the proper bearing, in the direction of your final objective.

If even this proves too difficult, you can actually follow
a bearing with compass in hand. With the map properly
oriented, point the direction-of-travel arrow from your present location on the map toward your objective on the map,
then turn the housing until it boxes the magnetic needle.
Where the direction-of-travel arrow intersects the compass
ring will give you your bearing. You can follow this bearing
without actually seeing the landmarks by keeping the magnetic needle boxed by the housing arrow as you move.
Traveling with one eye always on the compass is cumbersome, to say the least. If conditions are so poor that you
can't see even nearby landmarks, it may be wise to bivouac
and wait for the weather to clear or move to a better orienting site.

When you want to return to your original location, there
are two simple approaches. One is to keep the compass as
is but reverse your position: instead of pointing the direction-of-travel arrow away from you and toward your destination, point it toward you, box the needle, and walk the
line of the direction-of-travel arrow in reverse. Or you can
box the opposite end of the compass needle—the end that
points toward magnetic south—and proceed in the direction pointed by the direction-of-travel arrow.

When you are simply traveling back along the same route
by which you came, it's easy to get your "back" bearing. If
the bearing you traveled on was 180° or less, add 180 to
find your back bearing. If you traveled on a bearing of 180°
or more, subtract 180. You then line up the direction-of-
travel arrow with this number, box the needle, and proceed
in the direction indicated by the direction-of-travel arrow.

When you follow a bearing, write it down and mark it on
your map. If you accidentally move the compass housing
you can then correct it.

We recommend frequent references to maps when traveling in the backcountry. Glance at your map every fifteen
minutes or so to be sure you know where you are. If you
have doubts, use your compass to fix your location. A mis-

take in route finding that is not quickly corrected can cost you considerable time and hardship. Keep in mind that maps are not always 100 percent accurate: a prominent feature may not be on the map because of a mistake, a lake may have dried up, a marsh or meadow may now be a lake because of a beaver dam. Maps and compass provide an essential asset for any backcountry traveler; but your most valuable resource remains your ever-increasing ability to exercise good judgment.

Chapter **Six**

Traveling in the Backcountry

IT IS a fallacy to think that just because you know how to walk to the store, you know how to walk in the wilderness. Carrying a heavy pack, walking in boots over a variety of terrains, and hiking at high altitude take special preparation and skill.

NOLS instructors say that teaching travel technique is one area that often brings out leadership qualities and a spirit of teamwork in students. Bring the subject up with instructors who work in vastly different environments and the discussion becomes animated.

This was the case late one summer when Don and Donna Ford, directors of NOLS Baja, and longtime instructors Willy Cunningham and Tony Cullen joined us in the dining room at NOLS Lander headquarters, the old Noble Hotel, one evening.

The talk ranged over correct breathing and walking techniques, finding a rhythm for rest stops, and how to organize responsibilities in a small group in various types of wild country. Again and again we returned to the subject of leadership: whether you're part of a NOLS course or just out with a few friends, it's the gentle nudge of a good leader that gets a group thinking and acting in concert, and using techniques that assure everybody a rewarding, challenging experience.

The NOLS instructors admitted they themselves needed some guidance initially to learn various travel techniques. Once they got the knack, though, it seemed like good common sense. As a result, they don't teach travel techniques to novices like drill sergeants—they offer the basic information and let students discover for themselves how well the techniques work.

After a couple of hours of talk, Willy Cunningham grinned and pushed his chair back. "You know," he said, "nobody invented any of these techniques. Somebody just *realized* them."

On a NOLS course, we travel in groups of four or five. This lessens our impact on the backcountry; a large group of people coming down a trail together may harm the wilderness experience both for the group and for anyone they come upon. Small-group travel also encourages the development of good travel techniques. Everyone gets the opportunity to lead and to read maps, and rotating those responsibilities builds confidence and a better understanding of your companions. Relinquishing the reins and following another's lead is hard for some people to do—but good for them too.

Our goal in this chapter is to show you the two key elements of good backcountry travel: personal safety and efficiency of effort. Both will add greatly to your appreciation of the wilderness.

FOOT CARE

Good travel technique begins with good foot care. No amount of positive thinking is going to block out the pain of a blister. Damage your feet and the trip is over.

We have already discussed in Chapter Two the advantages of wearing two pairs of wool socks. The socks will absorb some of the friction of the moving boot and help cushion your feet on a rough trail. But even with two pairs of socks, if you walk in the wilderness the same way you walk on a city street, you won't last long. In no time, the rise and fall of your foot against the wall of the boot will cause blisters.

A good hiker walks flat-footed, and swings the whole leg so the foot lands relatively flat and the body's weight is carried primarily on the thick thigh muscles, rather than the calf. It's strange to think that one has to learn to walk all over again to do it properly in the backcountry, but habits that do you no harm on a city sidewalk can ruin your trip. If you edge your boot or walk "duck-footed"—with feet splayed—you will twist your foot with each step and cause the friction and heat that leads to a blister. If you rise up on the ball of your foot with each step, your Achilles tendon will rub the back of your boot and the top of your foot will become sore. If you tense your ankle instead of letting it pivot freely, your foot will strike the ground unevenly, causing friction.

Even when you avoid these pitfalls, you may develop, early on a hike, a "hot spot"—the name commonly given to the place on the foot that is about to blister. As the name implies, you usually notice a localized warm sensation. It is very important to catch blisters at this early stage. Beginners have to focus on their feet to feel a small warm spot through thick socks and a heavy hiking boot.

When you become aware of a hot spot, stop immediately. Don't be shy about slowing the group down—a few minutes of care now can prevent longer stops and lagging pace later on. A group leader should remind everyone in the first few days of the trip to check feet regularly.

All that may be needed is an adjustment to your laces, another pair of socks, or smoothing out your socks (a fold or a wrinkle can easily cause a blister). But if a simple adjustment will not solve the problem, if you can feel or see a red, tender area developing on your foot, you probably need to apply moleskin, molefoam, or Second Skin.

Moleskin is an adhesive tape with a soft cloth finish on one side. Molefoam is similar to moleskin but includes a thin layer of cushioning foam. Both products protect the foot from boot pressure and friction. Second Skin is a gelatin sheet applied to the foot which forms a layer that reduces abrasion and friction.

Once you've found a hot spot, do not cover the tender area. The goal of treatment is to build up a protrusion around the hot spot to protect it from direct friction, while leaving it open to the air so that it can heal. The best technique is to cut a small hole in the moleskin or molefoam that will fit over the tender area. Then cut another piece with a larger circle, a quarter- or half-inch wider than the inner circle. This will give you a small "donut" that can be placed over the hot spot. Or you can build up a layer of small strips of the material around the hole. If you are using moleskin, you may have to place three or four layers together in order to build up enough depth in the donut to protect the area from rubbing. Since molefoam is thicker, one layer will usually do the job.

If a blister has already developed, the treatment is the same. Always be sure that the infected area is left uncovered. Washing your feet regularly and putting on clean socks each day is particularly important when even the smallest infection develops.

Experienced backpackers, familiar with the tender spots on their feet, often place moleskin patches over potential hot spots before they hit the trail. This is particularly good practice if you have not hiked in heavy boots for a while and the skin on your feet has become soft. A piece of moleskin over a vulnerable area will give your feet a chance to toughen up on the trail.

NOLS recommends carrying both moleskin and molefoam; they are both lightweight and the combination gives you more flexibility in treating foot problems.

When cutting small pieces of adhesive and pulling the paper backing off, you may accidentally drop small pieces of trash. Be sure to police the area after you stop to treat foot problems.

"On the first three days of a course, at least once an hour I ask each student how their feet feel," says Tony Cullen. "If you can get through the first several days of tender feet without serious problems, there is a good chance that you can avoid major blisters for the rest of the course." Tony adds: "But you've got to keep asking. Most people are too embarrassed to ask an entire group to stop just so they can check their toes."

PERSONAL ENERGY CONSERVATION

You are ecstatic to finally be in the backcountry again. You are up early on a brisk morning, with the glow of sunrise flooding the valley floor below you. In among the trees, you and your companions have finished a breakfast of pancakes and coffee, broken camp, and are busily adjusting your pack straps in anticipation of a day on the trail. By

TREATING HOT SPOTS AND BLISTERS

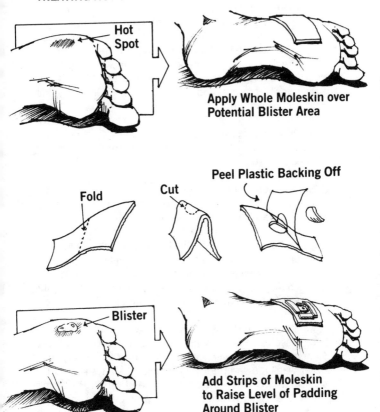

Apply Whole Moleskin over
Potential Blister Area

Fold   Cut   Peel Plastic Backing Off

Add Strips of Moleskin
to Raise Level of Padding
Around Blister

late afternoon you hope to reach Fiddler's Lake, just in time to catch your dinner while the fish are biting.

Off you go with great strides, bounding down through the green meadow to catch a winding trail. For a moment, you reflect back to the desk you left behind, the unfinished report, the telephone that won't stop ringing, a life that begins with a troubling morning newspaper. "It's great to be away from it," you think. A surge of energy wells in you as you reach the trail and you head into the lead, leaving your friends behind.

At the end of the meadow the trail becomes a series of steep switchbacks, little more than a narrow rut climbing the side of a high peak. It's just the sort of challenge you wanted and you make a dash for it, thinking of the view that awaits you on top.

Several hours later the heat of the afternoon sun bears down with unusual intensity. That first hill had a tricky slope to it, and that one small fall has an old knee injury acting up. You just took a break, but already you are thinking about another one. The likelihood of reaching Fiddler's Lake by dark has faded, and your three friends are arguing over who is slowing down the group.

You have just made a very common mistake. You let your energy get away from you. There is none left for the afternoon.

Conserving energy is one of the basic requirements of good travel technique. When you are in the backcountry, vulnerable to whatever nature might throw your way, you never want to use up all your strength. Always keep a reserve that you can draw on in a time of crisis. Becoming overly tired greatly heightens the possibility of injury or illness. It makes your judgment less dependable, and *you* a less than enjoyable hiking companion.

The ideal to reach for is a steady hiking pace which maintains a constant heart rate throughout the day. To accomplish this goal, you must develop an increased awareness of how your body functions on the trail and how you can make adjustments to accommodate your body's needs. The beginning of this awareness is learning to listen to and take charge of your breath—not an easy task for some.

Rhythmic Breathing

Rhythmic breathing is a method of monitoring and controlling your energy output while hiking. When you are breathing at your normal rate, your body is operating most efficiently. Heavy, labored breathing and gasping for breath are sure signs that you are wasting energy. Your muscles are not receiving enough oxygen to work at their peak efficiency. This causes your heart to pump faster, and you soon wear out.

While hiking, maintain an easy pace and a relaxed breathing rate. You can do this by synchronizing the rhythm of your step with the rhythm of your breath. If your breathing rate picks up with extra weight or at high altitudes, slow down your hiking pace.

On level ground, the average person carrying a 60-pound pack may take three steps per inhalation and three steps per exhalation. This is not a hard and fast rule; different bodies have different patterns. But this is a good place to start. Try it for five or ten minutes. If you feel short of breath, change pace to two steps per inhalation and two per exhalation. Or if you feel you can accelerate your pace to four steps per inhalation and four steps per exhalation, all the better. The important thing is to maintain a constant, comfortable breathing rate while hiking.

With a breathing rate established on level ground, you can gauge your needs as the terrain changes. On a steep hill you may shift to one step per breath. At higher altitudes you will find that the steps per breath vary; it is not uncommon to take two, three, or more breaths per step. Remember to breathe deeply, making every breath count.

Both the pleasure of being in the backcountry, with its fresh sights and subtle sounds, and the discomfort of carrying a heavy load on a long trek can distract you from rhythmic breathing. With concentration, however, conservation of energy can become a natural part of your technique in a very short time. Ironically, beginners often forget it when it is most needed—when the fatigue of the day has put them in a bad mood. Hiking is a skill like any other; it means taking mental as well as physical control.

Rhythmic breathing is much harder once you move off the trail. You leave behind the security of a path that you assumed was taking you in the right direction and suddenly you must continually orient yourself. You have to step up, over, and around things; all of this can interrupt the nice rhythmic pace you established on the trail. But rhythmic breathing is all the more important for off-trail hiking. It can give you a focus, minimize the difficulty of the terrain, and ensure that your energy is conserved for the long haul.

Pace

If you are just out for a stroll with no particular goal in mind, your pace comes naturally. You may saunter or walk briskly, but the pace is always comfortable, without pressure or discomfort. But when you have a goal and you are carrying a heavy pack toward that goal, you tend to push harder. The difficulty is compounded when you must find the right pace for a group of hikers, each with differing physical capabilities and hiking experience.

How do you know whether you yourself are walking at the right pace or not? There is a basic test. If you can keep it up all day with short rest periods every hour, you're moving at the right speed. It's the wrong pace if you need to stop or slow down a lot. Inevitably, beginners rush the pace and then spend the rest of the afternoon taking frequent breaks. At the best pace your legs and lungs work in harmony with each other. You should be able to carry on a conversation, not be sucking for air or dragging your feet. This is not to imply that you will never be short of breath or that your muscles won't ache. At times you will feel breathless and your muscles will hurt, but the strain should not be extreme.

Listen to your heartbeat. It will tell you if the pace is too fast. Your heart should not be racing; it should be steady, constant, adjusting to steep climbs and quick descents.

Starting the day's walk, begin slowly, giving your body a chance to warm up. As you get going, you'll notice that you will shift into an almost "automatic" gear. Some people call that a "second wind," but really it's your "first wind" because your body has just begun working at its optimum. The muscles have warmed up. The heart is surging blood through your arteries at a good rate.

No matter what the terrain, try to keep your pace steady. It's understandable that you will do a certain amount of trudging up a hill and walking quickly down, but try to minimize the gap between the two extremes. Recoup the extra energy you expended going up at a good pace, by coming down at a more leisurely pace. The steadier your pace, the longer you'll last and the more ground you'll cover.

It's normal for your speed and agility to decrease as the day progresses. If possible, plan the day's route so that the biggest challenges come in the morning. Don't expect that after five or six hours of walking you are going to be able to cross a boulder field, bushwhack through heavy ground cover, or negotiate rapid changes in elevation. If there's a choice between climbing a pass late in the day or camping and saving the assault for the morning, go with the latter. The pass won't look nearly as formidable with a good night's rest behind you.

Always keep in mind the evening itinerary and the schedule for the next day when you are deciding how much territory to cover. Leave enough energy, and daylight, to set up a good camp and cook an evening meal. Don't walk until you are completely drained. If you know tomorrow will require a lot of energy, lighten up the demands today.

One of the difficulties in finding a group pace is having to accommodate the slowest hiker. Before starting out on the trip, members should agree that the needs of the slowest and weakest will be given every consideration. If someone is barely making it from one rest stop to the next, the pace is too grueling.

Using up the energy reserves of the slowest member has many negative effects. It creates a situation in which there is a higher possibility of injury. It contributes to lower group morale. It creates unnecessary psychological tensions. And most important, it defeats the likely reason your group is in the backcountry: to have a good time.

Often the slowest hiker drops to the back of the line.

This is psychologically bad for the hiker, and makes it more difficult for the group to note and adjust to the slowest hiker's pace. It is better to put your slowest hiker near the front or in the middle of a line; the group will then set their pace based on the energy of its weakest element.

You may also wish to take some of the weight from a member who is having a particularly hard time. This might help him increase his pace, and it will slow down the hardier members of the group. Reassure the member who is giving up some weight that it is nothing to be ashamed of. It is a *practical decision,* not unusual, which should come at the suggestion of the leader.

If you are hiking in the high mountains, those who live at sea level are going to need longer to find their pace than those who are used to higher altitudes. People have different strengths, gaits, and lung capacities. It's important to let the capacities build at a natural rate for each person involved.

Establishing a good pace for a group, particularly in the early days of a trek, is a real test of leadership. Almost always there will be one or two members of the group who fall behind and need encouragement, and some who want to charge ahead. Setting the right tone in these situations is the leader's responsibility. Faster hikers will often become frustrated with being held back; indeed, many times a leader will become frustrated in the same manner. But establishing empathy so that slow people know that they have support is critical. As longtime NOLS instructor Willy Cunningham says, "It is a time like that when a lot of people realize that they are not cut out for a career in outdoor education."

If a leader senses that a fast-moving member of the group is becoming particularly frustrated, he or she should give that person more responsibility. In fact, there is no better way to develop empathy in a strong hiker who is a poor map reader than to assign him map-reading responsibilities.

The pace of a group may be significantly affected by weather. If a storm is brewing, you may need to pick up your speed in order to reach your camp or get off a pass. If you are forced to pick up speed, try to keep the new pace steady and reserve some energy for emergency conditions. Remember that if you push it too hard your weakest member may falter, and then you will all be stuck.

Heat is a good reason to slow the pace down. Overheating and dehydration are possible as temperatures climb. Make sure every member of your group is getting plenty to drink under these conditions.

Donna Ford stresses that with a group new to the backcountry, you must take it a day at a time. Keep people in the present; if they are having a hard time, they shouldn't be imagining two weeks of misery. Talk with them regularly. Ask how they are doing. Introduce them to the wonders of wildlife and weather. Every day on the trail, if proper energy-conserving techniques are used, each person will become stronger and more free to enjoy the surroundings.

The Rest Step

At NOLS we teach rhythmic breathing combined with what is called the rest step. Like any athletic skill, this basic technique requires discipline and practice. The rest step is what you use when the terrain begins to get steep and your breathing accelerates. It is a lot like shifting into low gear.

The rest step is, as its name implies, a step that gives your leg muscles the opportunity to rest. The beauty of it is that you can continue to move forward while regularly resting the muscles of each leg. To correctly use the rest step, follow this pattern: bring your back foot forward; plant the foot firmly on the ground and briefly lock the knee so that all your body weight shifts to that leg. This simple maneuver transfers most of the weight from your thigh muscles to the skeletal system, giving the muscles an opportunity to relax completely. Then reverse the procedure and bring the other foot forward. If with each step you lock your knee, your thigh muscles, which are doing most of the work, will have the opportunity to relax.

Because the rest step is rhythmic, it is quite easy to

coordinate it with your breathing. You may begin with one breath per step. If you find that the hill is becoming more difficult you can change to two breaths per step. In high-altitude climbing where heavy loads are carried up steep slopes at over 20,000 feet, it is not uncommon to take four or five breaths per step. With the rest step you can gauge your pace carefully, moving steadily toward your destination while ensuring that you do not become danger-ously tired.

Though simple, the basic rest step initially is somewhat "unnatural." It takes time to learn to employ it comfortably for a long period of time. A beginning hiker often can't learn to use it regularly until he gets very tired. As one NOLS instructor put it, "Many people don't learn it until right before they stop." But with practice the rest step becomes a natural, exquisitely simple part of your back-country techniques.

Layering for Climate Control

In Chapter Two we discussed the advantages of dressing in layers of clothing and the fabrics which fit into a good layering system. It is here on the trail that layering moves from a philosophy to practice. Maintaining a comfortable body temperature while hiking is an important part of con-serving your energy in the backcountry.

You should always be aware of the amount of heat your body is producing. Your goal is to remain as comfortable as possible while exercising strenuously. If you take a break after a long uphill trek and your body is hot, try to moderate the cooling process so that you do not chill. The key to accomplishing this is to wear clothing that will breathe and to make quick, simple adjustments to your clothing as your body dictates.

When traveling with a group, a critical time to be aware of climate control is in the early morning, five or ten min-utes after you start hiking. Mornings in the backcountry, even in the middle of summer, are often cool, calling for two or three layers of insulation as you cook breakfast and break camp. After five or ten minutes of hiking it is quite possible that the group will need to stop and take off a layer of clothing. A reluctance to slow the group can often interfere with this very natural need. It is important for a group leader to encourage people to respond quickly when their bodies begin to heat up. Waiting for the first rest break may be too late; your body may have become unnecessarily wet and uncomfortable, and you will begin your day with an undue drain of energy. An early-morning clothing break should be just that: a clothing break, not a rest stop.

Selecting clothing to wear when hiking in the rain is often a perplexing choice for a beginner. Unless you are carrying an outer garment made of one of the new breathable rainproof materials, you are faced with the choice of wearing coated nylon rain gear, which will prevent your sweat from evaporating, or wearing an insulating fabric on the outside, which will get wet but will remain warm and allow ventilation. The first thing a beginner should keep in mind is that standards of comfort are different in the backcountry than they are in town. The important thing when it is raining is to stay warm and not let your body chill. The method you choose to accomplish this is really a personal choice. Don't be disturbed if it means getting a little damp or clammy.

The Effective Rest Break

Extreme fatigue in the backcountry is dangerous. It leaves you vulnerable to accident and illness, and it weakens your most valuable resource, judgment.

All hikers need to rest, no matter how skilled or how strong they are. If you are barely making it from one rest stop to the next, nearly collapsing when you do, your pace is too fast or you are using improper walking techniques. Much will depend on the day's itinerary and how taxing the walk is. Rests must also be pegged to the fitness of the group.

In the early stages of a trip, particularly when there are neophyte hikers along, the group's leader needs to pay particular attention to the rest schedule. Inexperienced hikers often underestimate their capacity and tend to break too often. They hike a little and break too long. This type of schedule does not allow members of the group to build up strength, and it is physically debilitating. Try a set schedule, perhaps five minutes of rest per hour, and then adapt it to your group's abilities. Establishing a consistent pattern of rest stops can be very important to good morale.

A major factor in determining the length of a break is the natural process of lactic-acid production in the body. Lactic acid is a waste product of muscular activity. When you hike, the acid is produced and burned off, but when you suddenly stop, the acid continues to be produced for a while and remains in the system. If you stop for less than five minutes, the build-up is minimal and won't cause problems. If you stop for more than five minutes, however, it is best to break for twenty to thirty minutes to allow the excess lactic acid to clear out of the system. Rest breaks should include the opportunity to drink water, refill water containers, have a quick-energy snack, and relieve yourself. Accomplishing a break in five minutes with a large group often remains in the category of a worthwhile but elusive goal; nevertheless, it is a goal worth shooting for.

Find a good place to take a break, a site that will facilitate a restful and refreshing stop. Ideally a rest stop should be near a fresh-water source so that supplies can be replenished if necessary. It should be a sheltered area, protected from heat and wind. If you can, stop among trees or rocks so that there will be privacy for anyone who needs to relieve himself. Resting in an area surrounded by flat ground makes it much easier to start up again after your break; allowing the body to take a little time to get up to pace after a break conserves energy. Make sure you stop in an area with a clear view of major peaks, streams, or other prominent landmarks; a rest stop is a good time to check the map and compare opinions as to where you actually are on the trail. Use the rest stop to locate a good spot on the map for your next break. Psychologically, it is easier to hike toward a particular goal than to wonder when the next break will occur.

There are different degrees of rest. Depending on how much relaxation the group needs, the leader should call for a complete rest or a partial rest. A complete rest means taking off the pack. A partial rest could mean sitting on a rock or leaning up against a tree with the pack still on. A good leader will remember that the longer a group rests, the more motivation it requires to start up again. As the day wears on and muscle power wears down, a long break can be more debilitating than rehabilitating.

It is important that every rest break include some intake of food and water. Continually drinking liquids is essential to replenish the body's electrolytes and minerals. Trail food is always handy for a quick energy boost.

Your awareness of your own body should not go into recess on a rest break. Be particularly alert to your body heat. It is a good idea to put on an additional shirt or jacket while resting so that you don't lose too much heat.

Always take a break approximately fifty feet off the trail, out of courtesy for other backpackers who may be coming down the trail. In horse country, moving off the trail is also essential for safety. A horse can be spooked by people carrying large backpacks. When approached by a horse on a trail, move off to the lower side of the trail at least fifteen feet. If the horse reacts to the sight of backpackers, the rider can more easily regain control if the horse runs uphill. Have your whole group go off to the same side of the trail and avoid making loud noises. If you have a dog with you, be sure to keep it under control.

One final word on breaks: take them before they are desperately needed. Rest while you still have energy to draw on. The efficient and timely use of the rest break will extend the vitality of the hiker; it should not be held in reserve until near collapse.

Remember that these are only guidelines for rest stops on the trail. If five minutes after you start hiking you come upon a scenic vista that inspires you with its profound beauty, take a break, scheduled or not; that's one of the reasons you are out there.

ORGANIZATION FOR THE TRAIL

Old friends hiking together will probably know instinctively who is in charge at a given moment. Leadership, though informal, will be there when needed. Maps can be read jointly, decisions made collectively. In short, structure and organization evolve out of practice rather than conscious effort.

As group size increases, as you try to mesh strangers into a cohesive group, the need for organization on the trail increases, particularly if some members of the group are backcountry neophytes. An appointed leader becomes necessary. Tasks must be specifically assigned to build effective group dynamics.

As its name states, NOLS is not only an outdoor school but also a leadership school. After the first several days in the field, we divide the students into small patrols of four or five and assign a new leader for each patrol each day. Thus, every person learns to be sensitive to the needs of the group, deciding when to take breaks and when to keep walking. If there are conflicting interpretations of a topographic map, the group leader must decide which is correct and which direction to take. If an emergency occurs, there is no question who is in charge.

Some people who have been camping together casually for years routinely appoint one leader for the entire trip or a different person each day. It makes it easier on everyone if people know who is to make the decisions.

Leading a group requires accessibility above all, staying in touch with the individual needs of each member of the group. Sometimes it is best for a leader to be positioned in the middle of the line, or perhaps to circulate from the front to the back—whichever arrangement makes it easier to stay in touch.

In large groups, there are other tasks which can be assigned either formally or informally on the trail. Giving everyone a job helps keep the group alert and involved. It gives them something creative to concentrate on and keeps the mind off a sixty-pound pack. An end person should be appointed to make sure that slow hikers do not fall too far behind the main body of the group. This is particularly important in a large group with widely varying skills. The danger is that weaker members will be left behind. The end person can ensure that this does not happen and can assist the group leader in setting a proper pace.

Map reading is another function which can be assigned.

The map reader should be near the front of the group, selecting the route to the proposed destination. Few experiences can cause more division in a group than conflicting interpretations of a map. The appointment of a daily map reader helps defuse these problems. It is also a valuable learning experience to take on the map-reading responsibility.

When traveling through deadfall or deep underbrush, the second person in the line can be assigned to judge the condition of the trail. As the map reader sets the direction, the second person, a number of yards behind, can look for shorter, less taxing routes to move the group in the direction of travel. Moving the group a few feet in either direction to avoid a cumbersome obstacle can conserve a considerable amount of energy. The second person in line can also take primary responsibility for setting the group's pace.

Keeping a daily log of activities is another assignment which is useful on the trail. As we shall see when we discuss time control plans later in the chapter, a good record of starting time, major breaks, locations of water or major landmarks can be very valuable when it comes time to evaluate the trip and make future plans.

Every group entering the backcountry should give some consideration to its own organization. Keeping it entirely informal may be appropriate, although in an emergency one competent person must call the shots. The point is, structure and organization are tools which can be used unobtrusively to make a trip safer and more enjoyable.

There is one other common question about hiking with a group. What should be the normal distance between hikers? The best distance is probably between six and eight feet. For reasons of safety, don't bunch any closer, but don't lose visual or verbal contact either.

TIPS ON TERRAIN

The ideal environment for walking is well-spaced, tall conifers that dapple you with sunlight and cushion your feet with moss. This is nice to think about but rare to experience. You may instead find conifers that are only two feet high and intent on entangling you in their branches. Or you'll be walking in a valley that was buried in snow in the winter and is now a maze of brush. A boulder field can also be a threat to maintaining consistent pace and safe passage. For each terrain, NOLS teaches techniques which can help you navigate while maintaining a safe, healthy pace.

Trails

Getting background information is particularly important if you plan to use a trail. Trails have a way of starting out with bravado and then dwindling off timidly. Few trails were designed for today's backpacker. Many were blazed by miners seeking ore, or hunters and fishermen with only their prey in mind. A trail can give a false sense of security. It can make for delightful walking, but it doesn't always get you where you want to go.

If you find yourself on a well-used trail that you know is going somewhere, don't get lulled into a blind walk. Consult your map and be sure you are making the proper turn-offs. Check signs (with an eye out for those that may have been knocked down or obliterated by weathering), but remember signs can be wrong. There seems to be a breed of backwoods gnome that enjoys turning signs around.

If you are on an established trail, good conservation practice requires that you avoid taking short cuts, which can cause erosion and unnecessary marring of the natural landscape surrounding the trail. This is particularly important on switchbacks which zigzag up the side of a steep hill. When people begin to short-cut on switchbacks they create new trails, which are often too steep for safe travel and which wash out and widen during wet weather. Taking these short cuts will save a few steps, but you will be more tired and you'll leave behind a hillside marred by insensitive hiking.

When you encounter another group of hikers on the trail, either coming toward you or approaching from behind, it is common trail courtesy to move your group off the trail and let them pass.

You may find yourself relying on a blaze on a tree for your trail markings. This takes a keen eye; a season's growth of bark can cover a blaze. In an area that is not wooded, you can look for cairns, which are trailside stacks of rocks. These markings are not gospel; they are one person's or group's opinion as to the best particular route. That person or group might have been in the process of getting lost.

Trails have a tendency to encourage lazy hiking techniques, particularly when people have been hiking off-trail for days before. They reach a trail and suddenly they stop looking at their map. They begin walking too close together and walking at a blistering pace. Trails can make for pleasant, easy hiking, but they should not encourage lazy hiking.

Off-Trail

When you go off-trail you really begin to get a sense of the glory of the wilderness. Here there is no sign of man, only the natural, everchanging patterns of the wilds. Learning to be comfortable off-trail is a necessary prerequisite to this enjoyment.

Natural game trails often provide the best route through bushwhacking territory. Most game trails follow a path of least resistance; but keep a good eye on your map. The animals may not have been going to your destination.

You will occasionally find yourself in brush which can make walking an exhausting ordeal. Try to select the quickest route by looking ahead or on your map for heavily wooded, more mature areas where ground shrubs have died off and mature trees are the dominant vegetation. If you are proceeding through brush, always find out what is under it. It can cover holes, small streams, or rocks, giving a deceptively smooth contour to the rough ground beneath. Move with caution in brush. If there are adjacent snow patches, you may find it much easier to travel on those. The smoothness of the snow is preferable to the irregularity of the brush.

Try also to avoid traveling in avalanche tracks, a wide

swath of knocked-over trees, rocks, and rubble descending a steep hill. Walking through these areas is difficult and dangerous. You may have your best luck choosing slopes with a south or west exposure as opposed to north or east, where avalanching is more common.

Talus or scree is commonly encountered in off-trail hiking. Talus is a pile of rock fragments which have broken off cliffs or peaks. Usually talus is found at the base of a chute or gully on a slope steeper than 45 degrees. Talus fragments will range from the size of cobblestones to boulders and will often be sharp-edged, which makes a fall on talus dangerous. Descending a slope through a talus field is more hazardous than ascending; with your downward momentum, a fall is likely to take you farther. You have to be prepared to move precisely and lightly on talus; if you feel your footing giving way, move quickly to the next rock.

Scree is a pile of smaller rock fragments, loose and gravel-like, that makes for hard walking. If it is held in place by brush, scree becomes easier to maneuver on. Scree ranges in size from sand to the size of a fist and is generally more uniform than talus. Ascent is difficult on scree; it will slip under your feet and use up a great deal of your energy. Descending scree, on the other hand, can be much simpler: there are a number of common techniques, including quickly shuffling your feet to stay on the surface or locking your knees and using a "plunge step," which firmly plants your heel in the scree with each step.

On either talus or scree the major danger is falling rocks. It is very easy to kick loose a rock, which will quickly gain momentum as it travels downhill. Because talus is larger than scree, it presents a more dangerous potential for rock fall; but caution should be taken on both. On either talus or scree, keep your group close together so that rocks loosened by one person don't pick up speed before hitting the next person. Avoid walking beneath another hiker's fall line. Shout "Rock!" if any significant rock begins to fall. Remember that even a small rock can become a dangerous missile as it gains velocity barreling down a hill.

Sometimes you can't avoid scree or talus slopes. When hiking off-trail, you must often choose between a shorter route which will use more energy and a longer hike which is more energy-efficient. The more specific travel skills you can develop, the better you can make those decisions.

Hikers crossing a slope of scree on a horizontal line need to move stealthily and nimbly. If you plant your feet heavily in the scree, you will begin to slide. It may go against instinct, but you should never stop in the midst of steep scree and try to get "stable" footing. Keep moving until you're back on solid ground. Try to avoid moving on all fours; a rock kicked from above can easily maim a finger.

Walking Uphill

When you are going up a hill, stand straight. This is the best position from which to regain your balance if you lose your footing. You may fall forward, but you will be able to recover more quickly to an erect position.

In going up a hill, try to keep your steps small; aim for a maximum elevation gain of six inches per step. The energy you expend with two small steps is less than that consumed by one long one. Try not to waste your energy going up and down, stair-step fashion, over logs and rocks. If you can't easily step over a major obstacle, go around it and cut out as much unnecessary elevation gain and loss as possible.

The rhythm of uphill steps is critical: breath, foot placement, pace, all come into play here. Remember, the rest step was designed for efficient uphill travel. Use it.

Walking Downhill

Walking downhill is not always the relief it may at first seem. It is usually the downhill part of a journey that causes blisters, knee problems, and ankle injuries. Walking downhill causes much greater friction between the boot and the foot than an uphill hike. To help reduce friction and avoid blisters, tie your boots tightly. You will save your feet if you don't jam them into the ground as you put them down. Keep your knees slightly bent too, and resist the force of gravity pulling you forward. Walk with small, controlled steps, no faster than horizontal walking.

People build up the muscles required for uphill hiking much more than those needed to travel downhill. Therefore, there is a high risk of a recurrence of old injuries such as knee problems. Walk carefully. Control your foot placement. If there are rocks on the trail that are unavoidable, always step on their uphill side. Keep your eye on your next step.

Contouring

When hiking off-trail it is common to come upon the following situation. You are hiking on top of a hill and you approach a deep valley. The most direct route would be to go down into the valley, across it, and then up the steep slope of a far hill, there to resume your hike at approximately the same elevation at which you began. Although this route is the shortest as the crow flies, the crow would also fly it at the same elevation, while you would be walking down and then up steep slopes.

There is, however, an alternative. This particular valley is boxed in at one end by sloping scree fields at the base of high peaks which tower above you. Rather than taking the shortest route across the valley, you can hike at a constant elevation around the valley. This is called contouring.

Contouring routes are not always readily apparent and often require that you weigh a number of tradeoffs. Will it be easier to hike across a sloping field of loose scree which may be unstable but will allow you to maintain your elevation? Or is it easier to drop five hundred feet of elevation and then hike back up the same amount of elevation on a much more stable, shorter route? Only experience can provide a sound basis to make that decision; just be sure you consider contouring as an option.

Crossing a Slope

Contouring often involves a walking technique called traversing an incline: cutting across the slope of a hill rather than walking straight up or down it. Traverses are also used when you need to hike up or down a hill which is too steep to be approached directly. You then traverse back and forth across the slope of the hill, following a gentle zigzag pattern.

Before you start a traverse, visualize your route. If you are traversing up or down, use natural reference points to mark the points where you will make your turns. Keep your angle of ascent or descent gentle, under 45 degrees. If you are using your traverse to contour, take special note of natural obstacles which you'll have to go above or below. Make sure that you have a route fully planned before you start.

The critical skills for a successful traverse are foot placement and rhythm. Moving in a constant rhythm contributes to good balance, and careful foot placement will minimize unnecessary spills. It will spare you a great deal of fatigue if you can put one foot directly in front of the other to avoid walking with one foot on the uphill side and one on the down. The latter is bad for balance, and because it causes your foot to torque (twist) inside the boot, it is likely to cause blisters.

Adopt this stance for traversing: lower your downhill shoulder and lean out toward the base of the hill. Think of your spine as a plumb bob which hangs into the slope. If you slip from this position, you will reflexively catapult yourself into an upright position. Balancing your body while standing straight on an incline is difficult, but leaning out from the hill will make it less likely that your feet can be knocked out from under you.

When traversing a scree, talus, or snow slope in a group, keep everyone in tight formation so that no individual ends up walking on the slope below another. If this is impossible as in the case of switchbacks, stop the group at each turn before you proceed. If the size of your group prohibits this, be sure to keep your angle of traverse shallow enough so that any debris which may be kicked loose higher on the hill has little time to gain momentum. In scree it is a good idea to have the hikers follow in the same line and use the exact steps as the person ahead. This will take less energy and is less likely to cause a slide.

Even when contouring, it is wise to walk at a slight angle of traverse either up or down. When considering a traverse, think about the energy of the group, the weight of their packs, and your overall pace; out of these factors you must choose an appropriate angle of traverse.

Walking Over Boulders

When crossing particularly dense boulder fields, some NOLS instructors require their students to wear climbing helmets for protection. Or they may have students cross in pairs, spotting each other in order to break possible falls. Always, in a boulder field, you must be alert. Though your feet may be in one place, your eyes and mind are several boulders ahead, plotting the next move. The best technique is to establish a smooth, controlled movement. Standing in lengthy deliberation on a rock only complicates the matter. All the techniques we have discussed in this chapter—foot placement, breathing, and rhythm—are called into play in the agile maneuver of dancing with a heavy pack through a boulder field.

Going from one boulder to the next, aim for the most solid spot of the rock. Try to keep on as even a plane as possible; minimize your loss or gain of elevation. Direct downward pressure is a securing force for any potentially loose rock.

There is more chance of boulder movement in new fields than old. You can generally distinguish an old boulder field by the presence of vegetation: lichen growing on the rocks and plants having grown up through the cracks between the rocks. Remember, though, that lichen is *very* slippery when it or your boots are wet.

Rain or snow cover makes rocks slippery and dangerous. If these conditions exist, circumnavigate the boulder field if at all possible.

If you know a boulder field lies ahead of you and you have some spare time, take off your packs and play at boulder hopping for part of the day. It is an enjoyable exercise in agility and balance; a little practice without packs can encourage skill and self-confidence with packs.

Do not undo your waist belt when crossing a boulder field

with a pack. Balance is important here and your pack must move with you, close to your body. Boulder fields can be a real problem to a slow hiker with little confidence. It may be a good idea to take the pack from such a person and ferry it across. Groups should move across boulder fields with considerable distance between each person; crowding can interfere with balance and make a small spill dangerous. Finally, use your hands only for balance. Never reach up to grab a rock outcrop for support.

Crossing a Snowfield

Winter is not the only time hikers encounter snow. It hangs on through August in most high-altitude mountains, which is fine, because snowfields with a mild pitch can actually mean an easier, smoother trail and a shorter route to your objective.

We are dealing here with snowfields that have a slope of 25 degrees or less. Steeper slopes often require mountaineering equipment, such as ice axes and crampons, and that gear, in turn, requires individualized instruction.

When you encounter a snowfield, your first concern should be the time of day. In late spring, snow is melting rapidly; it turns to liquid on the surface, the water percolates down through the winter's powder, and eventually turns the underlying crystals to corn snow. In spring, the lower layers are wet slush, and a false step could throw you into a bottomless slurpie. The time to cross these snowfields is early morning, before they soften.

Later in the year snowfields develop hard corn snow underneath a hard, smooth, icy surface. At these times, snowfields should be crossed later in the day, when the surface has softened and your boots can get a grip.

Before crossing a snowpatch, look at it carefully. How long is it? What lies at the bottom? Is it too steep to cross safely without mountaineering equipment? Does it have level spots?

If the snow is firm and level, you'll have no problems; walk normally, the way you would on regular ground. If the snow is soft, be more cautious. When you take a step, put your foot down firmly, compressing the snow, but don't immediately put your full weight on it. Give the snow a chance to set up beneath your boot, then take your next step.

The object on sloping snow is to keep your weight centered over your foot, away from the slope. On traverses, lean your body out, away from the uphill slope; ascending a snowfield, try to stand erect; going down, lean forward over your feet. You want your weight to push down into the snow, not down toward the bottom of the slope.

When traversing a sloping snowfield you will want to use a kick step. Lift your leg as you would for a normal step, then swing the lower part of the leg, from the knee down, forward on a horizontal plane against the snow slope. This should make a horizontal shelf. Hard snow may make this difficult, but kick a few times before you give up. If you can't make a kick step, and the slope is steep, get off it.

Climbing up a snowfield, kick a step with just the toe of the boot. Take only short steps when ascending on snow—a few inches is plenty. Longer steps will make it difficult to dig in your kick step, will tire you out, and will force you to swing your body more, making a fall possible.

Unless you fear a long slide, most descents are made straight down a snowfield. Lean out over your feet, away from the slope, and plunge your heel into the snow, keeping your knee stiff.

Snowfields are not the place to take chances, particularly if you are not equipped with an ice ax and experienced in its use. Even a short slide down a snowfield can end in a pile-up of rocks with a twisted ankle—not what you want in the backcountry. If you start to feel unbalanced crossing a snowfield, stamp out a small flat space to stabilize yourself. Then get off it, taking the shortest, safest route.

River Crossings

A river crossing can be a refreshing splash across an ankle-deep creek, or it can involve a highly technical rope system across a white foam torrent.

In general, river crossings are considered one of the

more dangerous activities undertaken in the backcountry. In the mountains, riverbeds almost by definition are filled with slippery rocks, deep holes, floating timber, and dangerous hydraulics such as "keepers," holes in the stream bottom with powerful suction. The water may be full of blue-gray glacial "till" that will defy your attempts to see the bottom.

While most crossings on trails are little more than fords, you could be faced with a potentially dangerous crossing early in the season or during or after a storm. Especially if you want to travel off-trail, you should be prepared to encounter the most severe type of river crossings.

With this warning in mind, allow yourself plenty of time to think clearly and make wise decisions about the site and method of crossing. Thorough scouting for the safest possible site is essential. You might do well to split your group, sending one scouting party upstream and one downstream. Assign a time to reconvene and avoid wasting precious time.

When scouting, beware of snags, waterfalls, barbed wire, fences, rocks, holes, and other obvious dangers. Seek out a spot which is not only shallow and slow but also has an even, preferably gravel, bottom. Rivers are slowest in their widest spots; the outside of a bend contains the fastest and deepest water.

Does your crossing site offer a good view upstream which will allow you to see and have time to react to debris floating down at you? In the event that one of your group takes a spill, where will he land or be washed: three feet below a rock ledge in an unfathomable hole or in a quiet sandy stretch? Are the rocks on which you were thinking of stopping coated with slippery green slime?

Determine the limitations, strengths, and knowledge of your companions and choose the crossing site accordingly. If the river is wide and fast and you are concerned about the stamina of weaker members, you may want to select a spot downstream having some large boulders that will provide quiet eddies to rest behind. Be sure that these spots are not too deep.

If you find a place where you can cross dry by stepping

on boulders or traversing logs, check the rocks or logs for stability and slipperiness. Obviously, dry logs are the safest. If a log is slimy or wet, you can throw sand on it. When crossing on logs, select a spot where you can't fall far and won't land on jagged rocks or branches. Post several spotters downstream as a backup in case anyone falls or is washed downstream and needs assistance. Depending on the situation, the spotters might do well to locate a long stick or rope for reaching out to someone floundering in the water.

In all river crossings, undo the waist belt of your pack so that if you do fall you can get out of it quickly. When rock hopping, it is particularly important to plan your moves and then move continuously in order to maintain dynamic balance. He who hesitates gets wet.

Let's say there is no dry crossing and your best site will take you across a river flowing at mid-calf level. Most likely, you will be able to wade it easily. However, don't go barefoot. If it's sandy or light gravel, you can change to your sneakers or camp shoes to keep your boots dry. If the bottom is rocky, wear your boots. They will give your ankles support and protection from rolling rocks. Keep your boots laced loosely enough so you can pull your foot out if a boot becomes irretrievably jammed between rocks.

If the bottom is flat and you can see it, take your socks off to keep them dry and wear your boots over your naked feet. But if the water is cold and the river is wide, wear your socks to give your feet added warmth. You can cross in shorts to keep long pants dry and to reduce weight and water resistance. Wearing gaiters in a river crossing can be dangerous; if your boot gets caught in a hole, you want to get your foot out quickly. A gaiter would make this difficult, if not impossible.

In crossing, each person should carry a stick or ice ax to probe for holes and loose rocks. Pick a stick long enough to rest on your shoulder, raising your center of gravity. Face at an upstream angle for maximum stability and so you can avoid debris floating downstream. Stand well-braced with feet shoulder-width apart and move deliberately, one step at a time. This principle is absolutely critical when crossings are deeper and more dangerous. Whenever possible, a river crossing should be made on a diagonal, moving upstream. A diagonal movement provides less body resistance to the current.

Don't let yourself become mesmerized by the flow of the water as you cross. Look where you need to go, and go. If you do fall, don't panic. Dump your pack, get your feet pointed downstream, and swim or wade to one side or the other.

In a situation where the water is breaking above your knees and you can't see the bottom because of glacial till or suspended silt, one of your stronger members should cross first without a pack to test the footing and current. Have your spotters in place and ready to act quickly.

If the crossing is reasonably easy for most of the group but one member of the party is smaller or weaker, a stronger individual can ferry that person's pack across. At NOLS we sometimes have the weaker person link arms with two other people and cross as a threesome standing in a line parallel to the current. This way, the upstream person breaks the flow for the weaker one and both escorts lend stability.

If you decide the stream is so strong that most members need additional support, you could set up a taut hand line behind two trees on either bank. Again, this would only be to hold for balance—no one should actually be tied to it. If you use a taut line, make sure all crossings are made on its downstream side to avoid entanglement in the rope in the event of a fall. Some NOLS instructors have students clip the top of their packs onto the line with a sling and carabiner. This takes the weight of the pack off the student if he falls, and he can slip free if caught in the current.

For all river crossings, remember a cardinal rule: always unfasten the hip belt on your backpack. If you take a plunge, the first thing you need to do is quickly get out of your pack.

Tailor your crossing system to the weakest member of the group. And if you have persistent doubts about the safety of a crossing, don't do it. Spend more time scouting. Look at your maps, and chances are that you may eventually find some way to avoid it entirely or to cross in a safer place.

TIME CONTROL PLANS

NOLS developed the time control plan as a method of organizing all the information we have about wilderness travel into a useful form for daily use. Preparing time control plans while traveling in the backcountry reminds you to ask regularly the important questions we have addressed in this chapter. How much energy do you anticipate the group will have on a given day? What are the obstacles to be faced between point A and point B? What preparations are needed for the particular route you are taking? If you can answer these questions prior to setting out on the trail, your travel will most likely be more efficient and enjoyable.

The first step in preparing a time control plan is to look at your map and reaffirm where your current camp is located and what destination will be your goal for the next day's hike. Analyze your route of travel and note any interesting spots on the map which you might want to explore during your hike. Such exploration will take extra time, and this time should be anticipated in estimating your time of arrival at your next camp.

Figure out the linear distance of your route and estimate the travel time of the group. On the first days of a backcountry trip, two miles per hour is a fairly standard estimate. After a couple of days, if you are keeping a daily log, you will be able to estimate travel time more specifically.

Next, figure out the cumulative elevation gain of your route. This information needs to be factored into your travel time. NOLS has found the following to be a good rule of thumb. If you are hiking with full packs, add the time it takes your group to travel three miles to your total travel time for every 1,000 feet of elevation gained; if you are carrying a medium load, add two miles' travel time for each of these increments; if carrying a day pack, add one mile's time per increment.

Look at the map closely and identify any hindrances to

travel such as river crossings, snowfields, boulder fields, or heavy brush. Experience will help you to estimate the effect of these obstacles on your travel time; while you are gaining that experience, start by cutting your normal speed in half to accommodate travel hindrances.

Finally, factor in any breaks and meals which you will take on the trail. As mentioned earlier, it is a good idea to identify your break areas on a map, and use these as accomplishable goals during your hike.

Now add up your estimates of the time it will take you to travel on your next day's journey. Set a time to begin and an estimated time of arrival.

This time control process is much more than an exercise in map reading and backcountry paperwork. It enables you to think clearly about the capacities of the group with which you are traveling; its day-by-day use sensitizes you to a much more refined understanding of your own potentials in the wilderness, and it allows you to check your progress and anticipate any potential problems which may arise from a change in your schedule.

Chapter **Seven**

Backcountry First Aid

LEN PAGLIARO, a NOLS instructor and certified emergency medical technician, was climbing with some friends on Sunset Pass in Washington's Cascade Mountains eight years ago when one of his companions slipped.

Below the climbing face lay a 45-degree snowfield, and the fellow slid down it about twenty feet. He would have been all right but for a rock outcrop in the snowfield, next to which the snow had melted, forming a deep "moat." He fell into the moat, dropping about twelve feet, where he lay face down with his left leg broken just above the ankle.

It was a closed fracture—meaning the skin was not broken, which was lucky. But it presented special problems for his would-be rescuers. If the skin broke, the risk of serious infection would be high, yet moving him with the leg unbound, or taking off his boot, would probably break the skin. So one of the climbers descended into the moat and secured the broken leg using an ice ax for a splint. With splint securely in place, his friends carefully removed the injured man from the moat, and made him as comfortable as possible.

Three members of the group left immediately for help—a run to a ranger station that would take them more than six hours. From there they radioed for an emergency evacuation helicopter, passing along specific information about the injury and the exact location of the victim. Back on the snowfield, those who remained dug an icy platform 100 feet by 100 feet—a landing pad for a helicopter. Then they built a litter using pack frames and moved the victim to the landing site.

The accident took place at dusk. By 9:30 A.M. the following day the injured climber was being treated in a hos-

230

pital emergency room in Seattle. Without proper handling, the doctors later said, he could have lost a leg or foot.

He made a full recovery, reports Len, and continues to be an avid climber.

If you have an emergency requiring rescue, assistance, or evacuation in the backcountry, you should know ahead of time how to get help. Get the essential information before your trip into a wilderness area and take it with you. Whom do you contact for outside help? How do you get in touch with them? What equipment and resources do they have available? Emergency services vary from area to area. Knowledge of the capacities of emergency organizations that may come to your aid is as important as carrying a compass.

First aid is just that—help given to a victim *first,* often before the arrival of professional medical care. The primary rule of all first aid, backcountry or city is: "Do no harm. Do good if you can, but at least do no harm."

"It takes a special approach to deal with backcountry illness or injuries," says Len, who has taught NOLS courses since 1974. "They are usually different from what you find in cities or near civilization. In a city, an ambulance and hospital are only a few minutes away, while in the backcountry it may be twenty-four hours or more before an injury is treated by physicians. It is likely you will have to wait a long time for help to arrive. This alone will considerably alter your previous attitudes toward emergency treatment."

Knowledge of rudimentary first aid is an absolute necessity in the backcountry. You may unexpectedly find yourself called upon to deal with debilitating or life-threatening medical problems or injuries; you may have to organize a rescue or evacuation. This chapter will give you enough information to deal with some of the more common backcountry illnesses and injuries. It is *not* a substitute for thorough training in backcountry first-aid techniques. If you intend to spend much time far removed from society's health support systems, get competent first-aid training.

First aid courses are available through the American Red Cross, and often through local law enforcement, fire, ambulance, and mountain rescue organizations. Emergency medical technician training is usually provided by the state office of emergency medical services.

BACKCOUNTRY ILLNESS AND PREVENTION

Prevention is the best prescription for backcountry medicine. Preventing the occurrence of a serious medical problem avoids the rescue situation, a complicated and dangerous affair.

Prevention should begin before the trip. Know the allergies, medications, and special health concerns of the people with whom you are traveling. The group should have a frank discussion of these topics so that every member of the party can be alert to early symptoms of problems.

Attention to minor details is important in the outdoors. Extra care should be taken with small cuts and abrasions. A simple cut is not a problem. A cut that becomes infected *is* a problem. Keep minor wounds clean. Wash them carefully with an antiseptic soap and dress them. The same applies to blisters. A correctly treated blister, as described in Chapter Six, should heal well. A raw ugly blister, infected and painful, can mean a litter evacuation.

Bouts of intestinal discomfort, commonly referred to as the "mung," can be avoided by proper hygiene when cooking and camping. When they occur, the ill member of the party should be isolated to prevent the problem from running rampant through the entire group. His or her eating utensils should be boiled meticulously clean and kept separate from the rest of the group's. In effect, the victim is quarantined. This may be an ugly phrase, but with a little encouragement and explanation of the necessity of the actions, it can be well received.

General cleanliness can prevent the spread of noxious organisms through a group. Clean feet and socks reduce the occurrence of irritating foot infections. In general, addressing minor problems before they become major ones and adhering to the rules of safety are the first rules of backcountry medical care.

Mountain Sickness

Mountain sickness is a common backcountry illness involving a number of symptoms that occur with varying degrees of severity in individuals, usually at altitudes greater than 10,000 feet. Anyone is susceptible to the illness, though, for reasons unknown, some people are more prone than others.

The most common symptom is a headache, which may be accompanied by insomnia, loss of coordination, swelling of the eyes and face, lassitude, nausea, vomiting, loss of appetite, and reduced urine output. The condition seems to be aggravated by overexertion and dehydration.

When these symptoms occur in mild form, it's a signal that you need more time to acclimatize to the altitude. When headaches get severe and defy relief from aspirin, stop ascending, and if the condition persists beyond a few hours—or overnight, if you are camped—descend. Dropping 1,000 to 2,000 feet is usually sufficient.

Mountain sickness is a warning sign of lack of acclimatization to altitude. It can also be a prelude to the more serious problems of high altitude pulmonary edema (HAPE) and high altitude cerebral edema (HACE). In these advanced forms, mountain sickness can be fatal. Anyone venturing to high altitudes should familiarize himself with the medical problems he might face. Prevention is the best form of treatment, and you can avoid the problem by gradual ascent, preventing dehydration, avoiding overexertion, and maintaining a balanced, ample diet. Remember, if you begin to feel the first signs of mountain sickness, the best treatment is simple: Descend!

Cold Injuries

Humans are thermally sensitive creatures—homeotherms—and, as such, must pay attention to the temperature. If they don't, in many backcountry settings cold injuries are likely to occur. As we have discussed, heat is lost through conduction, convection, radiation, evaporation, and respiration. Heat can be gained by exercise and thermoregulatory processes, like shivering.

The best-known type of cold injury is hypothermia, a dangerous lowering of the body's temperature. It is a polite term for freezing to death. There are great individual differences in bodies' abilities to produce and conserve heat. When a body's loss of heat exceeds the ability to produce it, and the condition persists over time, hypothermia results. The symptoms are slurred, slow speech, incoherence, failing memory, stumbling, drowsiness, and lassitude.

A human functions normally when his or her body temperature is at 98.6 degrees. At 95 degrees, effective muscular action is weakened and the victim is not producing enough body heat to recover unassisted. At 93 degrees, muscular action is very difficult, and below 86 degrees, heart action becomes irregular.

To prevent hypothermia, hikers and climbers must be aware of the body as a heat source and the importance of clothes as insulation. If the body is to provide heat, it needs energy, and the energy is provided by food and drink. Eat when you are cold. Drink when you need to. Fatigue is a real danger. Ask yourself "Why am I cold?" and take steps to correct the problem. The greatest loss of body heat is through the head, so make sure you wear a hat. Find shelter early. The classic exposure cases involve people who waited too long to seek shelter.

However, if you've failed to prevent hypothermia, you must recognize it. Even severe cases can be difficult to detect, but early recognition is extremely important. According to one study done in Anchorage, Alaska, 48 percent of hypothermia cases are fatal. The victim often will say that there is nothing wrong with him. Believe the signs, not the victim.

Once afflicted, a hypothermia victim must be rewarmed. First, remove him from the offending environment, if possible (it should be, if you are properly equipped). Then provide external heat. Put him in a sleeping bag which has been warmed ahead of time, since the victim cannot generate enough heat to warm the bag himself. Put in hot water bottles and feed the victim warm, sugary drinks. Skin-to-skin treatment is most effective. If a double sleeping bag is available, place the victim inside between two stripped persons.

Although frostbite is quite rare in three-season camping, any hypothermia victim should be checked for its symptoms. Even in relatively mild weather, the hypothermia victim, who is already cold, may be particularly susceptible to frostbite.

Frostnip, which is the most likely type of frostbite that a three-season camper would experience, affects surface skin layers. The natural color of the skin takes on a gray or white tone, and small bumps cover the area. Frostnip, unlike the other types of frostbite, can be treated in the field, and does not require evacuation. If you find signs of frostnip, rewarm the frostnipped skin by placing warm hands on it. If hands or feet are cold, place the frostnipped area under an armpit or against someone's stomach. When the area is rewarmed, it will redden and sting. The tissue loss, if any at all, is similar to a sunburn and will be minor.

The other two types of frostbite occur almost exclusively in winter conditions. Superficial frostbite affects the skin and the tissue immediately underneath. The skin will be frozen on top, but soft and pliable underneath, the reverse of a half-thawed steak. This type of frostbite requires immediate evacuation. It is best not to rewarm the frostbitten area in the field, but that may be impossible to avoid, particularly if the frostbite is discovered after the victim is in camp. When the skin is rewarmed, it will be mottled and blue or purple in color. It may initially be numb, but will then sting for a period. Blisters will form in twelve to forty-eight hours after the thaw.

Deep frostbite means that the flesh is "frozen to the bone." Immediate evacuation is required.

Anyone with an interest in winter camping or high-altitude climbing, or who is contemplating entering a backcountry area where winter conditions are possible, should thoroughly understand how to prevent, identify, and treat frostbite. Several of the books and pamphlets referred to in the "Suggestions for Additional Reading" at the back of this book can provide you with the data you need for this required study.

Neither frostbite nor hypothermia is very common to three-season backpacking. However, because weather, one of the most unpredictable factors in wilderness living, is a major factor in the development of these serious problems, every backpacker should have some rudimentary knowledge of their symptoms and treatment. Most important, a knowledge of the severity of hypothermia and frostbite can reinforce how important it is to prevent either from occurring. Make sure you stay warm. Make sure your companions stay warm. The best prescriptions for preventing these serious problems can be found in the clothing and nutrition chapters of this book.

Snow Blindness

Snow blindness is a problem not to be taken lightly. At higher altitudes, the thinner atmosphere allows more ultraviolet radiation to reach your eyes, particularly when it is reflected off surfaces like water or snow. Don't think that you can simply wait until your eyes feel uncomfortable— be sure to wear sun goggles or glasses when you spend any time on snowfields. The actual onset of snow blindness doesn't occur until eight or more hours after exposure.

Your eyes can take only so much exposure; when radiation comes both directly from the sun and reflected off the snow, it can be too much. Roughly eight to twelve hours later, eyes become red and swollen, blinking and moving the eyes becomes painful, and exposure to light hurts.

If you suffer from snow blindness, don't rub your eyes. Treat them with cold compresses and shield them from bright light. Wet, cool tea bags placed directly over the eyelids can help to limit the itchiness and pain. It may take several days to recover.

Don't assume that just because the sun isn't out, you are safe from snow blindness. On a cloudy day you may be just as susceptible as on a bright day.

Sunburn

Again, the villain is ultraviolet radiation, and its favorite victims are the light-skinned folks with blond or red hair and blue eyes. If you get a sunburn in the wilderness, you can't just put on the lotion and lie low for a few days. Your skin will be further exposed to the elements, and good treatment may be difficult. You may have admired the tans of friends when they came back from a trip in the wilderness, but don't work too hard to match them.

A sunburn can mean a lot more than just skin discomfort. Prolonged exposure can lead to blistering, and you may suffer fever, headache, and chills if you burn severely. When your lips get badly sunburned you run the risk of herpes simplex infections, which appear in the form of cold sores.

Like the problems we've covered earlier, the simplest way to deal with sunburn is to prevent it. A good sunscreen lotion should be part of your standard gear, whether winter or summer in the backcountry. The best sunscreens for the backcountry are made with paraminobenzoic acid (PABA). If your skin is fair and sensitive, take along zinc oxide, which completely blocks out ultraviolet rays.

Heat Exhaustion and Heat Stroke

Heat problems can sneak up on you. In your desire to work your body hard in the backcountry, you may not realize when you are nearing heat exhaustion or heat stroke; symptoms that indicate danger may seem to you just a sign of good, tiring exercise. Keep in mind that illnesses associated with heat can occur regardless of what shape you're in—your muscles don't have to be tired.

When you work hard for several hours in a hot environment, be sure to take rest stops and drink fluids. Dehydration, coupled with hard exertion, salt deficiency, or difficulty acclimating to altitude changes, is a major contributor to heat exhaustion. Blood vessels react to the heat by dilating, trying to cool the blood by bringing it closer to the body's surface. But the dilation can go too far, slowing circulation and depriving the brain and other vital organs of essential nutrients.

A victim of heat exhaustion will feel faint, and possibly nauseated. The heart rate is usually rapid, and the person will become restless, suffer from headaches, and may even lose consciousness. Sweat and skin color will vary, but victims often feel clammy and turn pale.

If these symptoms appear, stop in a shady, comfortable environment and administer fluids. Do not rush back on the trail the minute the victim says he feels better. Take a real rest.

If you are susceptible to heat exhaustion, proceed cautiously. Stay out of the sun and rest during the hottest part of the afternoon. Take adequate fluids and salts. Consider traveling at night, if necessary.

Even more serious than heat exhaustion is heat stroke. Should a member of your party suffer from heat stroke, *immediately* treat him—it can be fatal.

When someone suffers heat stroke, the body's temperature-regulating system breaks down completely. The thermostat goes on the blink. The victim's sweat glands simply stop functioning—there is no sweat at all. He runs a high fever, his skin becomes warm, red, and dry, and he will likely be confused and disoriented. The onset of heat stroke is very rapid.

In treating heat stroke, try to cool the victim's body as rapidly as possible. Don't waste any time. If there is *tepid* water available, totally immerse the victim; if not, cover his body with cloths soaked in water or alcohol. Massage his limbs to keep the blood moving.

Make plans for an evacuation while you administer this treatment. If the victim's temperature drops to 102 degrees, stop trying to cool his body. Since his temperature is within the body's normal controls, you run the risk of overcooling. However, keep an eye on him to be sure his temperature doesn't rise again.

You can prevent heat stroke the same way you prevent heat exhaustion: by watching out for overexertion and overheating in hot weather, and by resting and taking plenty of fluids.

DEALING WITH ACCIDENTS

Setting priorities is the first rule of emergency care. Life-threatening problems must be dealt with immediately. Problems that are not life-threatening do not need action within minutes. The ambulance won't be arriving shortly, so take your time if the problem allows it.

Evaluate your patient carefully. Determine the extent of the problem. Having a book on emergency medical care available is a real asset. If you do, take some time to review it; it will give you a better understanding of your victim's problem and refresh your memory on the proper emergency treatment.

Your most crucial decision will be on the need for a rescue. Is the problem serious enough to require evacuation, or can it be dealt with in the field with a few days of rest and recuperation? Illnesses are often perplexing; a stomachache could mean a case of indigestion or a case of appendicitis. An outdoor leader, well versed in backcountry medicine, will be familiar with basic health problems, and with the aid of a reference book be able to determine if the problem requires evacuation or not.

In any accident or illness in the wilderness, stay calm and rely on your common sense. Excellent emergency care can be and has been given by untrained rescuers who display these qualities.

Approaching an Accident Victim

The first rule of rescue is that the safety of the rescuer comes first. Backcountry accidents often occur in precarious places; the victim of a fall may land on a ledge or an unstable scree field. Look around you and evaluate the dangers. You will not be an asset to the victim if you injure yourself as well.

Upon reaching the victim, do not move him until the extent of injuries has been evaluated, if possible. This is especially true if a neck or back injury is suspected. The victim can be protected from the elements by pitching a rain fly or a tent with the floor cut out above him. Clothing and sleeping bags can provide comfort and insulation.

When approaching the victim, introduce yourself and address him by name. This formality is important even if you know the victim; accidents often cause disorientation. Develop a rapport. One person, not two or three, should let the victim know who is treating him and who is in charge. Orient him to his surroundings; if possible, make him aware of what is occurring around him. Tender loving care —reassurance that everything is going to be okay—is fine, but do not mislead the victim. An accident victim can be remarkably perceptive. You want the victim aware and involved in his own care.

It is one of the peculiarities of going into the backcountry that victims may be predisposed to injury or shock. Says Len Pagliaro, "They may be tired, didn't sleep well, are hungry, cold, or whatever. The environment is a change, or it may be entirely new to them. Their condition may have precipitated the injury in the first place."

Immediate First Aid

There are three life-threatening priorities that must be dealt with immediately in any accident: absence of breathing, absence of circulation, and severe bleeding.

Check the victim at once for these conditions. If they exist they must be treated before any further examination or evacuation planning.

See if the victim's chest is rising and falling. Listen for his breath. The most common airway obstruction is the tongue. To clear this obstruction, simply reposition the head. Place your cheek next to the victim's mouth and nose and feel for air. If there is no breath, apply mouth-to-mouth resuscitation at once. To do this, place the victim on his back. With one hand on the forehead and the other gently lifting under the neck, tilt the victim's head back. Open the mouth and clear both the mouth and nose of any foreign material. Place your mouth over the victim's mouth, forming an airtight seal. Pinch his nostrils shut and blow air into the lungs. If there is resistance to the airflow, it means his airway is still obstructed. Clear it. Immediately resume mouth-to-mouth resuscitation, periodically lifting your head to observe whether the victim's chest is rising and falling on its own, the most obvious sign of breath. The natural recoil of the lungs will expel the air you have blown into them.

Repeat this procedure until the victim resumes breathing on his own. Normal breathing is twelve times per minute for adults and twenty times per minute for children. It may take considerable time, an hour or more, to restore normal breathing. Don't give up.

When the heart stops, it prevents circulation of vital oxygen and nutrients. Artificial circulation through external chest compression—cardiopulmonary resuscitation (CPR)—is the only corrective measure. If the heart has stopped, you must act immediately.

The procedure for CPR is fairly simple, but a thorough understanding and practice of the technique are essential. In order for CPR to be effective, it has to be done correctly. Only a CPR training program, available through local chapters of the American Heart Association or the American Red Cross, can give you the necessary background and knowledge.

There are two main types of bleeding: venous, which is dark and oozing, and arterial, which is bright red and spurting. As the blood spreads, it may appear that the wound is bleeding more severely than is actually the case. Examine the wound carefully to see if it needs your immediate attention.

To treat a bleeding wound, elevate the injured area above the level of the heart and simultaneously apply direct pressure to the wound with the cleanest material available, preferably sterile dressings. Pack dressings on the wound, taking care to keep it as clean as possible. These techniques will usually do the job. Tourniquets, the favorite remedy of the uninformed, are very dangerous and should be used only in extreme cases by one who is knowledgeable. Improper use of a tourniquet can cause severe problems and needless subsequent amputation.

The Physical Exam

A complete patient exam documented with thorough notes is essential to the care of an accident victim. Always make time to perform the exam; the results will provide a fuller understanding of the victim's condition and essential data for further evaluation. Backcountry evacuations are serious affairs. The decisions that have to be made require knowledge and judgment. Being fully aware of the seriousness of the problem will help you make a proper decision on the need for and type of evacuation.

The basic assumption behind the physical exam is that immediate medical problems have been treated and that the patient isn't going to die in the next few minutes. It is important that you take charge and create an atmosphere of order and calm. Put other people in your party to work at specific tasks: building a fire to warm water, inventorying equipment which might be used in an evacuation, looking at the maps to find the quickest and safest evacuation route.

These can be undertaken while the exam is in progress. The exam should be as thorough as possible in the circumstances. Make sure that your hands are warm. Shield your patient from embarrassment. Explain what you are doing. Warn the patient that you may cause him some pain.

The exam should be repeated at intervals. The changes may be more illuminating than the initial data. You may not completely understand the problem, or the symptoms the patient is manifesting, but you should still record them. In a case demanding evacuation, you act for a time as the eyes and ears of the physician who will eventually care for the patient. Any information that you can provide the doctor will be helpful. The physician can determine the value of the information, even if it seems insignificant to you. It is your duty to give the physician as much help as you can.

Include the following in your written report of the examination: name of victim, age, sex, level of consciousness, previous medical history, date and time of accident or onset of illness, description of accident, patient's complaints, findings from exam, pulse, respiration rate, pupil reaction, skin color and moisture, treatment. Using a flow sheet may be helpful in organizing this information, especially if the exam is repeated half a dozen times in the course of an evacuation.

The exam should begin with the head. Assess the level of consciousness. The rest of the exam will be modified by this assessment. Check the breathing passages to make sure that they are not obstructed. Move your fingers gently through the hair, feeling for bumps, blood, and irregularities. Look for facial asymmetry. Is one side of the face unequal to the other? Check the ears, mouth, and nose for blood or fluid leakage.

Now move to the arms. Look for irregularities, bruises, and asymmetry. If you suspect that one arm is not normal, use the other for comparison. Check for pain. Check the patient's ability to move hands, grasp, and feel.

Then examine the chest. Once again look for cuts, bruises, bleeding, and irregularities. Examine the collarbone, the sternum, and the ribs. Watch the victim breathe. Does the chest rise evenly or unevenly? Is there pain when the patient breathes? Does it occur on inhalation or exhalation?

Now move to the abdomen. Feel for excessive hardness or spasm of the muscles. Is there pain? Remember to continue to talk to the victim, be reassuring and comforting.

Feel the back for hidden injuries. Examine the entire spine for deformities and pain, from the base of the skull to the pelvis. This may be difficult if the victim is on his back, but with a little bit of work you will be able to gently slide your hands underneath without jostling the patient.

Feel the pelvis. Look for bruises, pain, deformity.

Examine the lower extremities. Feel around both legs from the hip to the ankle for pain, deformity, bruises. Check the ankles and feet for injury and determine if circulation is present.

While you are talking to your patient, you can get a better

idea of his level of consciousness, his orientation to time and place.

If the exam has been thorough, you have a solid basis for reference if the patient's condition changes. Remember, take notes on every aspect of the exam. If an evaluation is required, send a copy of the notes out so that the rescue party's response can be better planned. The exam also may have identified any number of conditions which may be treatable immediately.

Shock

In treating a serious injury, it is likely that you will have to deal with shock. This is a life-threatening complication; it is often shock that kills people who have a serious injury, such as a broken leg, which is not life-threatening in itself. You should *always* treat for shock when confronted with a backcountry injury.

Shock is a generalized depression of all body functions caused by progressive failure of the cardiovascular system, impairing performance of organs and tissues. It is characterized by pale, cool, clammy skin; weak, rapid pulse; weak, rapid respiration; dilated pupils, which are slow to react; unconsciousness or semiconsciousness; thirst, anxiety, and restlessness.

Shock must be treated vigorously and rapidly. You should anticipate it in an accident victim. Treat for it even if it does not appear to be present. Insulate your victim to prevent heat loss, but don't overheat him. If it is possible, elevate the legs eight to ten inches. This will aid the return of blood to the upper torso. If the victim is conscious, and does not have head or abdominal injuries, having him drink will be beneficial. Warm, not hot, drinks are good. Avoid dairy drinks such as milk and hot chocolate, as well as coffee or tea. Plain water is best. Light bouillon or fruit drinks are also beneficial.

Fractures and Dislocations

It is sometimes difficult to distinguish fractures from dislocations. The symptoms of a fracture are deformity around the injured bone, pain and tenderness at the injury site, crepitis—a grating sound or sensation at the injury site—and an inability to move or bear weight on the affected part. Dislocations are displaced joints which can display all the symptoms of fractures.

When in doubt, treat the injury as a fracture: that means the joint should be immobilized both above and below the injury with a splint. Pad the splint, both to ease the pain and shape the splint more closely to the victim's body. Splints should be used to prevent movement in the injured area, not to set or straighten the fracture. Tighten a splint snugly, but not so tight as to impede circulation or reshape the injured area. Leave some access to the hand or foot below the injury so you can check to be sure that circulation is not being cut off. Bandage open wounds or protruding bone ends. If you are inexperienced, practice placing the splint first by putting it on the victim's other extremity or on someone else's leg or arm.

For a forearm or wrist fracture, place the arm in a sling and immobilize it against the chest. The same treatment is appropriate for a break in the upper arm if you also place a rigid splint along the broken bone. Rib, shoulder, and collarbone fractures can also be immobilized by splinting the arm against the chest on the side of the injury.

A pelvic fracture is a very serious injury, because there may be internal bleeding and injury to the bladder. The victim should be immobilized on his back, preventing movement of the lower back and legs. Simply laying the person down is sufficient. It is good if you can initially lay the victim on an Ensolite pad and sleeping bag so that he will be more comfortable and the eventual transfer to a litter will be more efficient.

In a fracture of the upper leg, or femur, the powerful thigh muscles may displace bone ends, causing further bleeding, pain, and internal damage. Traction is the optimal treatment, but if you are unfamiliar with this procedure, immobilize the leg with rigid splints, tie both legs together, and pad between them. In a fracture involving the lower leg, ankle, or foot, a well-padded, rigid splint is sufficient.

Head Injuries

Major head injuries in the backcountry are very serious, and a large percentage—perhaps as high as 90 percent—are fatal. The head and spine are very sensitive areas, and the wrong treatment can cause further injury or death. Symptoms may be confusing or difficult to see. In addition, any action violent enough to cause a severe head injury is violent enough to cause cervical spine injury.

The first symptom is unconsciousness, though serious head injuries do not always knock a person out. The length of unconsciousness is roughly proportional to the seriousness of the injury.

Next, there may be blood or cerebrospinal fluid leakage. The pupils may be unequal in size or in their response to light. The victim will have a slow pulse and unusual respiratory patterns. The conscious victim will have a generalized, persistent headache and display irrationality, confusion, disorientation, uncharacteristic behavior patterns, and an unstable gait.

If there is any combination of these symptoms, the victim should be evacuated immediately. Treat for shock, but don't elevate the legs, because this increases the intracranial pressure. Assume there might also be a neck injury; a broken neck is frequently associated with a head injury. Head injuries in themselves do not cause shock and, if shock is present, look for another injury.

Spinal Injuries

The symptoms of spinal injury are pain and palpitation of the spine and disturbances of the sensory/motor function. The latter can be checked by testing the ability of the victim to voluntarily move hands or feet and to react to pressure from a pointed object.

To treat this type of injury, immobilize the neck with pads to prevent lateral movement, or improvise a cervical collar. All body movement should be prevented. Proper care and a rigid stretcher are critical to preventing permanent nerve damage. Without the proper training and equipment, you should not move the victim but simply treat for shock while arranging for an evacuation.

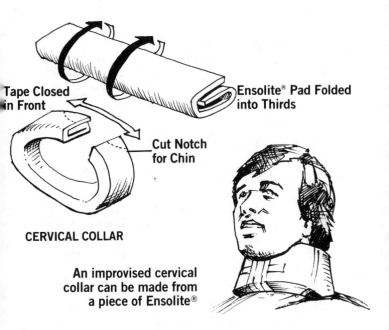

Tape Closed
in Front

Ensolite® Pad Folded
into Thirds

Cut Notch
for Chin

CERVICAL COLLAR

**An improvised cervical
collar can be made from
a piece of Ensolite®**

Sprains

A sprain is the stretching or tearing of ligaments around a joint. The most common is the ankle sprain. Sprains usually cause swelling, become discolored, and can be as painful as a break. A severe sprain, in fact, can mimic a fracture. If you're in doubt, treat it as a fracture with a splint and evacuation of the victim.

Mild sprains should be treated with I.C.E. therapy, that is, ice, compression, and elevation. Apply ice on and off for several hours. Elevate the foot eight to twelve inches and wrap with an elastic bandage for mild compression. Leave the bandage on for the first twenty-four hours. If ice is not available, use snow or a cloth soaked in cold water.

After twenty-four hours, put the injured limb through a range of gentle movements, applying the cold pack before and after until swelling and pain diminish.

Strains

A strain is the stretching or tearing of muscle fibers. To treat, apply ice, snow, or a cold pack for ten to twenty minutes, twice a day. This will help reduce the swelling. Passively stretch the injured muscle, applying the cold pack afterward, until the injury heals.

Dislocations

Dislocations are displacements of bone ends at a joint, for instance at the shoulder. The symptoms are deformity of the joint, pain or swelling at the injury site, and a loss of function of the joint.

Despite what you've seen in the movies—someone's arm being given a good yank to put it back in its "socket"—the treatment is the same as a fracture. Immobilize the bone above and below the injury. *Do not* attempt to relocate the joint. This procedure, performed by a well-meaning but unskilled rescuer, can cause further damage. Remember, the first rule of first aid is "Do no harm."

Bruises and Open Wounds

A wound is a disruption of the skin, and can be classified as either closed or open. Closed wounds—usually called bruises or contusions—make no break in the skin. In bruises, ruptured subsurface blood vessels cause a pooling of blood, which in turn causes discoloration, swelling, stiffness, and pain. A large bruise can be a sign of a fracture and, if in doubt, treat it as such.

Treatment of minor bruises is simple. Cold packs help reduce swelling and discomfort and should be applied first. After initial treatment, alternating cold and heat treatments is helpful in reducing stiffness and soreness.

Open wounds involve rupture of the skin. The main dangers from open wounds are infection and severe blood loss. The first step is to control the bleeding, usually by pressure on the wound. Keeping wounds clean to prevent infection is extremely important in the backcountry. A small wound that is untended can become infected and require evacuation of the victim. After bleeding has been controlled,

BUTTERFLY DRESSING

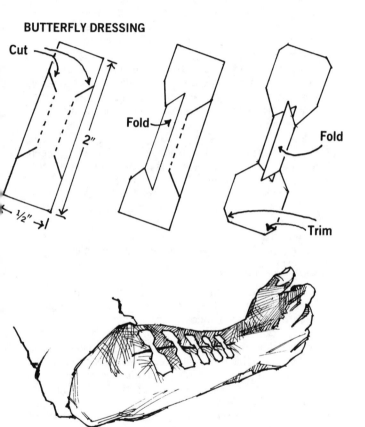

clean the wound with an antiseptic such as Zephrin or Phisohex. Scrub the area in a circular motion away from the wound. Clean your hands before doing any of this. Never try to close any wound that is grossly contaminated with dirt. Rinse it with the antiseptic, dress and bandage it, and evacuate the victim. A butterfly bandage, or a series of butterfly bandages for longer cuts, is the best dressing to close a wound.

Infection in a wound is demonstrated by pain, swelling, tenderness, heat or redness, or hot red streaks extending away from the injury. A severe infection can be a life-threatening injury. The presence of infection in a soft-tissue wound is cause for evacuation.

Specifically, a dressing covers a wound and a bandage holds a dressing in place. When applying a dressing, keep it as clean as possible, removing it from the package carefully. Cover the wound completely with it.

The bandage should be wrapped securely enough to apply pressure to control the bleeding, but not enough to constrict circulation. Remember, it will be in place for a good deal of time, so work slowly and carefully. A properly applied bandage will be comfortable for the patient.

Acute Abdominal Pain

Pain in the abdomen can be a serious and perplexing problem. Differentiating between severe indigestion and a more dangerous condition such as appendicitis requires medical skills usually beyond the knowledge of a first-aider or EMT. Abdominal pain can be a clue to a more serious underlying problem that may require surgery. Many times the proper diagnosis is difficult even for a physician.

One of the common abdominal problems is appendicitis. The patient will usually have a history of vague discomfort in the center of the abdomen that gradually moves and localizes to the lower right side. Other symptoms may be nausea, vomiting, and diarrhea. The lower right side of the abdomen will be tender. There may be muscle spasms. Even gentle pressure will cause pain.

Appendicitis is a surgical emergency, and evacuation should be undertaken immediately. Field treatment is to keep the patient warm and as comfortable as possible, and to give him nothing to eat or drink. The patient will have to be evacuated by the fastest way possible.

There are many types of acute abdominal emergencies other than appendicitis that require a physician's treatment. Anyone showing abdominal pain from either injury or unknown illness, with possible symptoms of shock, should be considered an emergency and evacuated.

Burns

Burns account for one-fourth of the accidental injuries in the United States. Over two million occur every year. Burns are classified as first-, second-, and third-degree burns.

First-degree burns are the most common. The skin is usually dry and reddened, but with no swelling or blistering. A sunburn is a first-degree burn. It will usually disappear in two or three days. Although it rarely requires medical attention, a first-degree burn should be considered serious if it covers two-thirds of the body's surface area.

There is no special treatment for first-degree burns. Immersing the burned area in cool water will lessen pain and minimize damage. Also, the application of a topical anesthetic, such as Solarcaine, will help.

A second-degree burn will be moist, and the skin a mottled white to cherry red, swollen, and blistered. The blisters are a key to second-degree burns. The burn goes deeper into the skin than a first-degree burn and is usually very painful.

A third-degree burn is characterized by dry, leathery skin or charred skin with a mix of colors from white to dark red. This burn reaches the full thickness of the skin. It usually involves little pain because the nerve endings have been destroyed.

Most second- and all third-degree burns require evacuation. When determining the severity of the burn, consider the age of the victim, location of the burn, extent of the burn, and any diseases or other injuries that may be present. Burns are particularly dangerous for children and the elderly. Burns of the neck and face may involve the respiratory tract. Burns of the hands and feet, because of the complexity of these structures, are serious. A sizable burn on a victim with heart disease or diabetes, or a burn associated with an injury such as a fracture, should also be considered serious.

The extent of a burn can be roughly measured by using your hand as a measuring tool. The hand covers about one percent of the body's surface area. Any second- or third-degree burn should be considered serious, particularly if it fits the following criteria: second-degree burns involving more than ten percent of body's surface area; and *any* third-degree burns. Patients should be evacuated as soon as possible.

The first step in treating a burn is to stop the damage. Cool the burn immediately in water. This lessens the extent of the burn and reduces pain. Beware of hypothermia during cooling. Wrap the burn loosely in a dry, sterile dressing. Do not use ointments or grease on a second- or third-degree burn. The main goal is to prevent infection and treat for shock.

Evacuations

"If it could be arranged," Len Pagliaro says, "I would insist that everyone who is doing backcountry first aid should have been a victim themselves. It is an incredibly insecure feeling. The psychological factors in this are important. You have to have confidence in your rescuers.

"To take one instance, suppose those who are moving someone in a rope litter have never been in one themselves. They tighten up and squash you, and don't realize how painful each bump can be. I was lowered off a cliff in a rope litter during a practice session. I was okay when I got in it and hurt when I got out."

Evacuating an ill or injured person from the backcountry can be a complex operation, requiring efficient organization of a network of people, equipment, rescue teams, and hospital personnel. It can also be a relatively simple maneuver, such as escorting or carrying weight for someone with a minor injury or illness to a car left at a roadhead, then driving the person home or to a doctor. Be it an easy one-hour stint or a harrowing multi-day undertaking, each evacuation will present a different set of problems and will require common sense, sensitivity, and at times imagination.

Having completed a thorough examination of the victim, the group leader must determine if an evacuation is necessary and what type of evacuation is the most efficient and appropriate. Calling in a helicopter to evacuate someone with a sprained or broken wrist is excessive, akin to cutting butter with an ax. On the other hand, a helicopter evacuation may be absolutely essential for someone suffering a fractured femur who is twenty-five miles across boulder fields from the nearest roadhead.

If an evacuation is necessary, one of the first jobs of the group leader is to put everyone to work. There is usually a lot of preparation to take anyone out of the mountains, particularly if outside help must be summoned and coordinated. Some individuals can take on the cooking responsibilities for the entire group. Others can prepare the litter or the pack of the evacuee, build siting markers if a helicopter is required, or help the runners get packed and ready to leave to request outside assistance. To keep records of the incident, your examination of the patient, your conclusions, and any treatment or drugs administered, you may want to request that someone be your scribe to accompany you and write down your comments on the case.

Such steps may at first sound excessive. But the record is essential, and as a leader, it is important that you delegate responsibility and do not get bogged down in the details of any one part of the evacuation procedure. Throughout, you need to remain somewhat aloof from the bustle of preparations and general anxiety that your group may be experiencing. This distance will help you objectively to evaluate your situation and coordinate efforts to devise the most efficient evacuation system using the available knowledge, manpower, and equipment at your disposal. A backcountry evacuation is likely to take considerable time—anywhere from several hours to several days —but this time can be minimized by careful planning.

There are a number of types of evacuation to consider. In each case, the severity of the injury or illness and the urgency of getting professional medical help are the overriding concerns.

Evacuation by litter involves carrying the patient out of the backcountry on some type of stretcher device. On trips in different locations, seasons, and climates, you will have different equipment and materials available for constructing litters, so it may take some improvisation. Commonly used materials include pack frames, packbags, ropes, nylon webbing, carabiners, Ensolite pads, skis, shovels, and even young, live trees. Backcountry preparedness means understanding the improvisational potential of your equipment before your trip. How far the victim needs to be carried, over what type of terrain, the size and strength of the party, and the time it will take to reach the roadhead are other important considerations in determining what kind of litter you need to build. Whether the victim can sit up or needs to remain prone is another key factor.

A victim with suspected head, neck, or spine injuries or one who is bleeding severely should be littered only with the greatest circumspection and carried, at most, a short distance to a helicopter landing site. If a qualified rescue team is coming with the helicopter, such an undertaking should be left to them.

Some options for litters are shown here. But in building a litter, don't assume that you can just look at the pictures and replicate them. You will be surprised how long it will take you, and how many little mistakes you will make your first time. Before you ever need to build one in the backcountry, practice in town and carry it around, loaded with a real person. Particularly with the pole and pack-frame litter, you may find you quickly scale down your ideas about using them very far off-trail in the wilderness. Even the best are awkward and heavy—litter bearers may need to rest every ten minutes or so.

With any of these litters, be prepared to make adjustments or adaptations that might be required as your evacuation progresses: boulder fields or streams are encountered, night falls, a rainstorm slickens the trail, your victim's condition changes, or your party tires.

If you decide a litter evacuation is impractical, your options are to use outside assistance with horses, helicopters, boats, or, in winter, snowmobiles. Before leaving for the backcountry you should explore the possibilities of summoning different types of assistance. Get the names, telephone numbers, and locations and put them in a secure place in your backpack.

A helicopter should be considered *only* when an injury is severe or evacuation alternatives impractical. Helicopter design has been refined to the point where the most advanced can now safely fly at high altitudes (10,000 to 20,000 feet) and in changeable conditions. Depending on where the nearest available helicopters are, this can be a quick but very expensive operation. Always keep in mind the limitations of helicopters. They can't fly at night in most mountainous regions and are also unusable in bad weather. They may be out of service because of mechanical problems. Remember that it often takes a considerable amount of time to arrange for a helicopter.

If you are planning for a helicopter evacuation, it is important to select and mark a good landing area. The ideal landing site will be a large flat area, preferably on a knoll that will give the pilot unlimited approach alternatives, depending on the wind direction. About 20 yards width and 100 yards length of the flattest land that can be found are recommended dimensions for a landing site.

Especially at higher elevations, helicopters should be able to take off into the wind to increase lift. Pilots will prefer flying in the morning, when the air is calmer and denser, for better lift. You may have to start a fire near your site to indicate wind direction for the pilot. After looking at your site from the air, the pilot may choose a different one, so the victim may have to be moved—preferably by the medical team on the helicopter.

Mark the landing zone with an H or Δ pattern, using brightly colored items such as sleeping bags that have been anchored well. Have all gear ready and anchored down when the craft lands. Helicopter rotors generate terrific wind speeds.

After the helicopter lands, do not approach until the pilot motions you to do so. Even if you think the rotors have stopped, always stay low, and never walk behind the craft. Always approach where the pilot can see you.

Because of the fickle nature of both weather and helicopters, you will always want to develop contingency evacuation plans in the event some problem does occur. But for certain life-threatening injuries, where other transport would itself be dangerous, a helicopter may be your only solution.

If outside assistance is necessary, you will have to send some of your party, your runners, to the nearest telephone to initiate the evacuation process and contact the proper authorities. The sheriff almost always holds the authority for rescues within a county, and must be notified of your evacuation needs.

Your runners should be selected from among your strongest members so they can get to a telephone in the shortest time possible. The leader of the group should always stay with the victim; he or she should never leave with the runners. The runners should be equipped with sufficient gear to travel safely, but as lightly and quickly as

ROPE LITTER AND FRAME LITTER

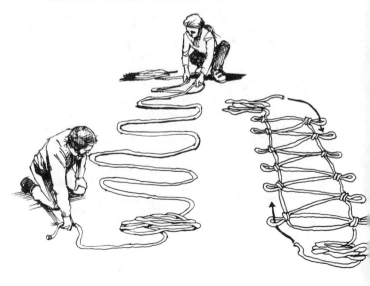

Sleeping Bag
for Patient

Pad

Frame Litter

Frame Litter Is Strapped
to Two Sapling Poles
which Are Then Strapped
to the Carriers' Pack Frames

Curvature of Three Pack Frames
Fits Together

possible. At least two and preferably four runners should be sent together, so that if one of them gets injured or slowed on the way out, one member can stay with this person while the other two continue on. The runners should be given change for a telephone call, appropriate telephone numbers, and a written list of instructions for the rescue party, including notes from the physical exam, marked maps, and all special requests and instructions for equipment, personnel, and any other important details. It is wise to write down the exact report to be delivered on the telephone—sometimes in the excitement of emergency situations, vital information is forgotten or distorted. It is important that the person making the calls stay on the phone until the person with whom he or she is talking indicates that all questions have been satisfactorily answered. The report should contain the following information:

1. The name and location of the caller, with time and date.
2. The name and sex of the evacuee.
3. A description of the injury or illness, including date, time, location, and signatures of witnesses.
4. A description of the patient's condition (critical, serious, unconscious).
5. Number of members in the main party, their location, and condition.
6. Location of the evacuee.
7. Number and location of runners.
8. Type of evacuation support requested, when, and where.
9. Extra medical/rescue equipment or personnel needed with evacuation support team.
10. Details of evacuation plan.
11. Contingency or backup plan.
12. Signature of group leader.

A copy of this report should be kept by the group leader.

In addition, the runners should carry maps marked with the following:

1. The location of the accident.
2. The present location of the group and the victim.
3. The runners' route out of the wilderness, their destination, and their estimated time of arrival.
4. The course chosen by the main evacuation party, including litter route, helicopter landing site, etc., with dates for each day of the evacuation.
5. Route for runners to follow after help is summoned.
6. Site for runners and main party to reconvene and dates.
7. Contingency routes.

Everyone on an extended backcountry trip should know how to administer basic first aid and conduct an evacuation. Even if you only go on shorter trips accompanied by qualified backcountry leaders, you should still have a working knowledge of emergency procedures. Always keep in mind the backcountry version of Murphy's Law: the qualified leader, the one with the first-aid training and experience, will be the one who gets hurt. Even on the most informal of wilderness outings, you may be the one who must deal with an accident or illness and organize an evacuation.

WOMEN'S MEDICAL CONCERNS

Both male and female leaders need to be able to comfortably discuss female health considerations. This is often an area which is overlooked in the preparation for a wilderness trip.

As with other backcountry medical concerns, the proper approach is preventive. If menstruation, possible vaginal and urinary infections, contraceptive use, and similar subjects are discussed and prepared for ahead of time, problems can be avoided.

But the first difficulty is open communication—a male outdoor leader may feel it's not his place to bring up the subject of menstruation to female students. He is wrong. If he has information that will make the trip easier, he should be frank and forthright.

The stress of backcountry exercise may induce major changes in a woman's menstrual cycle, or it may have no effect at all. The reasons for such changes are a subject of debate: it may be the physical strain, reducing fat in the blood; it may be the mental stress of facing backcountry challenges. Like many athletes in heavy training, some women experience temporary amenorrhea, in which menstruation stops completely. This can be troubling if it is unexpected. If it is anticipated, however, it may be a welcome relief from dealing in the field with tampons or pads.

Women generally report that the heavy physical exercise of backcountry travel lessens the severity of their periods —less pain, fewer headaches, briefer flow. Those who do menstruate during this hardworking time should know that medical research indicates no diminution of women's strength or endurance during menstruation.

Leaders of backcountry expeditions should be aware of "mittelschmerz," a cramping sometimes experienced by women between menstrual periods, during ovulation. The pain can occur on either side of the abdomen or in the lower back. Usually women who experience this are familiar with its symptoms and can identify and cope with mittelschmerz. The discomfort will generally disappear in about thirty-six hours.

When it occurs on the right side, mittelschmerz can sometimes be confused with appendicitis. The onset of appendicitis, however, is marked by diarrhea, vomiting, and low-grade fever. Mittelschmerz normally has none of these symptoms. If appendicitis is suspected, immediately evacuate.

The vagina normally maintains a stable pH level, slightly acid. When the balance is upset, by, for instance, a heavy intake of sugars or carbohydrates, the risk of vaginal infection is increased. Vaginal infections are classified in three categories: yeast, trichomoniasis, or nonspecific vaginitis. In the backcountry you cannot definitely specify which type it is, but the treatment for all will be similar.

Vaginal infections show up in the form of abnormal, often malodorous, discharge, redness or soreness in the vaginal area, itching and burning of the vulva, and often frequent, burning urination. They can occur when resistance is down, when medication such as birth control pills is being taken, in times of stress, and as a result of excessive sugar intake.

To avoid such infections, women are encouraged to wash regularly, wear loose-fitting cotton underpants, and, when possible, keep their sugar and carbohydrate intake down. Drinking extra water to flush the system is also recommended.

Vaginal infections can be cleared up or at least controlled by douching twice a day with a solution of two tablespoons vinegar and one quart warm water. Taking a portable douching bag makes this process much easier. Yeast infections, often characterized by a thick, white discharge that may look like cottage cheese, may not disappear even with this treatment, but it will keep them under control.

When you travel in the backcountry, remember that high altitudes increase the risk of blood clotting for both men and women. Women who take oral contraceptives are already running a higher risk of clotting. If you plan to spend much time above 12,000 feet and you are already taking an oral contraceptive, it is wise to discuss the possibility of risk with your doctor. If a woman has just recently had an intrauterine device inserted, she should wait a few months before going into the backcountry. If there are any problems, such as perforation or infection, they will probably show up within the first few months, and these are not problems one wants to deal with far from modern medicine.

NOLS courses carry several foods that are high in iron, and women with anemia problems should be sure to include these in their diets while in the wilderness. These include prunes, pinto beans, lentils, dried peaches, millet, split peas, raisins, dates, sesame seeds, pumpkin seeds, and wheat germ. Some of these foods when eaten in quantity can cause constipation, so their intake should be monitored carefully.

If a woman has a problem more serious than those discussed above, evacuation should be considered. Pelvic pain is difficult to diagnose in the backcountry. Bleeding that exceeds normal menstrual levels and continues for several days could mean a miscarriage, a tubal pregnancy, or severe stress. Infections associated with the bladder, with IUDs, or pelvic inflammatory disease (PID) require antibiotics and careful diagnosis, which you cannot do in the field; evacuation is essential.

Any woman who has questions or problems, or who feels pain or malaise that she is not familiar with, should be sure to speak up—this is not a time for reticence.

Similarly, group leaders should make it understood that any woman with problems will be treated sympathetically and knowledgeably, and without undue embarrassment. If a member of your party is having problems, talk to her one on one. Get a personal history, just as you would of anyone with any other medical problem. Ask specifically about menstrual history if that appears to be part of the problem. A woman may be suffering considerable anxiety, so be nonjudgmental and sympathetic. If rest is required, the group should adjust, just the way it does for a slow hiker or a blister problem.

Close friends in the backcountry rarely have any problem speaking up when something feels wrong. But in a group of men and women who are not that familiar with each other, there may be some hesitation. The time to overcome this is before the trip begins—by making sure that women in the group are aware of the preventive steps they can take to avoid discomfort in the backcountry. Frank discussion at that point can open the channels of communication should there be any problem once the trip is under way.

In the backcountry, used tampons and pads must either be burned in a very hot fire or carried out. When assembling their gear, women must be sure to include small plastic bags for this purpose. Women at NOLS have discovered handy tips to help eliminate the problem of odor from used tampons and pads: crushing a few aspirin and placing them in the bag, or wrapping the tampons in fragrant leaves.

FIRST-AID KITS

Whether you are hiking in a small group of three for a weekend outing or a large group of fifteen for a two-week trek, a complete first-aid kit is a necessity which should always be kept handy. Appendix I contains a list of sample contents of two first-aid kits, one for a large group, one for a small group. These basic items should be considered a minimal preparation for emergencies.

For larger groups, we advise dividing the large-group kit into several small kits. This ensures that the kits are available to all if the group is separated for any length of time.

It is a good idea to inform all group members how to use the various materials in first-aid kits and in whose backpacks they are being carried. It may be the least experienced camper who is immediately confronted with an accident.

At NOLS we package items for first aid in plastic bags. Sealable freezer bags work well and ensure that all items remain dry; soggy dressings are neither useful nor sterile.

In some cases, particularly when you will be traveling in extremely remote areas, it is advisable to consult a physician regarding prescribing a mild sedative or painkiller to be included in a first-aid kit. This should be analyzed on a case-by-case basis; it is not necessary for most weekend backpacking.

Chapter Eight

Weather

MARK TWAIN once said of the weather, "There is only one thing certain . . . there is going to be plenty of it." The other certainty we will add is that for the outdoor person, a healthy respect for and basic understanding of the weather is a necessity. Few factors can affect your safety and your comfort in the outdoors more dramatically than weather changes, and changing weather is one of the constants of living in the outdoors.

Most radio and television weather forecasts do not include wilderness regions in local forecast areas. Although the forecasts can provide a general idea of approaching fronts, they are not suited to the specialized needs of the backcountry traveler.

Prior to going into an unfamiliar area, it is useful to talk to the nearest National Weather Service office to obtain a more specific understanding of local weather conditions. Ask about regional extremes, including the high and low temperatures one should be prepared for, and average amounts of precipitation. It is often particularly helpful to talk with those involved in forecasting local forest fire conditions, since they will be most up to date on local situations.

Another preparation you can make to better anticipate the weather is to know the topography and altitude of the terrain you are entering, since local weather conditions can be shaped by these factors. Though not as overwhelming as atmospheric weather conditions, local weather variations can considerably determine wind direction, precipitation, and duration of storms.

Finally, simple equipment can be useful in backcountry weather forecasting. A compass can help you determine which way the wind is blowing. A pocket altimeter can tell you whether the barometric pressure is rising or falling (if you remain at one elevation and the altimeter registers an increase in elevation, the barometric pressure is dropping and a storm is probably approaching). And in the back-country, a thermometer is still the only accurate way to determine the temperature.

But if you are to be prepared for the "plenty of weather" which Mr. Twain assures us we will always have, you will also need to understand a few of the basics of weather information that determine whether it rains, blows, or shines.

THE ATMOSPHERE

Simply put, weather is the condition of the atmosphere in terms of heat, moisture, pressure, and winds. In order to understand the dynamics of weather, we have to understand some aspects of the atmosphere.

Until very recently, one of the problems with meteorological theories was that there was only one model, our own atmosphere, with which to work. Most other sciences had a number of samples, and thus could make comparisons, which ensured a better understanding of essential mechanisms. But today, as more planetary studies are undertaken, meteorologists are gaining a better understanding of our own atmosphere.

Our atmosphere is a collection of gases, primarily nitrogen and oxygen in the lower atmosphere, and hydrogen, helium, and ozone in the upper atmosphere. As gases are compressible, so is our atmosphere. This explains the fact that, while the atmosphere extends some 1,000 miles from earth, one-half of all the gases are contained in the first 18,000 feet above sea level. Over 90 percent of the atmosphere is contained in the lower 6 miles, an area called the troposphere, where the weather occurs.

The atmosphere consists of five layers. The troposphere is about 5 miles high near the poles and 11 miles high near the equator. The boundary between the troposphere and the stratosphere is called the tropopause. The stratosphere extends to about 30 miles above the earth's surface, the mesosphere to 50 miles, and the thermosphere to about 500 miles. Above this is the exosphere.

The "thick" atmosphere—particularly in the troposphere and the stratosphere—is responsible for the relatively moderate temperature variations the earth experiences between night and day. Without this atmospheric protection, the earth would have the same temperature variation as the moon.

Heat is the major factor affecting our weather conditions. Temperature changes through the atmosphere are what cause changes in the weather. The chief source of heat for the earth is the sun, which is 93 million miles away. The energy is transmitted as waves to the earth. Some of these waves are visible as light, some are not, and are instead transferred into heat by absorption with the earth. About 43 percent of the radiation reaching the earth is transformed into heat. Forty-two percent is reflected back into the atmosphere, and 15 percent is absorbed into the atmosphere.

Since the atmosphere absorbs little solar radiation, air is heated primarily by contact with the earth, which is easily heated by the sun. Very basically, the earth is heated in varying amounts in different areas. Mass movements of air occur as air is warmed and rises, and other air is cooled and sinks. In addition to this vertical movement, horizontal movement occurs as the cold air moves into the area vacated by warm air.

The amount of heat transfer and conversion is dependent upon the type of surface the sun's radiation reaches. On an average day—that is, with about 50 percent of the sky clouded over—water will absorb 60 to 90 percent of the sunlight that contacts it. This phenomenon is particularly important because 75 percent of the earth is covered by water. And, since water absorbs more of the sun's energy when that energy hits the water directly, the absorption by water is particularly efficient between the Tropics of Cancer and Capricorn.

Snow reflects about 75 percent of the sun's energy that hits it, holding only 25 percent. A grassy field retains 80

to 90 percent, dense forests 95 percent, dry sand 75 percent, and a plowed field between 75 and 95 percent.

Two conclusions can be drawn from these factors. Since
snow reflects much potential heat, polar regions stay cold.
Thick forests are located in the tropical areas, where they
catch and retain direct sunlight.

Water is always present in varying degrees in the atmosphere. The degree of water in the atmosphere is called
the relative humidity. This is the amount of water the air is
holding expressed as a percentage of the amount it could
hold at a particular temperature. Warm air can hold more
water than cold. So, when warm air is cooled without losing
water, the relative humidity goes up. If it is cooled beyond
its ability to retain water, it will release it as rain or snow.

Heat evaporates water from the surface of lakes,
streams, oceans, and plants. As the moist air rises, it
slowly cools until it reaches 100 percent relative humidity.
When the atmosphere is unable to retain the water any
longer, clouds form and, under the right conditions, precipitation ensues. The "dew point" is the point at which
the air becomes saturated and reaches 100 percent relative humidity, usually producing precipitation.

Beaufort Scale (estimating wind speeds)

Miles per hour

0–1	Smoke rises straight up, calm
1–3	Smoke drifts
4–7	Leaves rustle
8–12	Leaves and twigs move
13–18	Small branches move
19–24	Leaves blow over ground, small trees sway
25–31	Large branches move
32–38	Twigs break off
39–46	Large trees sway, difficult walking
47–54	Very hard to walk, some limbs break
55–63	Tree limbs and branches break
64 & up	Trees uprooted

THE SEASONS

The most obvious and sustained weather-causing factors are the seasons. The seasons result from the fact that the earth's axis is tilted at a 23½° angle to the plane of its orbit. When the North Pole is dipped toward the sun, the Northern Hemisphere has summer and the Southern has winter. At the summer solstice, about June 22 in the Northern Hemisphere, the sun has reached its farthest northern point, directly over the Tropic of Cancer. That is the longest day of the year in that hemisphere. The South Pole is then in the middle of its six months of darkness.

Conversely, the shortest day of the year occurs on or about December 22, when, from the Northern Hemisphere's point of view, the sun has reached its lowest point in the sky, over the Tropic of Capricorn. The North Pole now has its day-long nights.

At the fall and spring equinoxes, about September 23 and March 21 respectively, the sun falls about equally on the Northern and Southern Hemispheres.

There are two reasons why the sun is hotter in summer. First, since the relevant hemisphere is facing the sun longer, the sun has more time to heat it and the heat, once generated, has less time to dissipate at night. Second, the rays of the sun are reaching that hemisphere more directly, that is, more vertically. Analogously, the earth cools faster on bright clear nights, and stays warmer when it is overcast. Clouds in the atmosphere reflect heat back to the surface, keeping the planet warmer.

AIR MASSES

The earth is about 25,000 miles in circumference at the equator. Since the earth rotates on its axis once every twenty-four hours, the speed of the earth at the equator is a little more than a thousand miles an hour.

However, as the earth compresses toward the poles, the speed of rotation is slower. At the poles, there is no rotation at all. At 30° north latitude, around Houston, Texas, the earth is spinning at about 864 miles an hour. At 40° north latitude, a little south of Chicago, it's moving at about 770 mph.

The earth rotates from west to east, and all the things attached to the earth—the Sears Tower, Mount Everest, Death Valley, the continent of Africa, and the rest—move with it. The air, being relatively more independent, continues straight onward while the earth slides under it. In a vastly oversimplified way, this can be understood to cause prevailing winds, but other factors such as temperature, friction, and topography also affect them.

As the earth rotates in an easterly direction, air gradually assumes a motion from the northeast to the southwest. A large body of air, moving in a given direction in the Northern Hemisphere, will tend to move to the right of its path of direction. In the Southern Hemisphere, it will move to the left of its direction. This is known as the Coriolis effect.

The Coriolis effect can be understood in another way. Look at a phonograph record from above and imagine it spinning counterclockwise. This is analogous to looking at the earth from above the North Pole. Now imagine taking a piece of chalk and trying to draw a straight line from the center of the record to the edge as the record spins. Due to the rotation of the record, the line would form a curve that bends to the right. The direction of air movements on the earth is similarly affected by the earth's rotation.

An air mass is a volume of air, usually covering thousands of square miles, that has fairly similar characteristics at a given altitude. These characteristics are those of any weather pattern—that is, temperature, humidity, and pressure—but are representative of the region in which the air mass was formed.

Generally, air movements in the Northern Hemisphere begin at the equator and move northward. By the time this air reaches 30° latitude, it is moving eastward due to the Coriolis effect. As more air moves to this region, it literally "piles up," forming an area of high pressure.

Some of this air sinks to the earth. A portion moves south and west, becoming what is known as the trade winds.

Another segment moves north and east, becoming the prevailing westerlies.

Some high air continues north, cooling by radiation, then sinks near the North Pole. It then travels south and west, colliding with the prevailing westerlies at about 60° latitude. There it forms the polar front. The warm air, which is rising, moves up over the lower cold air coming down from the north. This results in unsettled weather conditions and is the origin of much of the weather in North America.

The unequal heating of the earth between the equator and the poles causes the north-south winds. These currents in turn cause the overall shifting of the large air masses, creating high- and low-pressure areas.

FRONTS

As air masses move, they come into contact with other air masses. These intersections are called fronts, and they are of particular importance in understanding large-scale weather patterns.

At the front, there is an area of transition, from one type of air mass to another. There are two basic terms used to describe these intersecting air masses, high pressure and low pressure.

"High pressure" refers to high atmospheric pressure, or the actual weight of the air on the earth's surface. High-pressure cells have relatively high pressure, and its associated winds blow clockwise and slightly outward from the center in the Northern Hemisphere. Highs usually represent fair weather, light winds, and relatively stable, unchanging temperatures. Technically, highs are called anticyclones. Generally, high-pressure cells move from west to east, driven by the prevailing westerly winds pushing low-pressure systems in front of them.

Lows, or cyclones, usually mean unsettled, cloudy weather with rain or snow. They move counterclockwise in the Northern Hemisphere, and are accompanied by strong winds. Tropical lows are very warm, others are cooler.

The leading edge of a cold air mass is called a cold front. Since the air in front of this advance is warmer (low pressure), the high-pressure mass moves in under the warm air, which rises, cools, and, if the dew point is reached, results in precipitation. As the warm air rises, it loses its stability and forms clouds of vertical development called cumulus.

Typically, as a cold front moves in, usually from the north or west, middle-altitude clouds form, sometimes including cumulonimbus. At this time, precipitation occurs, usually fairly heavily. However, as the front passes—which you can identify by an abrupt change in wind direction and pressure—a clearing trend starts. With cold fronts, you can generalize that you have about as many hours of precipitation after frontal passage as you did prior to frontal passage.

A cold front typically moves at about 20 to 30 miles per hour, and, as you can see from the illustration, it has a narrow weather band. Once you are in a high-pressure area, the weather is usually clear, cooler, and drier than the preceding weather. However, during the day, because of the great difference between air and ground temperatures, a lot of wind develops from the heating of the air, which rises as it warms. In this case, it's common for a lot of small cumulus clouds to form. Since the weather remains generally good, these afternoon clouds are called fair-weather cumulus, and with nighttime cooling, they disappear. This process is a clear indication of the presence of a high-pressure system.

A warm front occurs when a low-pressure cell moves in to displace a high-pressure cell. As the illustration shows, the warm air displaces the cold air more gradually, rises above the cold air, slowly warming it, and moves up over the frontal surface. This makes the warm front move quite slowly, 10 to 15 miles per hour, and also causes a very indicative cloud sequence.

Due to being forced up and over the cold air, there is a very gentle slope to the front, and the warm air is cooled gradually to the dew point, thus forming clouds. As much as 500 miles ahead of the actual front, you will start to see

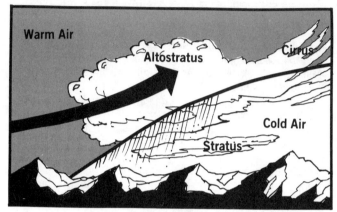

WARM FRONT

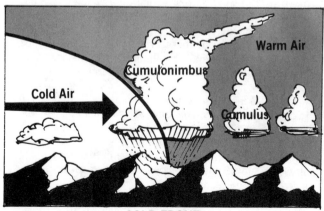

COLD FRONT

cirrus clouds, quite high. These will be followed by stratus clouds, of constantly decreasing altitude, and typically, near the front, precipitation.

A good rule to remember is that cirrus clouds precede the warm front by about two days. If you are watching the cloud sequence, you will have a good idea of when bad weather is going to occur.

Warm fronts typically do not bring the rapid, violent storms of a cold front. However, with the much greater volume of water vapor and longer duration of warm fronts, there is usually a lot of moisture, with possibilities of fog and prolonged storms.

CLOUDS

When the rising air reaches its dew point in the atmosphere, it forms clouds. On clear nights, the earth rapidly loses heat through radiation. Warmer air contacting the cold earth may form low clouds or fog. Clouds also form as warm air from the oceans or lakes moves across the land, which is often cooler. The lighter warm air may be pushed upward by colder air, as in the earlier example of the polar front. As the warm air is forced upward, it cools and reaches its dew point, forming clouds.

There are two basic types of clouds, cumulus and stratus, classified according to how they are formed in the atmosphere. Cumulus clouds are formed by rising air currents, and form at almost any altitude. Cumulus are the classic, constantly changing, puffy white clouds that people like to imagine as dinosaurs or dragons or dogs. They usually mean fair weather unless they gather into cumulonimbus, the towering "thunderhead" clouds. Cumulus clouds are formed by day in rising warm air and usually dissipate at night. Stratus clouds are formed by the cooling of air to the dew point without any vertical movement. They form sheets, or horizontal layers.

There are four families of clouds—high, middle, low, and towering—classified according to altitude. High clouds exist about 20,000 feet above the earth at their

TYPES OF CLOUDS

Cumulus

Stratus

Cirrus

Cumulonimbus

base and consist of ice crystals. There are three types of high clouds: cirrus, cirrocumulus, and cirrostratus.

Cirrus clouds are high clouds consisting entirely of ice crystals. They form at altitudes of about 25,000 feet. They are generally thin, wispy, and delicate in appearance. Though they contain no precipitation themselves, they can give twenty-four hours' notice of bad weather well in advance of a warm front. Mares' tails—scattered wisps of cirrus that look like their name—often signify approaching low clouds and accompanying precipitation.

Cirrocumulus clouds form the "mackerel sky" at 20,000 to 25,000 feet. They are often rippled and always too thin to show shadows on the ground. Cirrostratus clouds also form at 20,000 to 25,000 feet. They are thin sheets, much like a fine veil in appearance. The ice crystals that form them often reflect light to form a "halo" around the sun or moon.

The middle clouds are altocumulus and altostratus. Their bases average about 10,000 feet above the earth, but they can be as low as 6,500 feet and as high as 20,000 feet. They are usually composed of water droplets and may contain some ice crystals.

Altocumulus clouds are puffy or roll-like white or gray clouds. They do not completely obscure the sun. When they thicken, precipitation is usually indicated within eight to ten hours. Altostratus clouds are usually an unrelieved gray or blue in color. They can produce a fairly steady light rain or snow.

Low clouds range from near the surface to about 6,500 feet. This group includes stratus, nimbostratus, and stratocumulus. Stratus are low, uniform, thinly fibrous clouds. They are a water-droplet formation from which no rain can fall, but which may give off a fine drizzle. Nimbostratus are low, thick, dark gray masses. They are true rain clouds and can produce steady rain and snow. Stratocumulus clouds are thick, gray, irregular clouds which do not themselves produce rain or snow. They may, however, change into nimbostratus.

The towering clouds are cumulonimbus, which rise with tremendous vertical development from any low altitude to as high as 40,000 feet. These are the classic thunderhead clouds which, at their worst, produce tornadoes. They generally produce heavy thunderstorms, heavy showers of rain or snow, and sometimes hail. They are cauliflower-shaped with flattened, anvil-like tops.

RAIN AND SNOW

Rain falls to earth for the same reason that Newton's apple did: gravity pulls it. However, in most clouds, the water droplets that make up the clouds are so small—about 1/2500 inch in diameter—that gravity's pull on them is very small. Consequently, cloud droplets must form into rain drops large enough to fall, about 1/125 inch.

This coalescence occurs in three primary ways. Of the three, by far the most important is the merger of tiny ice crystals with water droplets. The water adheres to the crystals and changes to ice, until the crystal is heavy enough to fall. As it falls through warmer air, it melts into a raindrop. Raindrops fall at a speed of about seven miles an hour, depending upon factors such as the size of the drop, movement of air, etc.

The second method is more simple, involving essentially the collision of smaller droplets with larger ones. Droplets in a cloud are not of uniform size, and larger drops are not as severely affected by turbulence within a cloud. Smaller drops coming in contact with them are absorbed until the drop is large enough to fall.

The third method of rain creation occurs when lightning in a thunderstorm forms oxides of nitrogen, which are very water-absorbing. The exact nature of this cause is still undetermined.

Snow is formed when water vapor in a cloud is supercooled. Water can exist unfrozen in temperatures as low as $-40°F$. The water vapor is then spontaneously frozen around a nucleus, usually a small particle of dust carried aloft by wind. The snow crystal grows symmetrically, depending upon temperature for its shape. It then falls through an atmosphere cold enough that it does not melt the crystal on its way to the ground.

Most rain that reaches the earth starts out as snow in the atmosphere, though there are some clouds in the tropics that are too warm to allow for the formation of snow.

LOCAL WEATHER VARIATIONS

Up to this point we have been discussing large atmospheric conditions. These establish a base line for the type of weather you can expect in an area. Local variations are fairly insignificant, relative to atmospheric conditions. For this reason, one is most aware of local conditions as they modify frontal activity.

These local variations, which are created by the normal characteristics of the air mass modified by local conditions, may only contribute to a stable overall weather condition. But under the right set of circumstances, particularly when a warm, unstable maritime air mass is lifted up the side of a mountain, a lulu of a localized storm can be created.

In mountain environments, adiabatic cooling assumes a large role in creating local weather conditions. Dry air cools as it rises up the mountain slope by about 5½ degrees per 1,000 feet of elevation. If humid air is forced up mountainous terrain, precipitation and cloud formation result as the dew point is reached. This humid air cools at no more than 3½ degrees per 1,000 feet of elevation.

As the air moves down the opposite side of the mountain, it is dry, and warms adiabatically at a normal rate of 5½ degrees per 1,000 feet. Since it is warming, the relative humidity is further decreasing and there is no more precipitation. Therefore, the temperature will be warmer and the area will also be in a "rain shadow." Chinook winds are created by this phenomenon. Chinooks have been known to raise the temperature as much as 45 degrees in a quarter of an hour, and blow over 100 miles per hour.

Mountain and valley winds are a local weather phenomenon which may obscure more general weather patterns. As a result of adiabatic heating and cooling as air passes over the slopes, temperature changes and moderate winds may be experienced in the path of these air movements. Winds are especially strong in lower elevations through mountains, such as mountain passes, because winds will take the path of least resistance. They pick up speed as they "squeeze" through narrow passes.

Local low-pressure systems about 20 miles or so in diameter are also sometimes formed, frequently on the leeward side of mountain ranges. They occur when air under a large cumulonimbus cloud is rising rapidly. The low-pressure air is filled in by counterclockwise twisting air, caused by the earth's rotation.

Heat lows develop in deserts and other intensely heated places. The very hot air rises rapidly, and surrounding air rushes in quickly to fill the void. Dust devils are an example of small-scale heat lows.

STORMS AND LIGHTNING

The culmination of bad weather is a storm. Thunderstorms are the result of violent upward movements of air. This rise can be attributed to heating of the air by the ground, action of a cold front, or temperature differences between land and ocean.

The first stage of a storm is the cumulus stage, when air moves upward and extends the cumulus cloud structure to about 25,000 feet. This growth continues while the air in the cloud is warmer than the surrounding air.

The mature stage of the storm is reached when the cloud gets so high, at 40,000 feet or so, that the moisture reaches its dew point and precipitation begins to fall. Falling rain and ice crystals cool the air in the cloud, creating a counterforce of downdrafts among the updrafts in the cloud. Upper-air winds blow the top of the cumulonimbus cloud into the anvil-shaped top.

The final stage of the storm occurs when the cloud is entirely composed of sinking air being adiabatically warmed. Precipitation eases, then ceases.

One of the most serious dangers for the outdoorsman in

a thunderstorm is, of course, lightning. It can present a danger to hikers: about 300 people in the United States are killed annually by lightning or its ground current. However, as the earth is struck by lightning some 600 times a minute, the percentage of lightning which hurts humans is minimal indeed.

Lightning is produced during the turbulent creation of a cloud, in unstable air. The violent churning of the air charges particles with static electricity, and portions of the cloud become positively charged (usually the top, as positive particles are lighter) and other portions are negatively charged. With this electrical difference, lightning occurs in an attempt to balance the charges. As electricity will always follow the path of least resistance, most lightning occurs between clouds or within one cloud.

However, when the cloud is close enough to the earth, the negatively charged bottom of the cloud repels electrons in the earth, creating a positive charge. If the force is great enough, a stroke of lightning will reach for the earth, in order to balance the forces. Since air is a poor electrical conductor, any object higher than ground surface is likely to be hit first, as this minimizes the distance. If the object is a good conductor, such as metal or a tree (which contains water), this will be the target of choice for a hit.

Lightning is actually a series of direct-current "strokes," usually four, which together appear in such a short time that the eye can't distinguish them. The average flash of lightning is 1,000 to 9,000 feet long, has a diameter of 6 inches, has a charge of 30,000 amps, and releases about 250 kilowatt-hours of energy in a fraction of a second. Lightning is known to cause forest fires and explode trees. These effects are caused by two different "types" of lightning: "hot lightning" (lower currents, longer duration), which is apt to set fires, and "cold lightning" (higher currents, shorter duration), which can cause explosive effects.

Since it takes vertical formation to generate the turbulence necessary to create the large charges, lightning usually comes from cumulonimbus or cumulus clouds, and develops from a stream of electrons flowing to the earth. Once there, this current must dissipate, and it too follows the path of least resistance, often water, an excellent conductor. On land, this ground current may actually bridge some gaps of air, such as the mouth of a cave, and is the greatest cause of lightning-related deaths.

A lightning flash heats the air, which expands with great force. This expansion creates thunder. If you see a flash and count the seconds until you hear the thunder, you can tell how far away it was, each second representing 1,000 feet. If you hear thunder, it was caused by lightning, even if you didn't see it, and hence you should be aware of the possibility of an electrical storm approaching.

Since the discharge follows the path of least resistance, it will strike the nearest object, and since mountains and ridges rise closer to the cloud level, they'll be more positively charged (more repellent electrical force) and easier to hit, so they'll be struck a lot. So will any high objects: lone trees, the highest tree in the forest, and so on. This actually creates a phenomenon called a "cone of protection." Imagine a tree 50 feet tall. The area within a 50-foot radius of the tree will not suffer a direct lightning hit. Rather, the tree will be hit. This is how a lightning rod works. For the outdoorsman, however, this protection is not very useful, as trees often explode on being struck, and the ground current will emanate throughout the cone of protection.

In the event you find yourself in an electrical storm, move away from any metal substance. Avoid or leave any ridges or summits. Even moving off a short distance is better than being exposed. Stay away from streams or other bodies of water. Avoid single trees. Ideally, you should be in a forest. Stay out of shallow caves or overhangs; deep ones are okay if you don't touch a wall. Wherever you are, crouch, with your feet close together to minimize ground-current danger. If you can keep it dry, crouch on your sleeping bag to minimize conductivity.

Strange as it seems, certain trees are more susceptible to lightning strikes than others. Ash and beech are least likely to be hit, whereas poplar, silver fir, pine, and oak are most likely.

People are often stunned but not killed by lightning effects. Prompt CPR and treatment for burns and shock may well save a victim. For this reason, members of a party should disperse during a lightning display, to be available to render aid.

FORECASTING

Forecasting the weather is inherently difficult. Forecasting is an imperfect science in the first place, and experience is the best teacher.

The best way to maximize that experience is to formalize it. Before entering a region, learn the topography and altitude of the terrain. Orient yourself to the prevailing westerly winds and the general facing directions of the mountain ranges in the area. Once outdoors, stay attuned to changing weather conditions at all times, but set aside three points in the day, preferably at the same time each day, to observe the weather and make a written record of conditions. In the morning, around noon, and in the late afternoon, make a general review of weather conditions. Check the wind direction and speed. Note changes of direction. Watch pressure changes and humidity. Observe the clouds and take note of their type, altitude, and sequence. Then write down your weather forecast, and check it later against what happens.

Only by practiced observation can you develop a decent proficiency as a forecaster. And even when you begin to gain some confidence in your abilities, be sure to maintain some humility and humor about it: sooner or later, and generally quite often, the weather will prove you a fool. Remember, don't take it personally. If you are properly dressed and equipped, and have a good understanding of backcountry safety, only the severest conditions should prevent you from enjoying yourself.

Chapter **Nine**

Our Responsibility to Our Land

IN ONE of the few poetic pieces of legal language ever written, the U.S. Congress when passing the Wilderness Act in 1964 defined wilderness in the words of forester Howard Zahnizer: "An area where the earth and its community life are untrammeled by man, where man himself is a visitor who does not remain."

But like visitors in our homes who sometimes forget their coat, leave the bed unmade, and generally make us glad when they move on, not everyone is a good guest in the wilderness. As backcountry use increases—and it is increasing many times faster than the country's population —our wild country is becoming more and more "trammeled" by man.

Our efforts to hold on to the small percentage of genuinely wild lands left to us around the world raise several questions that are difficult to answer: We have to ask how much wilderness we will preserve from encroachment; we have to ask how often we will use it; and, finally, we have the issue of *how* we use it.

As an educational institution, NOLS has over the years increasingly addressed itself to the last question. We began as a school to teach wilderness skills and instill the less tangible commodity of leadership. Gradually we have evolved a definition of backcountry leadership that involves not only taking care of yourself and your companions, but also the wilderness resource itself. This is the essential mission of NOLS' emphasis on minimum-impact camping.

In twenty years, between 1960 and 1979, visits to our national parks increased from 136 million visitors to 282 million. In Wyoming's Teton Wilderness area, 115,800 people entered in 1981, up from 46,600 only six years before.

What are all these people after? Do they want the same sort of good times in the backcountry that they might seek on a Saturday night in town? Are they looking for a large country club? Do they want danger—a confrontation with a grizzly? Or are they seeking what former Missouri Senator George G. Vest called over a hundred years ago "a great breathing-place for the national lungs"?

It's a question often asked at NOLS. What is it that compels a fifteen-year-old from suburban Rhode Island to journey on a NOLS course within a primeval wilderness? Or a successful Houston businessman in his forties to kayak through the rain and cold on Alaska's Prince William Sound?

The answers are not simple, only essential. We must come to grips with our feelings about the wilds because of the age we live in—an age in which those wilds are not unlimited—and we must decide how to take care of them.

There seems to be in most people an intuitive sense that the manufactured challenges of the civilized world teach us little about what we must, in the end, know. In the wilds we find that life is otherwise: full of miracles, challenges, and illumination. That is the magic and the importance of wilderness in the modern world; echoing Emerson's words: "The whole of nature is a metaphor of the human mind."

Wilderness is a repository of values, particularly in this country where wilderness played such an important role in forging our ideals of freedom and independence. Just as cultures defend their history and mores against distortion or forgetfulness, so must we regard the wilderness. The aesthetic and inspirational qualities of the wilds are a key part of our national character.

Another element in that national character is self-reliance. We have no taste for staying on the beaten path, restrictions on our behavior, or bureaucratic regulations. A wilderness with a locked gate and a ticket-taker is a contradiction in terms.

At the same time, a wilderness where you share a campsite area with half a dozen other groups is no wilderness. A mountain peak marred with piton scars, a lake so abused that its water is undrinkable, a circle of blackened fire rings—none of these things bring us closer to nature. Backcountry from which the game has been driven by hunting pressure and too much human traffic is not really wild anymore.

How do we cope with these two problems: the increasing pressure on wilderness, and our desire not to set up another bureaucracy to limit access?

The answer at NOLS is that we learn to regulate ourselves using the minimum-impact techniques we have described in this book. If you choose and prepare your site properly, cook in a way that does not scar the ground, follow careful sanitation practices, and otherwise work to blend into the wilderness, you will have a gratifying and more enriching experience—and those who follow will not have to pick up after you . . . they won't even know you were there.

Rock climbers realized years ago that as their numbers grew, the scars they left were ruining the very landscapes they loved. Without anyone telling them they had to, they developed new techniques and equipment that did not harm the rock. Backcountry users of all sorts are making the same kinds of decisions today. Most people who go into the wilderness want to preserve it—they wouldn't be there otherwise.

But time is running out. If we want to save the wildernesses of the world, if we want to have biological enclaves that predate modern man, wilderness users must be educated now.

There are other issues to be resolved. Do we want to limit access to certain hard-pressed wilderness areas by lottery or first-come, first-served? Do we need more wilderness to create a larger natural buffer zone and, by sheer inaccessibility, keep human impact to a minimum in core areas required for sustaining wildlife? Do we want to give the energy and mineral developers one last shot at wilderness areas? Can we begin to reclaim wilderness areas whose timber or minerals have been ripped from the earth?

These are questions which follow naturally from a person's first experience of wilderness. Time and again we've seen students at NOLS return from a course invigorated with a new kind of confidence, and they want more. As they explore other of the world's wild areas—from the veldt of Africa to the wild waters off Baja, or perhaps just the myriad natural areas in their home states—they see the ever-increasing pressure on those wildlands. Then they start asking questions.

Educating ourselves to use the wilderness well and unobtrusively means a better experience for us, a better experience for the next person, and a better experience for us again when we come back. Good judgment and technique and a good minimum-impact philosophy come naturally to those who love the wilderness. It is to encourage and aid in the dissemination of that approach to the backcountry that this book has been written. Let the national lungs breathe deeply.

NOLS Three-Season Equipment List

You can use the following checklist as a guide to the clothing, gear, first-aid items, and repair materials you should take on your trips. For warmer weather with smaller groups you can take much less than is listed here. For cooler weather with larger groups you may need to expand the list. Planning your expedition, even if it is a short two-day trip, so that you take what you need makes for an enjoyable, safe outing.

CLOTHING

Socks, wool, Ragg type, 2 pairs short, 2 pairs long knicker type
Gaiters, 1 pair long
Hiking boots, 1 pair
1 rain parka
Upper-body insulation, 3 layers
Lower-body insulation, 1 layer
Roomy wool pants or knickers, 1 pair
Wind pants, 1 pair
1 cotton long-sleeved shirt
1 pair of shorts
1 pair camp shoes or sneakers
2 pairs boxer shorts
2–3 bandanas
1 wool hat
2 pairs mittens, 1 pair gloves
1 felt hat with brim or baseball cap
1 extra-long belt

SLEEPING GEAR

1 sleeping bag
1 sleeping pad
1 sleeping-bag stuff sack
1 ground cloth

PERSONAL GEAR

3 small stuff sacks
1 zip bag for food
1 backpack (able to hold 3500 cubic inches and 60 pounds)
1 day pack
2 pairs lash straps
Glacier goggles or sunglasses
Chapstick
Notebook and pencils
Foot powder
PABA sunblock
Hand cream
Cup, bowl, spoon (insulated mugs are great)
1-quart water bottle
Small pocketknife
Insect repellent
3 candles
1 compass
Toilet articles
1 small towel
1 swimsuit

TEAM GEAR

Shelter (tent, tarp, or bivouac sack)
1 stove, plus fuel, containers, and funnels
Matches
Maps
Whetstone

Shovel or trowel
Books
Cooking gear (pots, pans, pot grips, cotton gloves, spoon,
spatula, water carrier)

REPAIR KITS

(NOLS recommends these items be carried on any backcountry trip of one week or longer.)

Pack, Boot, and Tent Repair Kit: toggles, clevis pins, split
rings, spare tent pole, ripstop tape, 20-foot cord, wire,
screws, and brads. (For longer trips: extra shoulder
strap, Speedy Stitcher, thread, boot grease, and epoxy.)
Stove Repair Kit: wrench, fuel bottle cap and gasket, pressure cap. (For longer trips: one set of all stove parts.)

LARGE-GROUP FIRST-AID KIT

(adequate for twelve to fifteen people on a four- to five-
week trip)

2″ × 2″ gauze pads	18 or more
Useful for minor wounds, to clean small cuts, blisters, etc.	
4″ × 4″ gauze pads	18 or more
Large dressings for major wounds.	
3″ roller gauze	1 or more
Not a necessity but good for holding dressings in place. Brand names Kerlix and Kling work well.	
Eye pads	2
Used to dress the eyes. A luxury; can be improvised, but hard to beat the real thing. Also can be used as a regular dressing.	
Band-Aids	36

Butterflies   18
    Used to close minor wounds, especially
    wounds of the knees, knuckles, and
    elbows which are difficult to keep closed
    and thus hard to heal.

Ace bandages   1 or 2
    Two-inch width seems the most
    versatile. Can be used to hold dressings
    in place, wrap sprains, and hold splints
    in place.

Cravats   2
    Triangular bandages that have many
    uses for splinting, ankle wrapping, and
    bandaging; can be improvised, but do
    not weigh much and are useful.

Adhesive tape   1 or 2
    Two-inch width is the most versatile.
    Large rolls unnecessary.

Thermometer   1
    Knowing what a person's temperature is
    can be important; hand-on-forehead
    technique is very inaccurate.

Moleskin and molefoam   3 packages
    For the care of blisters and hot spots.

Aspirin   100-tablet
                                                bottle

Tincture of benzoin   1
    Good for keeping tape and moleskin on.

Antibiotic cream   1
    To protect minor cuts from becoming
    infected.

Scissors   1
    Useful for cutting tape and moleskin,
    and in dressing and bandaging.

Tweezers   1

    Great for removing splinters.

NOTE: The items that are listed in single quantities are not necessary on an emergency basis and should be in the leader's kit. The items in multiples can easily be packaged in separate kits to be distributed to a number of people in the expedition.

SMALL-GROUP FIRST-AID KIT

(adequate for three to six people on a five- to ten-day trip)

2″ × 2″ gauze pads	10 to 12
3″ roller gauze	1
Band-Aids	24
Ace bandage	1
Adhesive tape, 2-inch width	1
Moleskin and molefoam	1
Tincture of benzoin	1
Antibiotic cream	1
Aspirin	Small bottle
Thermometer	1

NOTE: If you have first-aid training, the following prescription drugs might be considered for long trips: antihistamine (for colds, hay fever, allergies), Lomotil (for diarrhea), antibiotic, painkiller, and epinephrine (if anyone is allergic to insect bites).

NOLS Recipes

BEVERAGES

Coffee

10 c. water
2 handfuls ground coffee
Pinch of salt

Bring the water to a rolling boil, throw in coffee and salt, and return water to a boil just long enough to get all the grounds wet. Take the coffee off the heat and let sit for a few minutes. Then tap the pot a few times to help settle the grounds. If tapping doesn't seem to settle the grounds, try pouring a cup of cold water into the coffee.

Milk

1 part milk powder
3 parts water

Variations: add honey, cinnamon, nutmeg, and/or rum or vanilla extract.

Hot Spiced Milk

3 heaping tbs. powdered milk
1 tbs. honey
½ tsp. vanilla extract
Pinch of cinnamon or nutmeg

Put ingredients in an 8-ounce cup. Add hot water and stir well. Try other flavors by substituting rum, almond, etc., for the vanilla extract. For cold-night variation, add 1 tsp. to 1 tbs. of margarine. The margarine will help keep you warm at night.

Home Mix Cocoa

6 parts milk powder
1 part cocoa
1–2 parts sugar

Mix milk powder and cocoa in a large plastic bag. Add sugar to taste.

Home Mix Drink

1 part Home Mix Cocoa
3 parts hot water
½ tbs. margarine

Prepare single portion directly in your cup.

Mocha

1 part Home Mix Cocoa
3 parts hot coffee
Pinch of nutmeg
Dollop of margarine (opt.)

Super Tea

10 c. water
4–6 tea bags
6–8 tbs. honey
4 whole cloves (opt.)
Pinch of cinnamon and nutmeg

Boil water. Steep tea and add other ingredients.

Russian Spiced Tea

1 lb. orange drink mix
½ c. instant tea
1 c. white sugar
1 tsp. cinnamon
½ tsp. ground cloves
½ tsp. ginger

Mix ingredients together. Use 2 spoonfuls for 1 cup. Add boiling water. You can make this mix at home ahead of time or scale it down and make up a pot for an after-dinner drink.

Hot Gelatin Dessert

2—3 tbs. gelatin mix
1 c. hot water

Add gelatin to boiling water.

Fruit Crystals

2—3 tbs. fruit crystals
1 c. water (hot or cold)

SOUPS

Basic Broth Soup

8 c. water
Flavoring base to taste (3—4 tbs.)
Seasonings to taste
Solid components (1—1½ c.)
4 tbs. margarine
Salt (if needed)

Boil water and add base until flavor desired. Add seasonings and solid components. Vegetables and rice take 20—30 minutes to cook, so add these first. Noodles, onions, and peppers take 10—15 minutes. Cook until solid components are done. Add margarine and salt if necessary. *Note:* When using tomato base, cook solid components first, then add tomato base.

Egg Drop Soup

Boil a couple of handfuls of pasta (noodles or spaghetti) in about 10 c. water. In later stages of boiling add chicken base, curry, salt, and pepper.

Mix together 1 part egg and 1 part dry milk, then gradually add water until it forms a rather thick paste. When pasta is cooked, drop egg mixture into pasta and water. Cook on low heat for a few minutes. For tasty addition, add slivers of Swiss cheese and melt.

Variations

SOUP	Base	Seasonings	Solid Components
Beef vegetable	Beef	Black pepper, chili powder, garlic (opt.)	Meat, bacon bits or ham bits, onions, peas, carrots, noodles or barley
Chicken vegetable	Chicken	Black pepper, dry mustard, curry powder (opt.)	Vegetables, noodles, onions, chicken pieces (opt.)
Chicken rice	Chicken	Black pepper, curry	Vegetables, onions, rice, chicken pieces (opt.)
Onion	Chicken	Pepper	Onions
Tomato–beef vegetable	½ beef, ½ tomato	Black pepper, oregano, dry mustard, chili powder	Meat, ham bits or bacon bits, vegetables, onions, noodles (opt.)
Lentil	½ beef, ½ tomato	Black pepper, chili powder (opt.)	Meat, bacon bits, lentils, onions, green peppers, barley (opt.)

Basic Cream Soup

8 c. water
Flavor base to taste (3–4 tbs.)
Solid components if any (½–1½ c.)
Margarine to taste (3–4 tbs.)
Salt if needed
Thickener if desired
Powdered milk to taste (½–1 c.)
Seasonings

Boil water. Add flavor bases. Add solid components and cook until done. Add margarine and salt if needed. Turn heat down to a simmer. Thicken, if desired, with potato flakes or a paste of 2 tbs. flour and 4 tbs. water, mixed

thoroughly until all lumps are out. Mix powdered milk with
½ c. water and add to the soup. Season to taste.

Variations

SOUP	Base	Seasonings	Solids	Thickener
Tomato	Tomato	Black pepper, oregano	None	Flour (opt.)
Tomato rice	Tomato	Black pepper, oregano, dry mustard	Rice	Flour (opt.)
Potato	None	Black pepper, dry mustard	Bacon bits	Potato
Corn chowder	None	Black pepper, dry mustard	Peas, corn	Potato
Mushroom	Mushroom	Black pepper	Onions	Flour
Split pea	None	Black pepper	Split peas, ham bits or bacon bits, onions	None
Chicken	Chicken	Black pepper, dry mustard	Chicken pieces, rice or noodles	Flour (opt.)

PASTA

Basic Recipe

2 parts water
1 part pasta
Salt to taste (1 tsp. to 1 qt. water)

Boil water. Add pasta and boil gently 10—15 minutes. Save any drained water for soups.

Variation: fry cooked pasta in margarine, or fry uncooked pasta in margarine before cooking.

White Sauce

3 tbs. margarine
3 tbs. flour
1 c. water or milk (4 tbs. milk powder to ¾ c. water)
Salt to taste

Melt margarine. Add flour, stirring to remove lumps. Add water or milk and simmer until desired thickness. To this sauce can be added vegetables (cooked), cheese, meats, flavor bases (do not salt sauce if base is used), and seasonings. Pour sauce over rice or pasta.

Basic Noodle Casserole

4 c. water
¼—½ c. vegetables and onions
2 c. noodles
1 tsp. salt (if needed)
2 tbs. bases and seasonings
½ c. powdered milk mixed with
    ¼ c. water
3—4 tbs. margarine, or to taste
Thickener (opt.)
Wheat germ garnish

Boil water. Add vegetables and cook 10—15 minutes before adding noodles. Add noodles, bases, seasonings, and salt if necessary. When noodles are mixed, add milk (making sure all lumps are dissolved). Add thickener if desired (either flour or potatoes as in soup thickener). Melt in margarine and top with wheat germ.

Variations: Add ¼—½ c. milk or water and bake 10—15 minutes in hot coals. Or add ½ c. mixed powdered eggs, then bake.

Variations

CASSEROLE	Base	Seasonings	Additional Solid Components
Chicken noodle	Chicken	Black pepper, curry	Chicken bits or ham bits, peas, peanuts
Beef noodle	Beef	Black pepper, chili powder	Bacon bits, peas, carrots
Fish noodle	Fish	Black pepper, dry mustard	Boned fish, wild onions (or freeze-dried), peas, carrots
Mushroom noodle	Mushroom	Black pepper, dry sour cream mix	Bacon bits

Sausage Stroganoff

5 c. water
2 tbs. margarine
2 tbs. beef base
2 tbs. dried onions
4 tbs. dried mushrooms
6 links sausage, cut into 1-inch pieces
4 c. egg noodles
5 tbs. dry sour cream mix
1 tbs. powdered milk
Parmesan cheese to garnish

Put first 6 ingredients in a pan, cover, and bring to a boil. Boil a few minutes until vegetables soften, then add noodles. Give noodles a quick stir to keep them from sticking together, then cover the pan and let them boil for about 10 minutes. In a bowl, mix sour cream and milk with some water. Add the water a little at a time until the mixture resembles cottage cheese. When noodles are soft, stir in the sour cream mixture and mix well. Simmer for 5 minutes, then serve. Sprinkle Parmesan on top.

Lentil Casserole

Lentils
Beef base

Instant potatoes
Margarine
Sliced cheese
Soybeans or sunflower seeds

Cooking time for the lentils will vary depending on altitude and how hot a fire you cook them on. If you won't have time to cook them from scratch at dinnertime, soak them during the day. And if you're going to be traveling to another camp, you can put them in a plastic bag with some water, put the bag inside a cook pot, and pack the pot very carefully in your pack (so it won't tip over).

Cook lentils and drain, saving the water. Dissolve beef base in water and then add potatoes. Make enough potatoes so you have equal amounts of lentils and mashed potatoes. Melt some margarine in a pan, then put in a layer of potatoes, a layer of lentils, and a layer of cheese. Pour in a little of the beef base juice to keep it moist and top with soybeans or sunflower seeds. Bake until cheese melts and ingredients are warmed through.

Macaroni and Cheese

4 c. water
2 c. macaroni
Salt (1 tsp. to 1 qt.)
2 tbs. dried onions, or to taste
1 c. cheese, cut into chunks
4 tbs. margarine, or to taste
¼ c. milk (opt.)
Black pepper and garlic to taste
Wheat germ garnish

Boil water and add macaroni, salt, and onions. Cook at a gentle boil 10–15 minutes or until done. Drain all but ¼ to ½ c. water. Add cheese and margarine. Turn down to a simmer and stir often. Add milk if desired (mixed well to dissolve lumps) and seasonings to taste. Cook and stir until cheese is melted. Sprinkle with wheat germ.

Variations

Add vegetables and cook with the macaroni.

Make a white sauce with cheese, onions, and spices; pour over cooked macaroni and garnish.

Spaghetti

4 c. water
2 c. spaghetti
1 tsp. salt
3 tbs. onions
4 tbs. margarine
3 tbs. tomato and mushroom base, or to taste (opt.)
Black pepper to taste
¼ tsp. garlic, or to taste
½–1 tsp. oregano, or to taste
½ c. chopped cheese (opt.)
¼–½ c. bacon bits or meat
Wheat germ garnish

Boil water. Add spaghetti, salt, onions and boil until done. Turn heat down to a simmer. Add margarine, base if desired, and seasonings. Melt cheese and garnish with bacon bits and wheat germ.

Variations: Add bases and seasonings to a white sauce and pour over cooked pasta. Or add 3 tbs. each dried mushrooms and dried bell peppers when adding spaghetti to water.

Cheese Barley

4 c. water
1 tsp. salt
1 c. grits or barley
1 c. chopped cheese

Bring water to a boil. Add salt and barley and cook until barley is soft, about 1 hour. Add cheese and stir until melted. Season to taste if desired.

Everybody's Barley Dinner

This is everybody's dinner because when it's done and served up, you pass around the seasonings and everybody gets to choose what flavor their dinner will be, depending on his mood and tastes.

4 c. water
1 c. barley
1 tbs. dried onions
1 tbs. beef base or miso (if you don't add beef base, add a bit of salt)
2 tbs. margarine
2–3 tbs. cream of mushroom soup base
½ c. diced cheese

Cook barley and onions in water over medium heat for about 1 hour. Keep pot covered. When barley is done (it will be "springy" when you chew it but not crunchy), add beef base, margarine, mushroom base, and cheese. Stir well. Let the heat of the barley melt the cheese—it should take a few minutes. Serve barley and pass around the seasonings. Here are a few suggested combinations:

garlic	Tabasco	garlic	curry
pepper	garlic	oregano	soy sauce
		chili powder	

Bulgur-Rice Pilaf

Bulgur is cracked wheat that has been parboiled and then dried. It cooks quickly and is very versatile. It can be eaten as a breakfast cereal (see recipe, p. 319), as a dinner food like rice, or can be added to breads and pancakes in place of part of the flour. Try to find the bulgur that has soy grits added to it. The protein of the bulgur and soy complement each other, making a complete protein.

4 c. water
1 tbs. dried onions
2 tbs. dried peas
1 c. bulgur-soy grits
1 c. rice
2 tbs. beef or tomato base (opt.)
3 heaping tbs. margarine
1 c. diced cheese

Bring water, onions, and peas to a boil. Add bulgur and rice; cover, and cook at a gentle boil. After 15 minutes, add base if desired. Cook an additional 5 minutes (or until all the water is gone and the mixture is light and dry) and remove from heat. Melt margarine in a frying pan, add rice mixture and cheese. Cook until cheese melts and rice is browned.

RICE

Basic Recipe

3 parts water
1 part rice
1 tsp. salt to 1 quart water
Margarine to taste

Boil water. Add rice and salt and stir once. Cover and simmer until done (20-30 minutes). If you prefer slightly crunchy rice, use 2½ parts water and do not cook as long.

Variations

Fried Rice: Cook rice. Rinse with cold water and drain well (optional step). Melt margarine in a frying pan, adding seasonings if desired. Fry rice until golden brown (15-20 minutes). Do not overload the frying pan with rice or else cooking time increases. Chicken and beef base both dissolve in margarine for chicken or beefy fried rice. Or, make a white sauce with flavoring base and seasonings and pour over rice.

Rice Casserole

All the following dishes can be baked. Cook rice and add bases, solid components, and seasonings. Add ½ c. extra water or milk (and eggs if desired) and bake 15-20 minutes.

Spanish Rice

4 c. water
2 tbs. dried onions

2 tbs. dried bell peppers
2 c. rice
½ c. tomato base
1 tbs. beef base
Chili powder, garlic, and Tabasco to taste
½ c. diced cheese
Bacon bits to garnish

Boil water with onions and peppers. Add rice and stir once. (Stirring rice while it cooks will make it gummy.) Cover pot and simmer about 20 minutes. Mix bases with enough water to make sauce consistency (use water from rice if there is any left). Add bases and seasonings to the rice and simmer a few more minutes. Remove from heat, add cheese and bacon bits. Stir and serve.

CASSEROLE	Base	Seasonings	Solid Components
Mushroom	Mushroom	Black pepper	Peas, carrots, powdered milk, wild mushrooms (opt.)
Cheesy rice	None	Black pepper, garlic, onions	Cheese, ham or bacon bits (opt.)
Spanish rice	3 parts tomato, 1 part beef	Green peppers, onions, black pepper, chili powder	Bacon bits or ham bits, corn (opt.)
Beefy rice	Beef	Onions, black pepper	Bacon bits, vegetables
Chicken rice	Chicken	Black pepper, curry	Peas, carrots, powdered milk
Curried rice	None	Curry	Vegetables, nuts, dried fruit
Fish rice	Fish stock	Black pepper, onions, curry (opt.)	Peas, carrots, boned fish, powdered milk

Sweet and Sour Curried Rice

3 c. water
1 tsp. salt
1 c. rice
½ c. raisins or other dried fruit (opt.)
2 tbs. dried onions
2 tbs. dried green peppers
½ c. dried vegetables
Bean sprouts (opt.)
¼-½ c. margarine
½ c. nuts and seeds
1 tsp. curry powder
¼ tsp. black pepper
¼ c. vinegar
½ c. brown sugar
3 tbs. soy sauce (opt.)
¼ c. water

In salted water cook rice, fruit, and vegetables until rice is done. (Drain rice if necessary.) Melt margarine in one or two frying pans. Spoon rice into pans. Add nuts and seasonings and fry 10-15 minutes. Mix vinegar, sugar, soy sauce, and water, and stir into the rice. Simmer 5 minutes with lid on.

Rice Pudding

3 c. water
Pinch of salt
1 c. rice
½ c. raisins or other dried fruit
2 tbs. margarine
½ c. milk
½ c. brown sugar or honey
1 tsp. cinnamon
Dash of nutmeg

Boil water with salt. Add rice and raisins, and boil gently until rice is done. Add margarine. Add milk, sugar, and spices to taste. Powdered eggs (equivalent to 1 egg) may be added for a more solid pudding. Simmer for about 10 minutes or place in greased pan and bake for about 15 minutes.

QUICK-COOKING BEANS

Before your trip buy dry beans (black, pinto, navy, lima, etc.) and soak them in water overnight. The next day put them on the stove and simmer until beans are soft all the way through. Drain the beans and dry them. If you have a food dryer, use it, or spread the beans on a tray and put them in a warm oven or out in the sun. Store the beans in jars or plastic bags until you need them. You may want to make a few dinners at home with the beans to see how they cook up. You may also find quick-cooking beans in stores that sell backpacking foods.

Bean-Rice Casserole

3 c. water
1 c. rice
½ c. quick-cooking black beans
1 tbs. beef base
3 tbs. margarine
½ c. chopped dried apricots
½ c. chopped dried pineapple

Put all ingredients in a frying pan and mix. Cover and cook over medium heat for about 20 minutes. Don't stir while it's cooking because that will make the rice gummy. When the water has been absorbed, test rice for doneness. If it's still a little chewy, add a little more water and cook a few minutes more.

Refried Beans and Tortillas

4 c. water
2 heaping tbs. margarine
1 tbs. dried onions
½ lb. quick-cooking pinto beans
3 tbs. tomato base
3 tbs. powdered milk
1 c. thinly sliced cheese
1 pkg. corn tortillas

Add margarine and onions to the water, cover, and bring to a boil. Once boiling, add the pinto beans, cover, and cook until soft (20 minutes). While the beans are cooking, put tomato base and powdered milk into a cup and add enough of the bean water to make a smooth paste. Stir tomato mixture into the beans. When beans are done, lower the heat and add cheese and seasonings if desired. Cover pot to keep beans warm and set aside. Fry the tortillas on both sides in a small amount of margarine. Fry a few minutes for soft tortillas or longer for crispy ones. Spoon beans onto tortillas and season with sunflower seeds, Tabasco sauce, or some sour cream (made from powdered mix).

POTATOES

Basic Mashed Potatoes

3 parts water
1½–2 parts instant potatoes
1 tsp. salt to 1 quart water
Powdered milk to taste
Margarine to taste

Bring water to a boil. Add salt and milk if desired. Add potatoes slowly, constantly stirring until potatoes are slightly thinner than desired thickness. Spoon in margarine and set on a very low heat until margarine melts.

Variations

Fried: make mashed potatoes as above but use 4 parts water to 3 parts potatoes. Fry in margarine.

Dry-fried: Fry dry potato flakes in a small amount of margarine until golden brown. Salt and use as a garnish. These taste like potato chips.

The bases, solid ingredients, and seasonings used in noodle or rice casseroles can also be used with potatoes.

Potato-Cheese Patties

4 c. water
1 tsp. salt or beef base
2–3 tbs. dried onions
3 c. instant potatoes
½ c. milk
½ c. biscuit mix
1 c. cheese chunks
Pepper to taste
Flour or cornmeal
Margarine

Boil water with salt and onions. Add potatoes and mix. Set aside to cool. Mix in milk, biscuit mix, cheese, and pepper until it forms stiff dough. Form patties and roll in flour or cornmeal. Fry in ¼ inch of margarine.

DEEP DISH PIES

Basic Recipe (for a 10-inch frying pan)

Crust

1 c. flour (or biscuit mix)
Pinch of salt
¼ c. margarine
1 tbs. water

Filling

3 tbs. margarine
2 tbs. flour
1 c. water
1 tbs. base
½ tsp. salt if a base not used
Seasonings
1 c. solid ingredients (cooked)

To make the crust, cut the flour and salt into the margarine until the flour is moistened; add water and knead into a ball with your hands. Flatten the ball and roll out with a fishing rod case or pat into the bottom of a frying pan with your fingers. Mix the margarine, flour, and water into a sauce, and add base if desired and seasonings. Add solid ingredients, and simmer until sauce thickens to a gravy consistency. Pour into the pastry shell and bake until the crust is golden brown (20–30 minutes). (Make another crust for the top if you wish.)

Variations

For other fillings, see the variations listed under noodle casseroles (p. 298) and rice (p. 303).

Basic Quiche

Make a Basic Recipe Crust (above) and bake.

Filling

3 tbs. dried onions
½ c. powdered eggs
½ tsp. salt

½ tsp. garlic
½ tsp. pepper
Seasonings to taste
½ c. powdered milk
1 c. diced cheese
1½ c. water

Soak the dried onions to rehydrate. Mix all dry ingredients together, then add water and onions. Beat until smooth. Cook over low heat, stirring constantly until smooth and mixture starts to thicken, then pour into the crust and bake until filling is solid and the crust is brown.

Quiche Lorraine

Make a Basic Recipe Crust and bake.

Filling

¼ c. dried mushrooms
3 tbs. dried onions
½ c. powdered eggs
½ tsp. salt
½ tsp. garlic
½ c. powdered milk
½ tsp. pepper
1 c. diced Swiss cheese
¼ c. Parmesan cheese
6 pieces cooked bacon, crumbled (opt.)
1½ c. water

Soak dried onions and mushrooms in a bowl of warm water to rehydrate. Mix other dry ingredients, then add water, onions, and mushrooms. Beat until smooth. Cook over low heat, stirring constantly until smooth. When filling starts to thicken, pour into baked crust and bake until the filling is solid and crust is browned (about 20–30 minutes).

BREADS

Dumplings

1 c. biscuit mix
½ c. flour or cornmeal
Powdered milk (opt.)
½ c. water

Mix ingredients and spoon over boiling soup or stew. Cover and steam 5–10 minutes. Dumplings are done when fluffy inside.

Biscuit Squares (for a 10-inch frying pan)

Pinch of salt
1 c. biscuit mix
¼ c. cold water
¼ c. powdered milk
1 c. White Sauce (p. 297) with flavorings

Mix first 4 ingredients into a stiff dough and pat into bottom of a frying pan. Bake until golden brown. Then either pour white sauce over biscuits or cut squares and dip in white sauce.

Grilled Cheese Sandwiches

2 parts flour
1 part Bisquick
1 part powdered eggs
½ part chicken base
2 tsp. Worcestershire sauce
Salt to taste
Cheddar and Swiss cheese, cut in thick slices
Margarine

Mix first 6 ingredients with water until thicker than pancake batter but thinner than biscuit dough. Dip the cheddar and Swiss slices in the batter. When slices are completely covered, fry them in margarine. A Swiss version of the grilled cheese sandwich.

Pizza

Crust

1 tsp. dry yeast
½ c. lukewarm water
½ tsp. sugar
¼ tsp. salt
1 c. flour

Quick Crust

½ c. biscuit mix
½ c. flour
½ c. cold water

Sauce

2 tbs. margarine
1 tbs. flour (optional for white sauce method)
½ c. water
2 tbs. dried onions (hydrated)
¼–½ c. hydrated vegetables
¼ c. tomato base
¼ tsp. black pepper
¼ tsp. garlic powder
¼ tsp. oregano

Toppings

Fish, wild mushrooms, wild onions, bacon bits, sausages,
    etc.
½ c. thinly sliced cheese

Dissolve yeast in lukewarm water, sugar, and salt. Add flour and mix into a stiff dough. Or mix ingredients of the Quick Crust into a stiff dough. Roll out dough with a fishing rod case or pat into the bottom of a frying pan. Turn up edges to hold the sauce. Mix the sauce. Either make a White Sauce (p. 297) and add spices, or just mix all the ingredients. Pour the sauce over the crust, cover with thin slices of cheese, add other toppings, and bake until the crust is golden brown. Top coals are not needed, so this can also be baked on a stove if low heat is used. Bake with a lid on.

Chapatis

Flat bread

½ c. flour
½ c. cornmeal
½ c. water
Pinch of salt
Margarine

Topping

Cheese, thinly sliced
Bacon bits or sausage

Mix all flat bread ingredients except margarine. Form into thin, flat patties and fry in a lightly greased frying pan until golden brown. Place cheese and meat on top and melt cheese by placing hot coals on the frying pan lid for 5–10 minutes.

YEAST BREADS

Yeast are tiny one-celled organisms dormant in their water-tight envelope. A good environment (warm water) and food (sugar or starch) to metabolize will activate the yeast. If the water is too hot it will kill the yeast, and if too cold, will not activate the yeast. Yeast can metabolize sugar directly or make sugar from other starches. As the yeast metabolize and multiply, gas (CO_2) is given off.

Flour, salt, water, and yeast are the basics of bread, to which other ingredients are added for variety. Wheat flour is best because it is high in gluten. The fibers of gluten become elastic when kneaded and hold gas pockets created by the yeast. Other flours such as graham or buckwheat can also be added but tend to make bread heavy if not very carefully used. We recommend beginners make very basic bread, which is usually successful even under less than ideal conditions.

Basic Bread Recipe

1¾ c. lukewarm water (110°)
1 package of dried yeast or equivalent amount
2 tsp. salt
2 tbs. sugar
1 lb. flour (3½–4 c.)

Dissolve yeast in lukewarm water. Add salt and sugar. Let set in a warm place about 5 minutes. Add half the flour and beat vigorously 2–3 minutes to help develop gluten. Then add the rest of the flour until the dough is thick. Lightly flour your hands and the dough and knead the dough either in a frying pan or on a cleaned rock. Knead for about 8 minutes, folding and turning so that all parts are kneaded evenly, adding more flour whenever the dough becomes too sticky to handle. Knead with the heel of your hand. The dough will be silky and springy when done. Shape into a loaf and place in a Teflon or well-greased pot or frying pan. Press into corners and grease the top of the loaf. Cover and set in a warm place about an hour. If it is very cold outside, let the bread rise by placing it on top a covered pot of boiling water.

Once it has risen, bake the bread 40–50 minutes. (Punching it down and letting it rise a second time will give a lighter texture but is not necessary.) When done, bread will be golden brown and will have a hollow sound when tapped. Remove from the pan and cool 5–10 minutes before cutting.

Beefy-Onion Yeast Bread

Add to Basic Bread Recipe:
1 tbs. beef base instead of salt
3 tbs. soaked onions
Onion water in place of water
2 parts flour and 1 part potatoes instead of all flour

Cinnamon-Raisin Yeast Bread

Add to Basic Bread Recipe:
Handful of raisins in yeast-water mixture
1 tbs. cinnamon with the salt
½ c. sugar

Cheesy Yeast Bread

Add to Basic Bread Recipe:
1 tbs. beef base instead of salt
1 tbs. softened onions
1 cup cheese, cut into chunks

Nut-Fruit Yeast Bread

Add to Basic Bread Recipe:
1 c. chopped nuts, seeds, and fruit.

Oatmeal or Cereal Yeast Bread

In Basic Bread Recipe use 1 part oatmeal or other cereal
to 2 parts flour instead of all flour.

Yeast Cinnamon Rolls

Basic Bread Recipe
4 tbs. margarine
¼–½ c. brown sugar
1 tbs. cinnamon
Nuts and raisins (opt.)

Mix bread and knead as in basic recipe. Instead of forming
into a loaf, roll dough out into a rectangle. Spread soft
margarine onto dough, sprinkle with brown sugar, cinnamon, nuts, and raisins. Roll up dough lengthwise. Pinch
edge of dough to the roll. Cut through roll every 2 inches,
place cinnamon rolls on their sides in a greased pan. Cover
with a damp cloth and let rise in the sun or near a fire.
When rolls have filled up the pan, bake them.

FISH

Boning Fish. If you need just meat and not bones, boil the cleaned fish, head and all, until meat begins to fall off the bones (10—15 minutes). Remove fish from the water and take off meat with a knife or fingers. Don't miss the piece of meat in the cheek. Use the water as stock for soup.

Filleting fish. Many fish are too thick to fry, so you must fillet them. Hold the fish by the tail and slice the meat off where it joins the bone. Slice toward the head. When one side is done, do the other. Use the fillet as a whole small fish. Because there is no skin on one side, bake fillet in a frying pan instead of directly on coals.

Fish Chowders

Fish, cleaned
8 c. water
4 tbs. dried onions
4 tbs. dried vegetables
Salt and pepper to taste
½ c. margarine

New England Chowder

¾ c. instant potatoes
⅔ c. powdered milk

Manhattan Chowder

4 tbs. tomato base
½ c. powdered milk (opt.)
Oregano

Cook fish in boiling water with onions and vegetables until fish is ready to bone (10—15 minutes). Remove fish, bone it, and return to the stock. Season to taste. Add margarine. Turn heat down to a simmer. Add potatoes and milk for New England chowder, and tomato base for Manhattan chowder. Taste and salt if necessary.

Fried Fish

Fish, cleaned and slightly wet
¼–½ cup cornmeal and/or flour
1 tsp. salt
Pepper, garlic powder, curry, oregano to taste
Margarine (as much as needed for frying)

Mix cornmeal, salt, and seasonings in a plastic bag. Put in fish and shake. Remove fish from bag and place in a frying pan with melted margarine. Fry the fish *slowly* until tender. To prevent curling, make several cuts on the back of the fish or turn the fish when it starts to curl.

Baked Fish

Place a cleaned fish directly on hot coals. Turn when done on one side. Take out of coals, peel away skin, salt to taste.

Creamed Fish

Pour White Sauce (p. 297) with vegetables and seasonings over fish that has been boiled, fried or baked. A tomato sauce with onions or a seasoned cheese sauce is very good.

Fish Patties

Fish
3 c. water
3 tbs. dried onions
⅓–½ c. powdered milk
Salt and pepper to taste
2–3 tsp. wheat germ
1½ c. instant potatoes
Margarine

Boil fish in water with onions. When done, remove fish from water and bone it. Mix with dry ingredients, form into thick patties, and fry in margarine.

BREAKFAST FOODS

Cooked Cereal

Instant flake-type cereals

1 part cereal
2 parts water
1 tsp. salt to 1 quart water

Granular-type cereals (non-instant)

1 part cereal
4 parts water
1 tsp. salt to 1 quart water

Boil water and add salt. Gradually pour in cereal while constantly stirring. Continue to stir while cooking, or take cereal off heat and steam with a lid on. Add margarine, milk, sugar, fruit, and nuts. Instant cereals take 2–3 minutes to cook, non-instant 10–15 minutes.

Granola

2–3 tbs. margarine
3 c. uncooked oatmeal or other flaked cereal
½ c. brown sugar or honey
½ tsp. salt (if salted nuts not used)
1 c. nuts and seeds
1 c. dried fruit, chopped into tiny pieces
½ c. wheat germ

Melt margarine in frying pan. Fry cereal until golden brown, constantly stirring. Add other ingredients and stir well. Eat hot or let cool and use as trail food. Granola can also be used as a breakfast cereal with milk (hot or cold) poured over it.

Pancakes

1½ c. self-rising biscuit mix
¾ c. flour or cereal (uncooked)
Enough water for a pourable batter (about 1½ c.)

Any self-rising mix may be used. High altitude causes over-raising, so some flour or other grain must be added. Mix all ingredients well. Lightly grease a Teflon frying pan and heat. Pour batter into the hot pan and cook gently over coals or on low heat until the bubbles on the top retain their shape. Flip and cook the other side. (Flipping is very easy and makes breakfast a spectacular event. Shake the pancake loose by gently hitting the pan on the side of a rock or loosen with a spoon. Then flip, without hesitation, using wrist action and watch the pancake so it can be caught when it lands. Practice with a glove if you need confidence.) Serve with Honey-Margarine Syrup, below.

Variations

Oatmeal, potato, cornmeal, fruit, or cheese can be substituted for the flour or cereal. Or, sprinkle any of the following on your pancakes: wild berries, dried fruit, nuts, chocolate chips, sesame seeds.

Syrup

1 part brown sugar
1 part water

Boil together 10 minutes, constantly stirring. Add soaked fruit, margarine, and spices if desired.

Honey-Margarine Syrup

3 tbs. margarine
3 tbs. honey
1 tsp. vanilla extract

Melt margarine in a pan. Add honey and vanilla, stir and cook until hot. Serve immediately over pancakes or pour onto cooked cereal. Once it has cooled, stir before using. Brown sugar can be substituted for the honey. Spice up syrup if you wish by adding cinnamon or nutmeg.

Cheese Grits

4 c. water
1 c. hominy grits
1 tsp. salt
2 tbs. margarine
1 c. diced cheese

Bring water to a boil. Add grits and salt. Simmer until grits are soft. Take off heat and add margarine and cheese. Stir until cheese melts. Serve hot, or let it cool and then slice into 1-inch-thick slices and fry on both sides in a little margarine. This is a quick breakfast that's not sweet like so many hot cereals.

Breakfast Bulgar

2 c. water
Dash of salt
1 c. bulgar-soy grits
1 heaping tsp. powdered milk
Raisins or dried fruit
Nuts or seeds to garnish

Boil water and salt, lower heat and add bulgar, powdered milk, and raisins or dried fruit. Stir, cover the pot, and simmer about 10 minutes. Serve cereal with margarine, brown sugar, and chopped nuts or sunflower seeds.

Cheese Omelet

1 part powdered eggs
1 part powdered milk
1 part Bisquick
Dash of salt
Sliced or diced cheese, as much as desired

Mix first 4 ingredients. Add water until the mixture has the consistency of pancake batter. Pour into greased pan and cook one side of the pan, then add cheese to the uncooked side. Flip the cooked portion on top of the cheese and finish cooking over medium to low heat with the lid on. Rehydrated onions, green peppers or bacon bits can be added.

BISCUITS

Basic Biscuit Recipe

1½ c. biscuit mix
½ c. flour or grain
½ c. cold water
¼ c. powdered milk
Pinch of salt

Mix all ingredients into a stiff dough. Drop or roll into balls and bake until golden brown in greased frying pan.

Cheese Biscuits

To the Basic Biscuit Recipe add a few onions that have been rehydrated and some garlic powder. Form into balls, putting a chunk of cheese in the middle. Bake them and eat them hot, or save them for trail food.

Skillet Biscuits

Basic Biscuit Recipe
Margarine
Soaked onions
Salt
Garlic powder

Mix biscuits as above. Fry in ½ inch margarine with onions and garlic powder. Turn until all sides brown. Cover and cook on low heat 8–10 minutes.

SWEETS

Muffins

Basic Biscuit Recipe
¼ c. extra sugar or honey
Nuts and dried fruit
4 tbs. melted margarine
2 tbs. water

Mix all ingredients in biscuit recipe plus additional ingredients into a sticky dough. Drop into a greased frying pan and bake until golden.

Fruit Cobbler

1–1½ c. water (varies with type of fruit)
Dried fruit, as much as desired
Sugar or honey to taste
Margarine and cinnamon to taste
1 c. biscuit mix
½ c. flour
Pinch of salt
½ c. water
¼ c. powdered milk (opt.)

Boil fruit in water until rehydrated and add about ½ c. extra water when the fruit is hydrated. Add sugar, margarine, and cinnamon. Mix biscuit mix with flour, salt, water, and powdered milk if desired, and spoon over boiling fruit. Cover and boil 5–10 minutes until the dough is steam-cooked.

Apple Crisp

½ lb. dried apples or other fruit
1 handful raisins
4 tbs. margarine
3 tbs. brown sugar
1 c. oatmeal
¼ c. flour
Pinch of salt

Put apples and raisins in a pot. Add just enough hot water to cover fruit. Soak until fruit is soft—about 15 minutes. While fruit is soaking, melt margarine in a pan and add oatmeal, flour, brown sugar, and salt. Mix well. Put fruit in a greased frying pan. If there is a little water left from soaking the fruit (½–1 c), pour it in too. Spread oatmeal mixture on top. Cover pan and bake over medium-hot coals until oatmeal topping is golden brown. Other dried fruits can be used in this recipe, or use a combination of fruits for a more colorful crisp.

Cinnamon Rolls

Basic Biscuit Recipe
¼–½ c. extra flour or biscuit mix
Margarine
Cinnamon
Brown sugar
Raisins (opt.)
Nuts (opt.)

Mix biscuit recipe and roll out (using a fishing rod case) into a rectangular sheet about ½ inch thick, using the extra flour when necessary to prevent sticking. Spread with margarine. Sprinkle with cinnamon, brown sugar, raisins, and nuts. Roll the dough lengthwise, pinching the dough closed so sugar does not fall out. Slice the column lengthwise into slices about 1 inch thick. Pinch together the side which will be on the bottom of the pan to prevent hot sugar from running out and burning. Bake 10–15 minutes until golden brown.

Basic Cake Recipe (for a 10-inch frying pan)

1½ c. biscuit mix
½ c. flour or grain
4 tbs. brown sugar or honey
½ c. powdered milk
Pinch of salt
1½ c. water
2–3 tbs. melted margarine

Mix all dry ingredients well in the same Teflon pan you will bake in. (If you do not use Teflon, mix in a separate bowl and pour into a well-greased pan.) Add water and mix until lumps are out. Add melted margarine. Smooth out batter and set on a flat bed of coals and bake 10–20 minutes until golden brown. Cool and frost if desired.

Variations

Chocolate. Use ¾ c. cocoa instead of powdered milk.
Cinnamon-Raisin. Add ½ c. softened raisins and 1 tsp cinnamon.

Peanut. Omit salt and add ½ c. crushed peanuts and
    ½ c. extra sugar.
Fruit Cake. Use ½ c. dry fruit drink in place of sugar.
Date-Coconut. Add ½ c. extra sugar, 1 tbs. extra
    margarine, 1 c. chopped dates and coconut, 1 tbs.
    extra water.
Boston Cream Pie. Make a plain cake. Cool and cut across
    its width into two layers. Mix pudding (see p. 325) and
    fill in between layers. Frost with chocolate frosting.

Quick Frosting

After the cake has baked, sprinkle brown sugar, cinnamon,
and margarine on the top of it. Put the lid back on and
bake until margarine is melted.

Chocolate Frosting

4 tbs. melted margarine
¼–½ c. sugar
½ c. Home Mix Cocoa (p. 293)
2 tbs. water (or 2 tbs. coffee for mocha frosting)

Combine all ingredients and cook on low heat, stirring vigorously. Add nuts, fruit, or coconut for variety.

Butterscotch Frosting

4 tbs. melted margarine
½ c. brown sugar
4 tbs. powdered milk
2 tbs. water

Mix as in Chocolate Frosting, above.

COOKIES

Basic Cookie Recipe

½ c. brown sugar
¼ c. margarine
¼ c. powdered milk
3 tbs. water
½ c. biscuit mix and ¾ c. cereal (or ¾ c. biscuit mix and
    ½ c. flour)
Pinch of salt

Mix sugar and margarine until well combined. Mix powdered milk and water and add. Work biscuit mix, cereal, and salt into a stiff dough. Drop into a frying pan and bake. Makes 9 3-inch flat cookies.

Variations

For chocolate cookies, use ½ c. Home Mix Cocoa (p. 293) and 4 tbs. water in place of the powdered-milk mixture. Add nuts, fruit, and seeds for variation.
Cinnamon and nutmeg go well in most cookies.

Cinnamon Thins

2 c. biscuit mix
⅓ c. flour
3 tbs. sugar
Pinch of salt
3 tbs. melted margarine
¼ c. powdered milk mixed with ½ c. water
1 tsp. cinnamon
¼ c. sugar

Mix the first 6 ingredients into a stiff dough. Roll into balls or flatten into squares. Cover with cinnamon-sugar mixture and bake until golden brown.

PIES

Easy Crust (for a 10-inch frying pan)

4 tbs. margarine
⅔–1 c. flour
½ tsp. salt
2 tbs. brown sugar

Melt margarine and mix in flour, salt, and sugar until the crust is the consistency of a graham cracker crust—not greasy, rather a dry crust. Pat into the bottom of the frying pan and bake 5–10 minutes until golden brown. Cool and add a cooked filling.

Rolled Crust

⅔–1 c. flour
4 tbs. margarine
½ tsp. salt
1–2 tbs. water

Mix flour and margarine. Add salt and water and knead into a ball. Roll out with a fishing rod case, adding flour to your hands, roller, and crust to prevent sticking. Bake, cool, and add a cooked filling.

Fruit Pie Filling

1–1½ c. dried fruit, tightly packed
2 c. water
2 tbs. margarine
Pinch of salt
½–⅔ c. sugar, or to taste
½ c. chopped nuts (opt.)
1 tsp cinnamon
¼ tsp. nutmeg
2–3 tbs. flour
4 tbs. water

Soak the fruit overnight or simmer until rehydrated. Drain all but ¼ to ½ c. water. Save drained juice for a drink. Add margarine, salt, sugar, and spices. Stir well. Mix flour and water (or use drained-off juice) until all lumps are gone. Pour thickener in the pot and simmer, stirring often, until thickened. Pour into an already baked crust. Garnish with wheat germ or granola.

Pudding Pie Filling

Instant and cooked puddings are both 4–5 parts water or milk to 1 part pudding. Under some conditions 5 parts will not set, so a 4-1 proportion is failure-proof. Use milk in all puddings except lemon. For lemon pudding use water and add sugar to taste. Bring cooked puddings to a boil, constantly stirring. Fill cooked pie crust and set in cool place about 2 hours to gel. For instant puddings, stir vigorously or shake in a water bottle and set to gel 15–30 minutes.

Jell-O Pie Filling

Mix Jell-O with boiling water (4 parts water, 1 part Jell-O) and let cool until barely gelled. Pour into a baked pie shell and cool again until Jell-O sets completely. Top with granola.

Apple Turnovers

1 c. dried apples, chopped
Pinch of salt
½ c. sugar
½ tsp. cinnamon
1 c. biscuit mix
4 tbs. melted or soft margarine
3 tbs. boiling water

Soak apples in a pot of water with salt. Drain, leaving ¼ c. water, saving the drained juice for a drink. Add sugar and cinnamon and simmer. While apples are simmering mix a dough of biscuit mix, margarine, and water. Pat into thin, oblong sheets about 5 by 8 inches. Place apples on one half of the dough and turn the other half over, pinching edges together. Bake until golden brown (10–15 minutes).

Peanut Brittle

1 c. sugar
2 tbs. melted margarine
Pinch of salt
1 c. peanuts

Dissolve sugar in margarine and cook, constantly stirring until smooth. When the hot sugar mixture forms a ball when dropped into cold water, it is done. Add nuts and cool immediately by placing pan in snow or cold water. (In the place of nuts, you can use seeds, dried fruit, or popcorn.)

Caramels

2 tbs. margarine
½ c. powdered milk mixed with 2 tbs. water
1 c. brown sugar
2 tbs. Home Mix Cocoa (p. 293) (for chocolate caramels)
1 c. peanuts, seeds, popcorn (optional)

Cook as directed for peanut brittle.

Sesame-Peanut Butter Balls (complete protein)

½ c. sesame seeds
1 heaping tbs. powdered milk
2 heaping tbs. peanut butter
3 heaping tbs. honey
Coconut to roll balls in

Mix sesame seeds, powdered milk, peanut butter, and honey together until a uniform ball can be formed. Break off spoon-sized hunks, form into balls, and roll balls in coconut. For a crunchy peanut butter delight, add ½ c. Grapenuts cereal instead of sesame seeds.

Popcorn

Oil or margarine
Popcorn
Salt to taste

Put enough oil in a pan to cover the bottom. Then put in popcorn—just enough to have one layer of corn in pan. Cover pan and cook on a *hot* fire. Shake pan a few times. When popping slows down, take pan off fire and wait a few minutes until popping stops. Then add salt. Popcorn is also good with powdered cheese sprinkled on top, or try sprinkling on some brewer's yeast for a cheesy-flavored nutritious popcorn.

Knots

Knot tying is an important backcountry skill. Knots will help you put up a tent, hang your laundry, or cross a river. The knots NOLS uses were selected because they are strong, and simple to tie and untie. Most of them fall into one of three major families: the overhand group, figure-eight knots, and bowlines. In addition, some other useful knots and hitches will be illustrated: the double fisherman's, the slippery taut-line hitch, and the prusik. Many of these knots were borrowed from the sailing world, while others, like the prusik, are unique to mountaineering.

Knots should be practiced until they become second nature. At NOLS, students are encouraged to tie every knot we teach over and over until they can make them properly with their eyes closed, or backward, or behind their backs.

When learning knots, try not to memorize ditties about rabbits and holes or drunks and bars. If you forget the saying, you forget the knot. Try instead to understand how each knot is put together and be able to recognize it even if it's upside down or pulled out of shape. Being able to look at a knot tied by someone else and assess its correctness is an invaluable skill.

Any knot weakens the rope at the point where it is tied. The amount that a rope's strength is reduced by a knot is determined by its "efficiency," which is expressed as a percentage. If a knot were 80 percent efficient, for example, it would weaken the rope by 20 percent. In general, the overhand family is 60–65 percent efficient, the bowline family 70–75 percent, and the figure-eight family 75–80 percent. This should not imply that all overhands should be shunned, however. With such a knot, a rope made to hold 4,400 pounds can still hold 2,640 pounds —a lot of force! Other criteria besides strength—ease of tying, untying after loading, and inspection—need to be carefully considered.

Some knot terminology needs to be explained. In knot tying, the rope can be conceived as having two parts: a standing end and a running end. The standing end is the actual end of the rope or webbing. The running end is the portion of rope that leads away from the knot.

Since much discussion will follow about loops and bights of rope, it is important that you know the difference between the two. A loop is a circle made by crossed strands of a rope. In a bight the strands of rope are pinched together so that the strands lie parallel and are not crossed.

In our experience at NOLS, knots seem to be more easily learned in families rather than singly. The overhand knot family includes the simple overhand, overhand on a bight, and the water knot or ringbend (also nicknamed the "overhand follow-through"). Simple overhand knots are not useful alone, but as a means of "backing off" other knots to

OVERHAND KNOT

OVERHAND ON A BIGHT

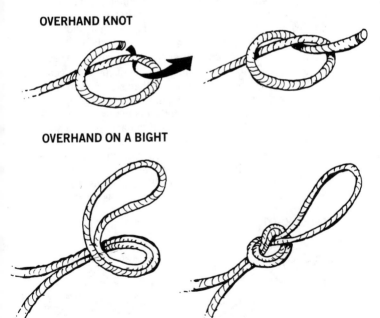

ensure that they do not work loose. The overhand is tied using the standing end of the rope after the other knot has been completed.

An overhand on a bight can be used for making loops in a Tyrolean haul line securing the end of a rope to an anchor or for any application that will not greatly load the loop. This knot can be tough to untie if it gets cranked tight.

The water knot or ringbend is one of the few knots that works well in flat or tubular webbing. Among other applications, it is used in making seat harnesses and runners for anchors. Avoid letting any twists in the webbing get inside this knot. Also make sure that it is good and tight, harboring no bulges of loose webbing. Knots in flat webbing tend to slip, so leave tails of at least three inches and inspect them periodically during use.

The figure-eight knot family is stronger than the overhand and bowlines and has come to dominate the climbing and mountaineering scene. They are extremely easy to tie and inspect. Tied on a bight, the figure-eight knot can serve the same purposes as the overhand on a bight, but is stronger and easier to untie after being severely tightened.

The figure-eight follow-through is one of the most common knots used by climbers to tie themselves from their seat harnesses to the end of a rope. Since rubbing the knot against the rock can be expected in climbing, for the security of the knot leave a three-inch tail and always hand-tighten the knot before climbing.

Another type of figure-eight follow-through, the Flemish bend, is used to tie two ropes together. It works best in ropes of the same diameter. At NOLS it finds common application in Tyrolean traverses and rappels. If the knot

WATER KNOT

FIGURE-EIGHT KNOT

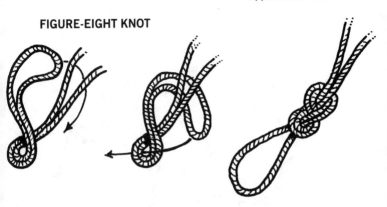

is expected to be heavily loaded, as in a Tyrolean for example, a stick can be poked through the knot near the center cross. Breaking the stick will later create enough slack to get the knot undone.

Although they have now been largely replaced by figure-eight knots, bowlines are still useful in situations where a loop of fixed size is needed. Bowlines are easy to tie, to adjust for tightness, and to untie after they have been loaded. They should always be backed off, however, as they have an insidious way of working themselves loose.

FIGURE-EIGHT FOLLOW-THROUGH KNOT

BOWLINE

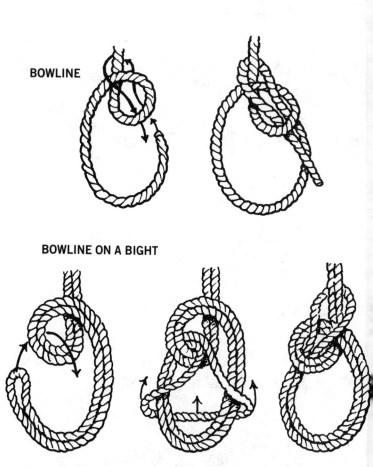

BOWLINE ON A BIGHT

Careful attention must be paid in the tying of bowlines so that the running end always faces the inside, not the outside of the loop. Otherwise the knot, which has a strength of 70 percent when properly tied, is weakened by about half. Other useful members of the bowline family

BOWLINE ON A COIL

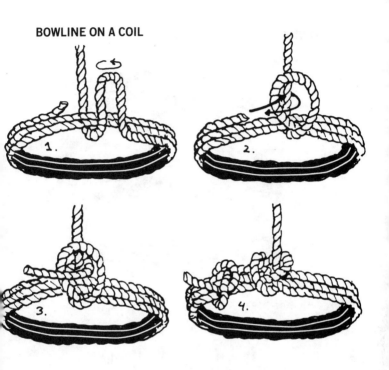

include a double bowline, which adds strength to a simple bowline, and a bowline on a bight, handy for making two loops side by side.

The double fisherman's knot is used to join two ropes together and works better on ropes of dissimilar diameter than does the Flemish bend. Also, prusik loops are typically made with this knot. It does have the disadvantage of being tough to untie after a load has been applied, however. When tying this knot, check that the two crosses are nested securely in each other.

The prusik knot is useful for ascending and descending ropes and making pulley systems for Tyrolean traverses and

DOUBLE FISHERMAN'S KNOT

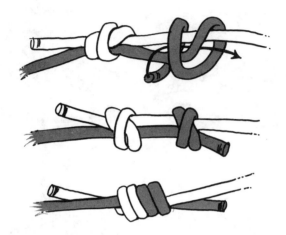

PRUSIK KNOT

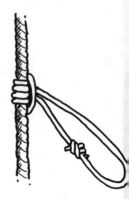

crevasse or cliff rescue. It is made with a prusik loop of about three feet of ¼-inch to ⁵⁄₁₆-inch laid or kernmantle rope that has the ends tied together with a double fisherman's knot. Using this knot the loop can be slid up or down a larger-diameter rope when it is loose, but will grip the rope securely when the knot is tightened or "set." Although three wraps are usually sufficient to create the friction needed to grip a wet or icy rope, some slippage may occur under these conditions.

The Programs of the National Outdoor Leadership School

The National Outdoor Leadership School is the nation's oldest and largest nonprofit wilderness skills training center, offering programs in Wyoming, Alaska, Washington State, Mexico, and Kenya. All NOLS courses are designed to encourage proficiency in four major outdoor-skills areas: minimum-impact camping and travel; leadership development; outdoor living skills such as cooking, first aid, and nutrition to ensure comfort and safety in outdoor pursuits; and specific outdoor recreational skills such as mountaineering, skiing, hiking, climbing, kayaking, caving, and fishing.

WILDERNESS COURSES are the heart of the NOLS curriculum, the standard course, to develop competent, well-versed, outdoor men and women. These courses provide thorough training in camping, hiking, navigation, minimum impact, fishing, and natural history. They also provide an introduction to technical climbing and rope systems. Wilderness courses are offered by NOLS Wyoming in the Wind River, Beartooth, and Absaroka ranges; by NOLS Alaska in the Talkeetnas; and by NOLS Washington in the Pasayten Wilderness. A number of specialized courses also fall within this family, including Wilderness/Natural History Courses, which emphasize the ecology of the backcountry; Adventure Courses for fourteen- and fifteen-year-olds; and Wilderness Seminars, two-week versions of the basic wilderness courses targeted for business and professional people.

MOUNTAINEERING COURSES cover the same materials as wilderness courses, as well as teaching technical climbing skills on rock and snow. These courses are offered by NOLS Wyoming in the Wind River Range, by NOLS Washington in the Cascades, and by NOLS Alaska in the Alaska Range. Specialized mountaineering courses include Advanced Mountaineering Courses for people who want to perfect their skills and the Mount McKinley Course for those interested in learning high-altitude mountaineering.

NOLS SEMESTER COURSES offer the most thorough wilderness training available. Running in length from ten to fourteen weeks, semester courses cover all the outdoor skills taught in the NOLS basic curriculum, plus considerable advanced and specialized training. NOLS Kenya offers semester programs throughout the year. Its curriculum includes hiking and climbing on Mount Kenya, cultural and natural history components in the Great Rift Valley, Masai Mara, or Nguruman Escarpment, and snorkeling in the coastal areas around Malindi. NOLS Alaska offers a summer semester program which includes sea kayaking, snow and ice climbing, and tundra hiking. NOLS Wyoming has both a fall and spring semester program in the Rocky Mountains which, in addition to basic NOLS mountaineering training, provides special instruction in technical rock climbing, caving, desert hiking, and cross-country skiing.

SEA KAYAKING COURSES are offered by NOLS Mexico along the Baja Peninsula and by NOLS Alaska in Prince William Sound. These are much like the wilderness courses except all travel is done in one- or two-person kayaks. Students receive special training in seashore minimum impact, fauna and flora identification, navigation, and seamanship.

SKIING COURSES are designed to introduce winter camping and ski-touring training to experienced summer hikers who want to extend their time in the outdoors. Students learn to construct snow shelters, analyze avalanche potential, prevent cold injury, and enjoy the remarkable silence and rigor of the winter wilderness.

NOLS offers a number of *professional courses* for outdoor recreation professionals who want to learn all aspects of leading groups and teaching in the outdoors. In addition, *special advanced courses* are available for those who want to fine-tune specific backcountry skills such as fishing, climbing, kayaking, and skiing.

For information about the training programs of the National Outdoor Leadership School, write for the NOLS catalog. Address your inquiry to NOLS, P.O. Box AA, Lander, Wyo. 82520, and mark the envelope "Wilderness Catalog." Or call NOLS at (307) 332-6973.

Glossary

adiabatic cooling—air cooling due to rise in altitude

altimeter—a device for measuring altitude

anklet—a gaiter covering only the ankle

approach shoes—ankle-high boots for trail walking

billycan—a handleless metal can used in camp cooking

biodegradable—capable of being broken down organically

blaze—to mark a tree by removing some bark

boulder field—an area with a concentration of boulders, so dense you must walk on the rock

bushwhack—to travel off-trail, often in brushy or forested areas

cagoule—a pullover rain garment that reaches to the knees

carabiner—aluminum snap link used in rock climbing and technical mountain systems

cell—in weather parlance, an air mass

Chinook winds—strong warm, dry winds in valleys and canyons on the leeward side of mountain ranges

clevis pin—a metal pin, held in place by a split ring, commonly used in attaching backpacks to external frames

compass bearing—a direction in degrees measured by a compass

contour lines—lines on a map outlining all areas of equal elevation

corn snow—pebble-like snow found during late spring and summer.

Cordura—a heavy weave of nylon

Coriolis effect—an effect on air movement caused by the earth's rotation, curving to the right in the Northern Hemisphere and to the left in the Southern Hemisphere

CPR—cardiopulmonary resuscitation; a way of artificially providing breathing and heart action

cravat—a triangular cloth used in bandaging

dew point—the temperature at which relative humidity equals 100 percent, thereby causing condensation of the moisture in the air into rain

duff—the layer of dead plants, needles, and leaves covering the ground in forested areas

ecosystem—a system of living things and their relationship with the environment

EMT—emergency medical technician

fruit crystals—instant fruit drink

grommet—a brass eyelet used in tarpaulins, garments, backpacks, etc.

guy line—cord from the side of a tent to a stake, used to steady the tent

leeward side—the side sheltered from the wind

litter—a homemade stretcher

lug soles—a sole with a deep cleated tread

mineral soil—earth with no organic content, such as sand or gravel

molefoam—a padded form of moleskin used to lessen foot abrasion

moleskin—a thick adhesive plaster used to prevent blisters

off-trail boot—a stiff ankle-high boot

plant recolonization—when plant species which have died off move back into an area

pot grip—a pliers for handling hot pots

ripple sole—a sole with a very shallow tread

roadhead—the end of a road leading to the backcountry

rucksack—a pack with no frame

scree—a loose collection of small rock fragments

scree collar—a padded rim to prevent debris from entering a boot

60/40 cloth—a fabric of nylon and cotton threads

split ring—a ring of metal split so it can be put through a clevis pin (like a key ring)

squeak heel—an inflammation of the Achilles tendon

sternum strap—a buckled strap that crosses the chest holding the pack's shoulder straps in place

switchback—a path following a zigzag pattern on a steep hill

till—powdered rock deposited by a glacier

toggle—a metal or plastic device commonly used with tent guy lines to secure them and prevent slippage

topographic ("topo") maps—maps which reveal the topography of an area with the use of contour lines

tubular webbing—a woven nylon strip

tump line—a cord that crosses the forehead and attaches to the bottom of a load, putting the weight on one's neck

turnbuckle—a metal coupling with threaded ringbolts at each end, used on some backpacks to tighten or loosen backbands

Velcro—a type of fastener using two pieces of woven plastic that fasten to each other on contact and separate with a tug

welt—stitching between boot soles and uppers

wick—to transfer moisture from one layer of clothing to another

widow makers—standing dead trees

Suggestions for Additional Reading

Advanced First Aid and Emergency Care. American Red Cross. Garden City, N.Y.: Doubleday, 1980. *The* textbook for first aid, and a good book to have along.

Aviation Weather. Federal Aviation Agency and U.S. Department of Commerce Weather Bureau. Washington, D.C.: U.S. Government Printing Office, 1975. Although written for pilots, this book has a wealth of weather information for hikers.

Backpacker Magazine. The best periodical for keeping up to date on new equipment and techniques.

Backpacking on a Budget, by Anna Sequoia and Steven Schneider. New York: Penguin Books, 1979. The prices have become quickly outdated, but the book has some good ideas.

Backwoods Ethics, by Laura and Guy Waterman. Boston: Stone Wall Press, 1979. An excellent work on land use, the wilderness ethic, and "no trace" camping.

Be Expert with Map and Compass, by Bjorn Kjellstrom. New York: Charles Scribner's Sons, 1976. The best book on how to use a compass. Describes the Silva orienteering system.

Contours, by C. Boxhall and E. J. P. Devereux. London: George Philip & Son Ltd., 1965. The clearest explanation of topographic maps written.

Diet for a Small Planet, by Frances Moore Lappe. New York: Ballantine Books, 1975. *The* book about complementary proteins, and an essential part of a serious outdoorsman's library.

Gorp, Glop, and Glue Stew, by Yvonne Prater and Ruth Dyar Mendenhall. Seattle: The Mountaineers, 1982. A fun collection of recipe favorites of noted outdoorsmen.

Hypothermia, Killer of the Unprepared, by Theodore Lathrop, M.D. Portland: Mazamas, 1975. An extremely valuable pamphlet.

Knotcraft, by Allan and Paulette MacFarlan. New York: Bonanza Books, 1967. A stylistically dated but useful work on knots.

The Lightning Book, by Peter E. Viemeister. Cambridge, Mass.: MIT Press, 1972. Without doubt the most thorough description of lightning and its effects available to the general reader. A fun book to read on stormy nights.

Medicine for Mountaineering, by James A. Wilkerson, M.D. Seattle: The Mountaineers, 1975. An in-depth study of medical-care requirements for mountaineering expeditions. Essential for any group.

Modern Rope Techniques in Mountaineering, by Bill March. Manchester, N.H.: Cicerone Press, 1976. Written specifically for climbers, but useful knowledge for any serious backpacker.

Modern Snow and Ice Techniques, by Bill March. Manchester, N.H.: Cicerone Press, 1974. While of great use for climbers, the sections on snow are also handy for backpackers.

Mountaineering First Aid: A Guide to Accident Response and First Aid Care, by Dick Mitchell, et al. Seattle: The Mountaineers. A small pamphlet explaining priorities when administering first aid.

Mountaineering: The Freedom of the Hills, 4th ed., edited by Peggy Ferber. Seattle: The Mountaineers, 1982. Though aimed at climbers, this is the truly classic work, with a breadth of information for any mountain hiker.

Movin' On, by Harry Roberts. Boston: Stone Wall Press, 1977. An equally valuable winter addition to the following.

Movin' Out, by Harry Roberts. Boston:Stone Wall Press, 1975. Perhaps the best analysis and description of hiking equipment ever written.

The New Complete Walker, by Colin Fletcher. New York: Knopf, 1974. A good book for solo backpackers.

Pack to Nature, by Frank Ford. Fort Worth, Tex.: Harvest Press, 1974. A good little work on nutrition and recipes.

Ropes, Knots and Slings for Climbers, rev. ed., by Walt Wheelock. Glendale, Cal.: La Siesta Press, 1967. The simplest, clearest book written on knots.

Topographic Maps. Department of the Interior, Geological Survey. Washington, D.C.: U.S. Government Printing Office, 1976. A quick, simple summary of topographic maps.

Weathering the Wilderness, by William F. Reifsnyder. San Francisco: Sierra Club Books, 1980. A fine work on weather. Of particular note are analyses of local weather patterns for many sections of the country. Highly recommended.

The Wilderness Handbook, by Paul Petzoldt. New York: W. W. Norton, 1974. A fine book by a great man. The first book to describe the NOLS experience and early techniques of minimum impact.

Wilderness Search and Rescue, by Tim J. Setnicka. Boston: Appalachian Mountain Club, 1980. A technical, highly detailed, excellent work on search and rescue.

About the Authors

Peter Simer is Executive Director of the National Outdoor Leadership School. Born in Minneapolis, he is a graduate of the University of Southern California, and completed his graduate work at UCLA and Southern Connecticut State College. Mr. Simer became a full-time NOLS instructor in 1971, and participated in the first NOLS climb of Mount McKinley. He has since participated in courses and trips in Washington State, Alaska, Wyoming, Kenya, the French Alps, and Soviet Caucasus. He became the Executive Director of NOLS in 1975. Mr. Simer is married, has one son, and lives in Lander, Wyoming.

John Sullivan is a writer who has taken numerous NOLS courses in Wyoming and Alaska. An alumnus of the University of Southern California, where he completed graduate work at USC's film school, he has created material for television, including films for the Academy of Television Arts and Sciences' Emmy Awards program, and films for the educational market. He has directed theater at the Los Angeles Music Center's Mark Taper Forum, where he was a resident director, and at the Circle Repertory Theater in New York. He has served as a communications consultant to many organizations including NOLS and has held positions with the Rand Corporation and the University of Southern California. Mr. Sullivan, his wife Mónica, an attorney, and their son Peter reside in Lander, Wyoming.